Roy,

I appreciate so much your helping us out this week. You have shown a generous spirit that should also make you appreciate the life of this man who was also generous and courageous. Best wishes for your future.

Lib Sears

FOR FREEDOM

THE BIOGRAPHY OF
JOHN NELSON ARMSTRONG

The Biography of John Nelson Armstrong
For Freedom

L.C. Sears

Professor of English

Harding College

 Sweet Publishing Company · Austin, Texas

LIBRARY OF CONGRESS CATALOG CARD NUMBER: 79-94236

STANDARD BOOK NUMBER: 8344-0058-8

Printed in the U.S.A.

CONTENTS

PREFACE

Strange are the ways of Destiny. Who could have foreseen that the man who would free an enslaved people and bring unity again to a nation torn apart by hatred and bitter war would come from a wretched log cabin in Kentucky?

In a far less spectacular role, in a century which has increasingly magnified centralized power in government, in economic and social organization, and even in religion, who could have dreamed that one of the foremost champions of the freedom of conscience and the unity which Christ sought would come from another log cabin in an undistinguished section of West Tennessee?

In giving to the world the biography of John Nelson Armstrong, I have been keenly aware that it is impossible to present his personality, his ideals, convictions, hopes, and dreams as vividly and forcefully as he revealed himself to those who knew him. For this reason I have chosen to let him speak as often as possible directly to the reader.

The conversations here recorded are taken from his letters and writings which are in my possession and from his own dictation and the memory of his family and friends.

Since Armstrong taught in six Christian colleges beginning with the Nashville Bible School shortly after its opening, and since he was president of four of these colleges, his life reflects more clearly than that of any other man the growth of the Christian schools among the churches of Christ from their infancy to maturity. As an evangelist his work extended from Florida to California.

As an educator, evangelist, editor, and writer he was involved in the gravest crises facing the church and the nation in the first half of the century, and his story is a heroic struggle to preserve the Christian ideal of personal freedom in a world increasingly obsessed with dreams of power. I hope that the insight and the courage with which he faced the problems of his time will inspire a deeper reverence for the principles that are eternal and that will help us solve the problems of our day.

I am deeply indebted to Mr. Virgil Bentley and Mr. Jim Bill McInteer, to my sons Dr. Jack Wood Sears and Dr. James Kern Sears, and to my wife Pattie H. Sears for many helpful criticisms and suggestions, and to a host of friends and former students for their encouragement and cooperation.

Lloyd Cline Sears
Harding College
Searcy, Arkansas

Chapter 1

AS THE TWIG IS BENT

THE DAY John Nelson Armstrong was born, January 6, 1870, broke clear but stinging cold. The cabin was still dark when Robert Armstrong raked the live coals together, laid on kindling topped with sticks of dry oak and hickory, then hastily dressed as flames lighted the darkness and pushed back the cold a grudging distance from the rude stone hearth.

The cabin was solidly built for its day and kind. Four years before, soon after the war ended, Robert Armstrong and Elizabeth Hathaway, his wife, had bought the little farm near Gadsden, Tennessee. There was no house. Together they cleared the hazel bushes and blackjacks from a high point overlooking the valley to the north and east. With days of back-breaking toil Robert cut the trees, and with broadaxe and adze shaped them for the walls—heavy beams eight inches thick and ten to sixteen inches wide. With the help of neighbors he raised the walls and roof, and secured the notched and fitted corners with strong oak pegs driven into holes laboriously drilled through the solid beams.

Despite the rude simplicity of his birthplace John Nelson Armstrong received from his parents a remarkable heritage of personality and character. From his father Robert came his deeply emotional nature, his warm friendliness, a fine sense of humor, and perfect integrity, for Robert Armstrong's name was a local synonym for honesty. From his mother Elizabeth came his penetrating insight and his shrewd good judgment. From both came his purity of heart, his high sense of responsibility and depth of conviction.

In a large family young John Nelson Armstrong learned unselfish sharing and loyalty to others. In addition to the two older brothers, James David and Thomas Isaac (called Tom Ike by his brothers), there were two younger brothers, Robert Edgar and Stark, and three younger sisters, Ora, Nannie, and little Chippie who died of diphtheria at the age of six. Added to these were the two grandmothers who spent their last years in the home—altogether a family of twelve.

Needless to say, the log cabin became too small. The family bought an eight-room house and a hundred-acre farm only a mile from Gadsden, and later added a forty-acre woodland adjoining. It was a creek bottom farm, and the principal crops were corn, strawberries, and tomatoes. They grew no wheat, and since flour was nine dollars a barrel and dollars were hard to come by in those days, they had biscuits only on Sunday morning—for other meals plain cornbread. But this could be served in a variety of ways—with cracklins after hog-killing times, as mush, fried or with butter or sweet milk, or as hoe-cake or hush-puppies. There was always plenty of pork, potatoes, black-eyed peas, turnips, and greens. Homemade sorghum was a daily dessert, Christmas was a special season for each one got an orange and some striped peppermint candy.

Strawberry time was also a special season. There may have been certain qualities in the soil, or a combination of soil and climate, but no berries surpassed those of West Tennessee in delicacy of aroma and flavor.

At strawberry time the poorest farmer could feast his family on a delicacy that even the tyrant King Richard III had to beg as a favor from his henchman. The Armstrongs had always more berries than the market could take. Mother Armstrong cooked gallons of them into rich waxy jam, and the family ate additional gallons. Young Nelson (nicknamed Nelse), like the other children, learned to hoe and weed and pick, but he also learned the deliciousness of fresh berries with sugar and rich cream. Even the cornbread gave way to hot buttered biscuits when strawberries came in. At one time in a race between the brothers Nelse ate thirteen bowls of berries and Tom Ike eleven.

The two big magnolias in the front yard and the old-fashioned breezeway through the new house were cool places to play. As a child Nelse loved to crawl under the loom and watch the shuttle glide back and forth as his mother wove. At other times, when his mother picked the geese, he held fearfully their writhing heads to prevent their biting protests against the indignity and pain. Sometimes he and his brothers slipped off Sunday afternoons to the swimming hole a half mile away in a neighbor's field. This had to be done with care because his mother always objected. Sometimes their wet hair gave them away. Once, after a week had safely passed, Nelse unthoughtedly mentioned what a fine crop the neighbor had.

"When did you see that crop?" his father asked. And the secret was out. With such restriction it is a tribute to young Armstrong's initiative and persistence that he finally learned to swim.

But there was little idle time on the farm. At the age of six or seven Nelse helped carry the corn to mill, riding the mule and sitting on the sack across its back. On one eventful day, as they crossed the creek, the mule, with the perversity natural to its kind, suddenly stopped to drink. The rear end high up the bank and the head down to the water made a steep slide down which the boy tumbled heels over head into the creek and was sent home to dry. His embarrassment was complete when he crept into the kitchen and recognized the voice of his little sweetheart, talking to his mother in the living room. They blocked the only access to his bedroom and dry clothes. So he spent the afternoon hunched up, wet and miserable, in the kitchen.

If this first experience did not teach him the trouble women can bring, the second must have finished the lesson. The little girl was visiting again. He was to plant peas in the corn, but he decided to hide in the trundle bed under the high bed until his father gave up the search, and he could then spend the afternoon with his girl. But it is uncanny what eyes fathers have. One pull on the trundle bed, and there he was. While his sweetheart looked on his father tanned his jacket well and sent him to the field. So he got a whipping and the privilege of planting the peas too—a double blessing. But, he was learning discipline, duty, work, obedience, and even a painful humility.

This was the only time his father ever whipped him. His mother, however, had a more volatile temper, but her whippings never hurt. Sometimes if the children saw the lightning coming, they could dart around the table and out the door till her temper cooled. But even these escapes were weighted with suspense and possibly painful consequences. The morning she saw her good quilt torn in two from end to end the boys thought the lightning would surely strike.

"You boys have been fighting, and look what you've done!" she cried angrily, as she held the pieces of quilt before them. But all protested there had been no fight; they were sound asleep all night. Then Nelse suddenly remembered.

"Well, Ma," he said, sheepishly, "I guess I'm the guilty one. I dreamed I was coming up a hill, and suddenly there were snakes all around. I began killing them as fast as I could, but one big one just wouldn't die. I had to kill it inch by inch, and I had to yank and yank to get its head off." That evidently was the thick hem at the edge. At sight of the boy's embarrassed and sorrowful face the lightning and clouds slowly vanished. All in all, the children learned genuine respect for parental authority as well as faithfulness to duty.

Gadsden in 1870 had fewer than a hundred residents. A half dozen one-story brick or frame stores stretched along one side of the Louisville and Nashville Railroad out of Memphis. With the cotton gin and depot they nestled sleepily in the narrow valley. On a little hill rising sharply on the west stood the school, the church of Christ, and the Baptist church. On a second hill to the north lived Dr. James. On a third hill across the track to the east were the Methodist church and immediately above the depot the local hotel, a small two-story frame building. The outstanding event of each day was to watch the train come whistling and clanging in, unload a little express or an occasional passenger, and go chugging and puffing out. In summer there were usually a few loungers around the depot, and storekeepers and neighbors sat on the front porches of the stores whittling and talking politics or the weather and exchanging jokes and local gossip. Like most small towns Gadsden offered few opportunities. As the children of the community grew up they left for other places. But if attractions had been many, the Armstrong children had little time to spend in town, and only an occasional trip to Humboldt, the county seat.

Nelse's introduction to school was distinctly unfavorable. Two children were seated together at each homemade desk. His older brothers told how hard the teacher whipped, and he expected an unpleasant time. His fears were not allayed when he saw the stack of first-class, seasoned hickory switches standing in the corner. They had all the appearance of business, ready and eager for the unfortunate victim.

But J. R. McDonald proved to be an excellent teacher. He seated the little fellows, whom he called "Know Nothings," behind him, and the larger students in front where he could keep a sharp eye on them. Some boy near Nelse once irritated him, and forgetting where he was and the bunch of switches in the corner, he banged the other boy over the head with his *Blue-Back Speller*. The blow cracked like a shot, and McDonald whirled round and demanded why he had hit the other boy. There must have been something appealing in the white-faced terror of the child's face, for

McDonald merely said, "Don't ever do that again, Nelse," with not even a glance at the whips in the corner.

During all the years he was in school he was never whipped, though he had to stand in the corner once for not knowing his spelling lesson. McDonald always closed the day with the spelling class. He used not only the famous *Blue-Back Speller*, but for upper grades he took one page a day in Webster's *School Dictionary*. His method was most thorough. In addition to spelling, students learned the sounds and diacritical marking of letters, the meanings of words, and how to use them in sentences of their own. These were lessons the child never forgot. Years later as a college president he took over the seventh grade spelling class for one year and surprised the students with ultra-modern techniques which he had learned from McDonald fifty years before.

The school contained all eight grades, and as Nelse and Fred James, Hiram Reeves, Willis Reeves, Theophilis Humphreys and others finished these, McDonald carried them on through the high school course. Needless to say, it required a genius to cover so many levels of work and do it with the old-fashioned thoroughness for which McDonald was noted. His students were not spoon fed. He encouraged them to work independently. Some classes were necessary, and for these, students of the different grades marched up to a recitation bench, and after the recitation back to their seats again. But much of the work was done individually. The morning was spent on arithmetic with no classes. If a student could not work a problem he could go up to the teacher and get help, usually in the form of a question or a mere suggestion that would start the student on the right path but never give him the whole solution. McDonald demanded of each student all he could do.

Both parents recognized the importance of education. Even if they had to do without necessities, they always managed the money for books and school supplies. Taxes paid only three months of the term; the rest was paid by tuition. But the Armstrongs always managed the tuition.

Nelse loved all his work, but delighted most in arithmetic, in which he led the class. As he and the little group of boys finished the eighth grade, McDonald instructed them in Latin, rhetoric, and physics, or "natural philosophy." McDonald often made short but stimulating speeches. For the older students he organized a debating society on Friday afternoons. Here Nelse got his first experience in speaking. Later he took part in a community Literary Society which met in town. But he had agonizing difficulty overcoming his natural timidity. He told McDonald once that he never wanted to be called on to speak again.

"I'm not a public man, and I never intend to be," he declared.

But he was McDonald's favorite student. The master had seen in him qualities which he himself had never guessed. Like all great teachers he worked tirelessly to bring them out. When he felt that he had given him all he could in the little school, he urged him to go on to college. But before he went McDonald arranged for him to spend one year as his assistant at Gadsden. The experience and the money he could save would both be helpful when he went to college.

Two other experiences in the little school made lasting impressions on him. The boys had a custom of lining up in two opposing lines and daring each other to cross a certain point. The older boys usually egged on the younger until accepting the dare became a matter of upholding the honor of their side. The result was some very spirited fighting. Nelse never liked to fight; nevertheless he felt compelled to uphold the honor of his group, and he flailed about him energetically if not scientifically. The experience, however, turned him strongly against violence and force.

On the other hand, he thoroughly enjoyed the "athletic program" of the little school. They played "town ball," "cat," "base," and "fox-in-the-hole," or "fox-and-geese," with hot and red-faced vigor. They were health-building sports. Years later, as a college president, disgusted with the extremes in college athletics, he said, "That was as good a system of athletics as we have ever had since." To him it had the only justifiable reason for athletics—health and clean sport—with none of the evils and excess.

One other influence entered into the preparation of the boy. Not until years after their marriage, when the boys were growing up, had his father and mother belonged to any church. Then after the war they attended a brush-arbor meeting held by some preacher of the group derogatively called "Campbellites"—a group pleading earnestly for the restoration of the Christian faith as it was preached and lived by the apostles and Christians of the First Century. They were both deeply moved and were immediately baptized. As the child stood on the bank of the creek and saw his father and mother go down into the water to be immersed, he did not understand the meaning of it, to be sure. But he saw the two whom he loved and trusted most and to whom he was obedient go through an act which, even to his childish understanding, indicated submission to something greater than themselves. When he came to understand, he too followed them in the same expression of submission.

His parents took him regularly to church, and there he saw the same reverent regard for a higher than human authority. His father's extreme timidity prevented his taking a lead in the church. He never learned to speak in public or to lead a prayer. But his mother read the Bible to the children in the home, and also the *Gospel Advocate*, the independent religious weekly which they always took. She had attended school only three months in her life, but she read well and kept up with the children as they learned.

Both in the church and in the Armstrong home there was always a reverence for goodness and truth and the Will of God, which the children understood must be supreme. The church services were quite informal—singing, the reading of the Scriptures, prayer, the Bible lesson, and always the Lord's Supper, when in a period of silence they remembered his death and his resurrection and sat at table with him "anew" after nineteen hundred years and broke the bread and drank the wine with him "in his kingdom." These acts left deep impressions of reverence.

Mr. McDonald was a leader in the church and urged the boys to take part in the church services. In spite of his timidity Nelse learned to read the Scriptures, lead in prayer, and even make short talks. The church had no regular preacher, only annual revivals and occasional visiting preachers, some of them outstanding men. The one who had most influence on him was Jesse Phillips, who later sacrificed his own life in rescuing his daughter from their burning home. He was a self-made preacher, but a polished gentleman, a genuinely good man, and an inspiring speaker. More than any one else in these early days he seemed to Nelse the ideal of the unselfish Christian minister.

Many forces combined together to help the boy grow up, forces from his home and his community. But added to this physical heritage was the power of spiritual ideals, dimly felt at the baptism of his parents, more vividly experienced as he listened to the reading of the Scriptures and the prayers, and reaching a richer development in the recognition of a Higher Will to which he should submit his personal impulses and desires. How great this power was we can only gather from his later life.

Chapter 2

A COUNTRY SCHOOL TEACHER

IT IS FORTUNATE that in choosing a career a boy's vision broadens with experience, and he has time and the right to change his mind. In isolated communities, with no stimulus from outside, life tends to remain static. Children follow the pattern of their elders with little variation—except for farmers. Children of farmers leave the farm in flocks, partly because their education leads from the land and excites interest in other ways of living.

This was true in the Armstrong family. None of the children carried on the farm after the parents died. J. D. owned an attractive grocery in Obion until his death, Ed operated a drug store, and Stark became an accountant. Perhaps in reaction against the meager allotment of Christmas candy, Nelse's first ambition was to be a clerk in a candy store. When a cousin visited the family this dream changed to law. J. W. Williams had become a very successful lawyer in Saint Louis and was later to become an able and distinguished judge. He talked enthusiastically of the opportunities in the legal profession and of the income and prestige which it could bring. He opened up to Nelse and the family a new and golden world, free from the poverty and sweaty toil of the land. The family had already recognized in Nelse exceptional ability. He was the one who loved books and study. While he was especially fond of mathematics, he did equally well in other studies. In spite of his timidity, which led him often to vow he would never make another public speech, he had already become the outstanding speaker in the school and in the community literary society. So it was concluded that he should prepare himself for law.

Many years later Judge Billups of Cordell, Oklahoma, commented on the outstanding success he would have made in the legal profession had he carried out his early resolve. He had a penetrating, far-sighted vision, and could usually guess far in advance what others would plan to do. He was never content with a superficial knowledge of any problem, but kept probing and turning it over and over until he understood every phase of it. He had great faith in men, but a keen understanding of human weaknesses. With his students he was warmly sympathetic and for-giving and those who might lie to others were frank with him, but when one violated the principles of right and decency and tried to hide the truth, he could examine as penetratingly as a prosecuting attorney. He seemed almost to read one's mind, and usually discovered any deception. As a speaker he inspired conviction and the confidence of men.

It was to prepare for law that he left for college. But already a different influence was at work within. The prac-tice of law was open to many temptations and pressures. He was aware of the disrepute which some had brought upon it and which was reflected in the story of the man who saw in the cemetery a tombstone with the inscription, "Here lies a distinguished lawyer and an honest man." Looking up in wonder, he asked "Why bury them both in one grave?" He had no doubt of his cousin's integrity; he accepted only cases in whose justice he had complete faith.

But he questioned whether he himself could always adjust the practice of law to his ideal of what a Christian ought to be.

This consideration, however, may have been less important than the new sense of values which had been growing within him. The practice of law was still a far-away dream, but he had already been taking part in religious activities—the kind of work to which on a larger scale a minister would devote his life. He had come to feel its importance. To settle disputes of men over property was a necessary service and valuable for the present, but to instruct the souls of men was vital both for the present and for eternity. He had apparently come to feel as Jesus did when the young man said, "Master, compel my brother to divide the inheritance with me." And Jesus replied, "Man, who made me a divider of property?" Others could devote their time to the settling of estates, but Jesus had more vital work to do. Like him, even at the early age of seventeen, Nelse felt that he must be about his Father's business.

Some foreshadowing of the decision may have been subconsciously reflected in the college he selected. He entered West Tennessee Christian College, which was later called Georgia Robertson, and still later Freed-Hardeman College at Henderson, Tennessee. Its church affiliation even more than its nearness was the reason for the selection.

At the college he found the students divided into two groups—preachers and non-preachers. No one studied the Bible but the preachers. It may have been this factor which helped him reach a decision. He wanted to study the Bible. Consequently he enrolled in the preacher class and began to "study for the ministry," as they spoke of it then. He took outlines of sermons and studied Milligan's *Scheme of Redemption*. But he also studied college algebra, plane geometry, psychology, then called mental philosophy, Latin, rhetoric, and moral philosophy.

But his study for the ministry was short. When he returned home Christmas, Jesse Phillips, who had encouraged his religious activities, took him aside and told him what a preacher ought to be. Until that time Nelse had thought of the ministry as a profession like medicine or law, a profession in which one could serve, to be sure, but which would also set one apart and give a measure of prestige and honor and even security. Phillips explained to him that a preacher of the gospel was nothing more than a developed Christian. All Christians were to preach by word or deed according to their ability. It was a life of humble service, not apart from the people and above them, not for prestige and security. It was to give one's body a living sacrifice for Christ, as all other Christians were bound to do, each in the way he best could give. This conception removed the professional glamour, and when he returned from the holidays he left the "preacher class," gave up his ministerial scholarship, and took his place among those who would be simple Christians serving in any capacity they chose.

His roommate at Henderson was Fred James, son of the doctor who had brought him into the world eighteen years before. He was beginning the work which would lead eventually to his own medical degree and his long service as physician in his father's place. The two boys had been close friends and classmates. Years later Armstrong spoke of him with the greatest affection, and paid him the unusual tribute, "He was good through and through, and as pure as a girl." The commendation reflects the high opinion of women which Armstrong held through a lifetime, but which the cynical today might consider quaint and amusing.

The second year the group from Gadsden roomed together at the home of a Mr. and Mrs. Booth, who lived where the Freed-Hardeman College Administration Building now stands. Mr. Booth was a preacher often away from home. The couple were deeply religious but informal in their expression of religious interests. Sometimes in the evening Mr. Booth called the boys into the living room and announced, "Boys, Fanny would like to have prayers tonight," and the group would read the Scriptures and kneel for a short period of prayer. This might occur again in a few days or sometimes not for two weeks. Mr. Booth explained that they did not want their prayers to become a matter of mechanical routine. This informality in prayer made a deep impression on Armstrong, who came to feel that people should pray, not at set times, but for what they needed when they needed it. It was simply a matter of talking with their Father.

At the Booths Hiram Reeves and Moses Dunlap joined Armstrong and James. The Booths followed the dignified custom of having the head of the table carve the meat, and when Mr. Booth was away preaching, as frequently happened, the task fell to one of the boys. None liked it. To escape the penalty all made a rush to the table and the slowest had to sit at the head and carve the roast. While Nelse, who was now over six feet tall, could never have contended in Olympic races, he and James and Dunlap always reached the table first and Reeves had to do the carving. On one occasion the race was so close and Hiram's disappointment so lugubrious that the three competitors burst into uncontrollable laughter and had to leave the table. Outside they hung over the paling fence and laughed it out, until they were suddenly sobered by realizing that Hiram was inside enjoying a good dinner and they might have to go to bed hungry. Although Hiram was large and slow of foot, he learned to do an excellent job of carving, a grace which Armstrong always avoided.

At Henderson for the first time Nelse became acquainted with one of those broad eruptions which, from the time of Martin Luther, have disturbed the unity and peace of churches. The famous old North Church of Boston had been divided a century before by the introduction of instrumental music in the worship. An organ had been used at Saint Louis in 1867, but it was unknown to the little group at Gadsden. Since a college was located at Henderson, however, the leaders of the new movement sent their state evangelist, A. I. Murrell, to Henderson for a long meeting. At its close the elders of the church announced that they were installing an organ to assist in the worship. Many of the members and some of the elders were opposed, but one elder was set on it, and the organ went in. Those who opposed submitted and continued to meet though they did not approve the action.

R. L. Whiteside, one of the students at the college, was already an experienced preacher. Though he was older and more mature than Armstrong, the college contact was the beginning of a life-long friendship.

When the organ was introduced in the worship at Henderson, Whiteside and two other boys left. Teachers had meetings with the boys and tried to keep them. To the Gadsden group the question was entirely new, and they stayed on. Mr. Booth later explained the issues to them. He was strongly opposed to the change, and as the four boys studied the question they came to the same point of view. This was young Armstrong's first experience with a movement which was dividing churches all over the country, leaving bitterness and faction where peace and brotherly love had once prevailed. It was a forerunner of other developments which were to bring sadness to his later years.

During the two years at Henderson he took part in a literary society, and at the close of the second year was on the commencement program for the class oration, a distinction which indicated his growing ability.

At the end of the year Armstrong left college. Out of money, but with his interest in books and the year of apprentice teaching under McDonald, he turned naturally to teaching. He applied for the Matthews school about four miles from Gadsden. The summer term opened with thirty-five students, which quickly grew to sixty-three. He had all eight grades. He had never taken a course in education and had to learn by experience how to manage, organize, discipline, and keep everybody quiet and busy while he taught group after group. But he was a born teacher, inspired respect, and never had trouble with discipline. Even the change from student to teacher at Gadsden was easily accomplished. At first students called him "Nelse" as they had the year before, but after he explained to them kindly that he was now their teacher, they addressed him with the respect due the new relationship.

That year's experience with McDonald was invaluable. Besides methods of instruction and organization he learned from McDonald one lesson in English which he never forgot. He was directing the Friday afternoon program and criticized one of the student speakers.

"John, you drug your feet all over the floor when you went up to speak. Try to pick them up next time," he said.

McDonald looked quickly around but said nothing till the students were gone, then turned to him, "Nelse, that wasn't 'drug'. That's a regular verb."

So in spite of his childhood habit "drag" was a regular verb the rest of his life.

With his natural good judgment, his understanding and love of others, and his exceptional ability as a teacher he quickly won the respect and love of his students. After finishing the year at the Matthews school he was employed by the Jackson school, by another school in Madison County, and at Gibson Station, continuing to teach in summers even after he had entered the Nashville Bible School.

His first year at the Matthews school was naturally his most trying experience. The day the county superintendent made his visit, however, everything was in order and the children were cooperative and quiet. All went well until the biggest girl in school, whose very size attracted attention, decided to go to the rear of the room for a drink. It was in the day before sanitary fountains, and the water bucket contained two long-handled dippers. To attract the attention of their visitor the girl decided to try an experiment which no one in that community had ever dreamed of. She took a dipper in each hand, put one inside the other, and filled them both with water, then attempted to drink from both dippers at once. The water poured down her chin and the front of her dress while the superintendent looked on in amused wonder and her teacher in horrified silence.

Since the time his childhood sweetheart saw him whipped it was thirteen years before he was again entangled in a love affair. In one of the rural districts, however, he met a very attractive young lady with natural, platinum blond hair. She was also an excellent housekeeper, who could cook to suit the taste of a king, which is also one way of reaching the heart. He boarded at her home during the term, and before the close of the year they were engaged to be married. But he explained that he must first finish college, and that would take at least two more years.

It was a fortunate delay. He was a lover of books with the heart of a scholar. He loved to learn and he loved to teach. With this kind of interest he soon became concerned about his sweetheart's lack of education. She had quit school in the grades. He thought of his mother who had gone to school only three months, but who had kept abreast of things and had given herself a measure of education by her constant reading. He attempted to interest his sweetheart in books, but she could not be bothered. He talked to her about a correspondence course and purchased one for her. She could not bring herself to finish the first easy lesson. In his discouragement it began to dawn upon him that he had made a serious mistake. If his life was to be devoted to teaching and study, how far might they drift apart in the years to come if his wife cared nothing for intellectual pursuits? Did they have enough in common to make a happy marriage?

He fought against the idea, but it persisted. He re-entered the college at Henderson for a third year, but was disappointed. The college had changed, and the work was poor. The president, G. A. Lewellen, and his vice-president, Hershell Thomas, were in a feud and would not speak to each other. President Lewellen, a scholarly man from Lexington, Kentucky, begged him to stay and graduate in the spring, but he was too unhappy with conditions. After Christmas he transferred to Union University at Jackson, where he found the work much better. But the religious atmosphere was different. Although students and teachers were friendly, he felt like an outsider.

In the summer he again returned to teaching, and that fall and winter taught at Gibson Station. After a long struggle between his sense of obligation to his fiancee and the growing certainty that marriage would only bring unhappiness to them both, he finally had a frank talk and asked to be released. To some the break would have been a small matter, but he shrank from causing pain, and he had to be honorable in seeking release. He was thankful in later years that never at any time had his conduct with the girl been different from what it would have been in the presence of her parents. He was glad when later she was happily married. But this narrow escape from a life-long tragedy led him to speak often to students about the seriousness of marriage and the care and good sense necessary in planning for it.

After his term at Union University he had decided to go to Lexington, where J. W. McGarvey's influence was strong. But that summer Jim H. Morton held a meeting at Gadsden and the Armstrongs invited him home. He had become acquainted with Nelse during the meeting and recognized his possibilities. At the table he suddenly asked, "Why don't you send this young man up to Lipscomb's school?"

It was the first knowledge they had about the Nashville Bible School, established by James A. Harding and David Lipscomb only two years before. As Morton told of the men who headed it and the work it offered, his words kindled a warm glow of enthusiasm. To Nelse it seemed the answer to his need. Morton's suggestion became a turning point in his life. It was to lead through experiences which would expand and deepen his heart and mind and qualify him for the profound influence he would later have on thousands of young people who came in touch with him.

Chapter 3

THE COLLEGE INSTRUCTOR

WITH OUR BEST judgment we plan our lives, reach our decisions, and many ask no other counsel. But those who live in touch with a Higher Wisdom receive a guidance better than human judgment. It comes naturally through close association with the Scriptures, but it comes also from influences we may not see, combinations of circumstances which close old doors and open new. For God "shapes our ends, rough-hew them how we will."

For John Nelson Armstrong conditions at Henderson closed one door. Union University was not satisfactory, and Lexington was not the happiest prospect. Then unexpectedly came information about a new college, and the right door opened. For in spite of Mr. Phillips' explanation about the ministry, young Armstrong still felt strongly drawn to it. He enjoyed teaching, but he could not be content filling a country schoolroom. Phillips was a good man and an excellent leader in the church. He had always refused to serve as an elder because he believed elders must be appointed to their office with a ceremony in which other elders or ministers conferred the responsibility by laying their hands upon them. But with the simple informality to which the church was accustomed, most members hesitated to use such ceremony. So without the title of elder he, nevertheless, did the work of one.

With his encouragement Nelse preached his first sermon. The subject, "What It Means to Be a Christian," he later developed into a week of sermons. This early theme revealed the emphasis which would later be found in all his teaching—the practical but penetrating insight into the Christian's responsibilities in daily living. With this first sermon the die was cast. He had again decided to preach. That he had not yet discarded the idea of professionalism is indicated by his purchase of the customary ministerial garb. Before going to Nashville he had bought the long Prince Albert coat, high turned-down collar, and square-toed shoes designed to set ministers off in a class apart and give them a dignity above the common man. Added to this was the usual mustache— and his was a splendid example of masculine glory—long, sweeping, black, always carefully trimmed and kept.

In this regalia he arrived at the Union Station in Nashville, October, 1893. Carrying his suitcase out to the streetcar, he waited patiently for the conductor to hitch up the mule, when suddenly the car started off and left him staring in disappointed amazement. It was his first experience with the electric trolley. Not wanting to show his ignorance of city ways, he walked nonchalantly about, assuming an air of sophistication, until another car stopped. This time he did not wait for the mule, and was soon zooming along the track at a speed he had never experienced before. He commented later, "I don't see how a fellow could possibly be as green as I was then." But the greenness quickly passed. He was soon to become acquainted with a new world and a different quality of culture. The bare simplicity of his childhood, however, gave him an enrichment of life which made it easy for him to associate freely with the poorest of men as well as with the educated and well-to-do. It led him to appreciate people for what they are, not for what they have or what they can show.

He had written the president of the college when he was to arrive, addressing him as the Reverend James A. Harding. Uncle Billy Dodd, who kept the boys' dormitory, met him and conducted him immediately to the little chapel, which would seat about forty or fifty people. Thirty-two students enrolled that morning.

After chapel he remained for President Harding's Bible class, during which the question of calling people "reverend" came up. Harding explained that the title "reverend" suggested an attitude which men should have only toward God. After the class Armstrong asked, "Brother Harding, did I understand you to say it was wrong to address preachers as 'reverend'?"

"Yes, that's right," Harding replied, and explained his reasons again. It is doubtful if he remembered the letter from the tall young man, but the young man remembered it always. It was the beginning of a profound change in his understanding of the status and work of a preacher.

After class Uncle Billy took him over to his room in the old Reed mansion. It was a dark red brick, gloomy and somber, dating from long before the Civil War and used during the war as a hospital. In its youth, it no doubt rang with the laughter of children, in its middle age it had groaned with the wounded and dying, and now in its tottering old age it enwrapped the eager young learners in the cold and gloom of its final decay. Built in the day when materials were cheap, slave labor abundant, and heat available for the mere cutting of trees and hauling of wood, the rooms were spacious, the ceilings high, and the windows large. The boys roomed on the second floor. The room assigned to Armstrong contained an iron bedstead, a small table, and two chairs. There were cracks through the wall, and the bricks had fallen out from beneath the great window, leaving a hole large enough, he said later, to throw a feist dog through. Bricks had also fallen from the back of the big fireplace, and most of the heat went up the chimney. Added to this the boys in the next room had to pass through his to get in and out, creating a constant disturbance.

To the old mansion the school had added a projection at the rear which served as dining room and kitchen. The administration building was a mere three-room wooden structure, one room of which was used for chapel and classes combined. President Harding and Dr. Grant lived in modest houses nearby.

Armstrong had been used to no luxury at home, but his accommodations here were worse than anything he had ever known since the family left the log cabin in his childhood. He became violently homesick and would have left at once, but he had paid the school nearly every cent he owned. There was nothing to do but stick it out.

When classes started, however, homesickness quickly vanished. In winter the wind whistled beneath the window and through the walls. Inside he studied in his overcoat and took it off when he went out. But he soon forgot the gloom and the chill, for he had found the greatest teachers it was ever his privilege to know. He said later that Union University was well equipped for the time, his teachers in English and Latin were Yale graduates, and his teachers in mathematics and science were outstanding.

"But Nashville, with no grounds, no buildings, no equipment (as men measure things) gave me the very best training I ever received in my life. I was electrified. There was something about the school and the men, intangible, indescribable, but deeply felt. Their vision, their courage, their humanity, their love of students, of people, of God and his word was immediately contagious, and we all responded."

He took Latin, Greek, and Bible with Harding, English with Dr. Grant, physiology with Dr. Ward, and another Bible class with David Lipscomb. They were all superior teachers, but Harding was a daily inspiration. He could double the lesson any time and make the students love it. He had no equal in leading students to feel they could do anything they set their hearts to do. He had a perfect faith in God's immediate presence and instant help. He was fond of quoting Paul's statement, "I can do all things through him that strengtheneth me." And as he spoke, with an intensity of feeling and conviction that was contagious, no one doubted that God would help him also as he had helped Paul. It is no wonder the little school sent out so many men of outstanding ability. Little men became big, timid men grew courageous under his teaching. In comparison with the inspiration from such teachers physical discomforts were as nothing.

Though less inspiring to many, Lipscomb was greatly esteemed by all thoughtful students. Armstrong especially appreciated him for his sound judgment and practical teaching. He had the older, more mature and experienced men. But most of these early students were mature. Many had been preaching for some time and had come for further study. Among them was John E. Dunn, one of Armstrong's roommates and a life-long friend, Sim Jones from Canada, who later started Beamsville Christian College in Ontario, Webb McQuiddy, L. K. Harding, J. A. Harding's oldest son, R. C. White, another roommate of whom Armstrong always spoke with affection, Lewis Yeagley, A. D. Rogers, Trahern, Rutledge, and William J. Bishop, another roommate who later became a missionary to Japan. All these were dedicated students. Armstrong usually tried to be in bed by ten, but he often awoke at midnight or after to see Bishop asleep over a book at his desk.

But not all were as mature as this group. There was young Shaube, who was preparing to preach, and whom Trahern and Rogers convinced, in his innocence, that they were a committee to pass on the licensing of young ministers. They compelled him to preach for them the same sermon three times before agreeing to "pass" him. There was also good-hearted Abraham Foster from Glory, Texas. His fellow students had great fun teasing him about a maidenly school teacher who, they declared, was "going to Glory to lay her head on Abraham's bosom."

L. K. Harding, son of President Harding, was an exceptionally brilliant student. A few minutes before a Latin class he could rush in to Armstrong and Rutledge and say, "Boys, let's get this Latin lesson." They may have worked on it two or three hours, but in a few minutes he harvested the results of their labor and always made one of the highest grades in the class.

While Armstrong enjoyed all his courses, he was most deeply impressed by his Bible and Greek. Greek was the joy of his life and he buried himself in it. Under Harding he read Xenophon, Thucydides, Plato, Homer, and other Greek classics. He loved the *Apology* especially, both for the integrity of Socrates and for the grace and beauty of Plato's language. As his knowledge of Greek became richer he called it "the most perfect instrument with which to express thought ever used by mortal tongue, the language that could express the most delicate shades of meaning, the language in which we can almost read the very impulses of the heart of the writer." It was the perfect instrument for God to give men a revelation of himself.

A regular college activity was a meeting each Monday night in which young men discussed any questions of interest. The meetings were usually closed by Harding himself with an enthusiastic speech which might sometimes last an hour. But under the spell of his voice no one grew tired. Often on controversial questions leaders on both sides of the issue were brought in for a discussion or a series of discussions. At such times, though men spoke their convictions freely and vigorously, and emotions might run high, the meetings usually closed in a spirit of friendship and goodwill.

In one such meeting Armstrong, who loved simplicity, had strongly condemned the tendency to create a formal organization, like a Dorcas Society, to do the work which all are obligated to do, simply as individual Christians. Another speaker heatedly charged him with exaggeration and misrepresentation. Armstrong replied with a quotation from his critic's speech that was equally exaggerated. The air became

highly charged and all felt the tension. The next Monday
night Armstrong arose and apologized to his critic for
having been too severe with him. Everyone expected the
other to apologize also, or at least respond, for he had
been equally severe, but he remained silent. Armstrong rose
instantly in the estimation of the audience. But in such
free discussions he was learning to differ from others even
heatedly and yet, with humility, to respect and love his
opponent, experiences which influenced profoundly his whole
life.

Harding constantly influenced his students to undertake
new tasks. Preachers were few and the churches constantly
in need. When calls came, Harding sent boys out whether
they had much experience or little. They would gain experience by going. So when a call came from the Tenth
Street church, Harding said, "Yes, Armstrong and Foster
will preach for you—one in the morning and one at night."
It was the second time Armstrong had preached, but the
place and the occasion were completely different. This was
not Matthews country school but a city church in the state's
capital, and his mouth went dry and his mind closed up. He
had used an hour for the sermon at home. At Tenth Street
he ran through his material in twenty-five minutes and with
a sense of shame and defeat had to sit down. Walter Harding, J. A. Harding's brother, who was in the audience com-
plimented him highly, but Armstrong felt disgraced. It did
not occur to him that perhaps the very shortening of time
may have increased the effectiveness of the sermon. But he
could not, even in later years, forget the sense of embarrassment, and never felt completely at home when speaking
at Tenth Street.

The first year at Nashville Armstrong paid all his expenses. But the second year his treasury was empty. He
could pay board and room, which in those good old days
was ten dollars a month, but with characteristic generosity
Harding waived the charges for tuition and fees. At the
close of the second year, through Harding's recommendation

he had obtained a teaching position in Mississippi which would have paid a hundred dollars a month. But on the last night of school Harding said, "If you'd rather come back and teach three classes in Greek for your room and board, we should be very glad to have you." It did not take three minutes for him to decide. As an instructor in Greek he would gain invaluable experience, have an opportunity to continue advanced studies, and enjoy the rich friendships he had formed.

Two people, however, had grave doubts about the appointment. Harding was such a brilliant teacher that Lipscomb doubted if any instructor could successfully follow him. When Armstrong's work began, Lipscomb slipped quietly into the room to listen. After several days he said to Harding in his drawling way, "Well, Brother Harding, that Greek is all right. Armstrong can do it."

Lipscomb had a genuine affection for the young instructor, but he also had a dry humor which he often used to puncture the ego of his students. When Armstrong, uplifted a little by the thought of his new responsibilities, came to explain that he would have to drop his Bible class, Lipscomb drawled, "Well, Brother Armstrong, I guess we'll have to try to get along without you." And the young instructor felt suddenly deflated.

The other doubter was Harding's own daughter, Woodson. The Nashville Bible School was established for men, but even the first year it was invaded by girls. A Miss Mamie Griffin and a Miss Lily Elam insisted on coming. They lived off campus, and since the school had no library or study hall, the two came to the Harding home between classes. The second year there were no girls, perhaps because the school had moved to new quarters. The third year, on a new campus, Woodson Harding was admitted with two friends, Jennie Hammond, a beautiful girl who died of tuberculosis a few years later, and Essie Odom, who later became Mrs. John E. Dunn.

Woodson had first year Greek with her father, but when she learned that he was turning the Greek over to the young assistant, she was highly indignant.

"Why do you want to give your Greek to that long, lanky boy?" she demanded. "I want to take Greek with you."

"Just wait, my dear," her father replied. "I think he can teach you all the Greek you can learn."

He was right. From the beginning students saw no lack. Their young instructor knew his subject thoroughly and was both an exact and an inspiring teacher. In the years ahead his students were heading the Greek departments at David Lipscomb College, Thorp Springs Christian College, and Abilene Christian College as well as Harding College.

At the end of the year, 1896, he was graduated along with John E. Dunn, Webb McQuiddy, and R. C. White, receiving a diploma, with the degree to be conferred later. He now entered upon full-time teaching, but also continued his advanced studies. Along with Greek he taught Latin, and John T. Glenn, one of his first students in Latin, was a constant source of delight. He said of Glenn later, "He and I learned the first rule: i.e., to love one another. In a little while he took my place in the teaching of Latin at Nashville. It is not exaggerating the fact to say that Glenn has never had a superior in all the Bible school faculties as a teacher of Latin, and I think only one equal." The unnamed "equal" was Dr. L. K. Harding.

Armstrong now gave up summer schools around Gadsden for evangelistic work in and around Nashville. He spent one summer preaching for the church in Scottsboro, Alabama, holding their meeting in the days as he said later, "before I knew how to preach." It was a valuable experience. The congregation was small and in the absence of men to take the lead a Sister Stewart and a Sister Gregory had invited him to come. Mr. Gregory loved the church, partly because he was devoted to his wife who loved the church, but he was a successful lawyer and his profession claimed most of his interest and time.

Armstrong's introduction to his summer work at Scottsboro was a surprise which one with less sense of humor might have found disconcerting. He arrived late at night and the Gregorys had their servant meet him at the station and take him to his room at their beautifully furnished home. The next morning Gregory knocked at his door and took him down to breakfast. He looked him over carefully and then said in his brusque, hearty voice, "Well, Armstrong, I believe you'll do. Stewart was talking to me yesterday. You know his older daughter ran away with a fellow a few months ago, but he has a younger daughter still at home. When he learned you were coming, he said, 'Gregory, I hope that new preacher is so ugly my daughter won't even look at him!' And by golly he has sure got his wish."

"Why, Mr. Gregory," exclaimed his wife, "I wouldn't say that."

"Well, it's the truth," he said.

A slow quizzical smile lighted their guest's eyes and he said, "I'm glad Mr. Stewart won't have to keep his guns loaded and his doors locked at any rate." And Mrs. Gregory burst into a relieved laugh.

But Armstrong was never sensitive about his appearance. At first many people may have had Gregory's impression, but in a few minutes the plainness of Armstrong's face dissolved in the warmth of human interest which lighted the eyes and softened the features with a radiance of inward beauty. A student once wrote that when he first saw Armstrong's picture he thought he was extremely ugly. "But when I arrived on the campus and walked into the administration building, he was the first person I met. He greeted me and inquired where I was from. When I told him Wills Point, Texas, he replied that he had held a meeting there some thirty years before. There was something about that first meeting that changed everything. From then on Brother Armstrong had the most lovely face of any man I ever knew."

Others were similarly impressed. One has written, "There was nothing about him attractive on the outside, but you soon forgot that as you saw the beauty of the inner man shining through." And Dow Merritt, many years after he was a student, said, "At a distance he looked gray and lonely and forbidding. Near at hand he was pink and his personality was magnetic and irresistible. His memory is sweet. In all my fifty-seven years I have never had any other feeling for him than love."

Armstrong's features were Lincolnesque in ruggedness, the nose long and with a suggestion of Roman strength, the mouth firm but sensitive and generous, the chin strong and well formed, the brow high and crowned in earlier years with a heavy mass of wavy black hair, the legacy of two grandmothers. The eyes, deep-set under cliffs of straight black brows, were at times calmly placid, but in the heat of discussion could flash with fire or glow with animation, and in friendly conversation could light up with kindly humor. It was a face whose intelligence, strength, and inner glow of human kindness instantly won the confidence of men, and students sought him for advice about their most intimate problems.

The meeting at Scottsboro was sluggish and the attendance small. Mrs. Stewart was worried but tried to encourage him.

"I don't want you to be discouraged about the crowds," she said, for there simply were no crowds.

"But why is the attendance so small?" he asked. She hesitated a moment, considering.

"I think one thing is that Brother Gregory is the leader and his language is not what it ought to be. Then the Gregorys and the Rorexes play cards nearly every night. I love them both, but this has been a block to the church for years."

The Gregorys and Rorexes did not gamble. Though members of the congregation disapproved the use of cards associated with gambling, they had made no protest. The condemnation was from people outside who felt that such conduct was inconsistent with Christian living.

When Armstrong returned to his room, he found Gregory reading the paper while his wife was arranging flowers on the table. He was a guest in their home. His innate courtesy shrank from any rudeness; he disliked to cause unpleasantness or pain, and especially to those who had treated him with such kindness. The easiest course was simply to remain silent and hope conditions might gradually change. But he had a conscience that strangely never considered his own ease or advantage, that had to act even if action was unpleasant and hard. Here an ulcer was affecting the health of the church, and those involved had not recognized it. As a minister was he not, like his Lord, a physician to heal the illness of his people? He could defer the matter till later; but he knew what he must eventually do, and he was never one to postpone unpleasant tasks. Still it was with much fear that he hesitated, and then sat down.

"Sister Gregory," he began, "I have just heard that you and Brother Gregory and the Rorexes play cards nearly every night, and that this has brought reproach upon the church and hindered its growth."

"Well," said Mrs. Gregory, slowly, as she dropped her flowers and came toward him, "if it is a reproach to the church, we won't play cards any more."

Mr. Gregory, who was always outspoken and blunt, but was also generous and big-hearted, and welcomed the frankness of others, threw down his paper and looked up. "Well, Daisy, there's no doubt about that," he said.

"Then we'll not play any more in my house," she declared.

And the card playing stopped. With his knowledge of the world Gregory understood the attitude of people toward their playing, but he loved good games and good company. To have these pleasant evenings banished might have caused resentment in a different kind of person, but Gregory was perfectly fair. He could not blame the young preacher for telling him what he already knew.

During the summer Armstrong often drove into the country to preach to another little group. The weather was hot, and Mr. Gregory, who loved his ease in the cool of the evening, could not understand him.

"I wouldn't work my head off going out to that place to preach. Those people are not worth saving anyway," he remonstrated.

But secretly he admired the persistence and earnestness of the young man. It showed a faith and a zeal he did not posses and could hardly comprehend, but which he respected. The contributions of the little church were small, and Gregory became ashamed of what they were giving the preacher. But instead of appealing to the members to do more, with characteristic brusqueness he walked in one day, threw him a five dollar bill, and said, "Here's some filthy lucre for you," and walked out.

But no one can estimate the power of goodness, of a deep and sincere faith, of unselfish love, when we associate with these qualities day after day. In spite of his gruffness Gregory was more deeply influenced than he knew. One day he asked Armstrong if he believed in prayer.

"Yes," Armstrong replied, "I certainly do."

"I don't," he said, shortly, "except for one's sins."

Months later, however, his wife Daisy became desperately ill and grew rapidly worse. The doctors finally gave up all hope. Gregory was stunned with grief, for he loved Daisy more than his life. Up to that moment he had felt no lack in meeting any emergency. With his brains and ability he needed no help against opponents at the bar. He had always given his wife anything she needed, anything money could buy. He would have fought the world to protect her against the smallest pain. But now he was helpless; he was struggling with an invisible enemy against which money and brains had no power, and he knew no other weapons with which to fight. In his despair he did what all others finally do—he thought of God. But with his long skepticism about prayer he doubted if he was on speaking terms with him. But he knew one who was, and he went down the street to Sister Stewart, whose faith and consecration he knew. It was a shaken and humbled man who stood at her door.

"Sister Stewart, the doctors all say that Daisy has to die," he said. "If there is any one in Scottsboro God will hear, it's you. I want you to pray for Daisy."

Sister Stewart did, and the whole church did. Daisy got well and outlived her husband many years.

Armstrong recognized that what the little church at Scotts-boro needed most was a dedication of their own hearts to the Christ. In spite of himself Gregory felt the impact of his preaching, and he said with a hint of humor, "Armstrong, I'm going to write Lipscomb that you have spent the whole summer preaching only to the church."

The summer ended, but its memories always remained in the heart of the young preacher. They remained also in the hearts of the people he served. Some years later when he was president of the college in Missouri, he was asked to return to Nashville to speak at a reunion at the school. The Gregorys made the trip to Nashville just to see him again. As Gregory greeted him, he said with his usual bluntness, but with a hard, warm clasp of the hand, "Armstrong, I came all the way up here just to see some of your sort again."

On the same reunion program James A. Harding, then president of Potter Bible College, Sim Jones from the college in Canada, and Lipscomb of the Nashville Bible School all spoke. Sister Lipscomb said that Armstrong had the best prepared speech on the program. But he was terrified at the thought of speaking on such an occasion and had practiced incessantly, stealing over to the chapel at night and speaking in the dark until he knew perfectly what he wanted to say. Joe S. Warlick, who was always a great wit as well as a great debater, remarked,

"I wondered before I came to this reunion, just what a reunion was. Now I find it's just preaching."

"Yes," said Elam, "but there's preaching, and *preaching*."

Armstrong in these early years was learning the difference between "preaching and *preaching*." It was a time of rapid growth, from the years when his words, as he later said, simply "fell at his feet," to the years when they moved powerfully the hearts of his hearers. Under the teaching of Harding and Lipscomb he had learned what simple un-denominational Christianity was and the real responsibilities of a gospel preacher. He became ashamed of his Prince Albert coat long before he had money to buy a new one.

Although from habit Lipscomb continued to wear the Prince Albert till he died, and Harding till after he retired from teaching, Armstrong threw his away as soon as he could purchase an ordinary suit. He also shaved the handsome long mustache. He wanted nothing to separate him from the people he loved and served.

But this was only a symbol of the transformation which was taking place. As he saw the picture of the Christ in his studies and in the lives of the men with whom he worked, he came to love the sincerity, the deep humility, the utter unselfishness, the singleness of purpose, the deep conviction, and the perfect trust which were reflections of the glory which John saw, a "glory as of the only begotten son of God." And these qualities were also growing in him.

Chapter 4

THE PROFESSOR'S ROMANCE

LOVE IS THE most familiar of emotions, but its ways are strange past finding out.

Second year Greek was in session—six mature men and one slip of a girl. There was R. L. Whiteside with his hair already thinning and with his great dome of forehead projecting over his sharp eyes, giving the impression of gigantic intellect. He was a mature preacher at West Tennessee Christian College seven or eight years before. With a wife and children he was again trying to advance his education in the face of almost impossible financial difficulties. There was Lewis Yeagley, small, with black eyes, black hair, generous nose and mouth, gentle and impetuous, preparing to preach in Michigan.

With men like these Miss Woodson Harding seemed strangely out of place. She was sixteen, and her girlish face, sparkling, roguish eyes, and vivacious laughter were a striking contrast with their somber earnestness. But President Harding believed that the mastery of Latin and Greek, but especially Greek, would give the mental discipline, the habit of logical, clear thinking which would enable one to solve almost any problem. Woodson shared her father's faith in Greek as well as his great love of reading. She could hold her own with anyone in the class. But it was not easy, for this new instructor, now twenty-five, expected his students to know everything. E. G. Cullum relates that in the examination on the verb *luo*, with its hundreds of forms, he accidentally omitted the letter *upsilon* in one word. Armstrong first gave him a hundred, but since so few had perfect papers, he checked again, found the one error, and changed the grade to ninety-nine and nine tenths.

He was never satisfied with a free translation, no matter how smooth. He wanted to be sure his students understood every construction and the implication of the language. One morning "Woodie" was translating a difficult passage from the *Memorabilia*.

"But assuredly," the accuser said, "he [Socrates] made those who talked with him to take no notice of the established laws, saying how foolish it was to elect the officers of a state by beans, when nobody wants to take a pilot elected by beans, or an architect, or a flute-player."

"Let's stop a moment, Miss Woodson," interrupted the instructor. "What does Socrates mean by electing officers by beans?"

"It must have been some way of voting, but it was a funny way—using beans."

"That's right. Instead of marking ballots as we do in our country, the candidates drew beans out of a jar. Those who reached in and drew out a white bean were elected; those who got the black lost. Actually people did not vote; they merely used a lottery."

"Brother Cullum, why did Socrates consider such selection foolish?"

"It took no brains or ability for a man to put his hand in and draw out a bean. The most incompetent might get the white beans."

"True. In defense of the Athenian custom, however, all candidates were screened by the city fathers to be sure they possessed the qualifications necessary for the office. With such screening the Athenians felt the selection by lottery prevented unscrupulous candidates from bribing the people for votes, either by outright gifts of money or by promises they never intended to keep, as sometimes happens in our country. But, Miss Woodson, you translated *huperoran* as 'take no notice of' the established laws. Do you suppose there may be a better rendering of the term?"

"I suppose so, but that seemed to make sense."

"Yes, in the sense that if you take no notice of a person you may be deliberately insulting him. Your lexicon also suggests the term 'despise.' That would actually represent the charge against Socrates."

"But did you notice the form of the word *nomoon*? What case is it?"

"It's accusative, isn't it?"

"I'm asking you. Is it?"

She looked up quickly, but could tell nothing from the slow, mischievous smile that lighted his eyes. He would tease the same way if she were right or wrong. He must not scare her into making a mistake. She looked at the sentence again.

"Yes, it's accusative, the object of *huperoran*."

"I guess that's from Miss Woodson's grammar, class," he smiled. "But if you check the one we are using, you'll find the accusative spelled with an *omicron—nomon*. Here we have the genitive. It is the object of the verb, but if you'll consult your lexicon and also the rule for the partitive genitive in your grammar, you will find a long list of verbs, including *hupereroo*, which take the genitive under certain conditions.

"And this is one of many instances which show the extreme exactness of the Greek language. If the accuser had meant only that Socrates kept his companions from *noticing* or *seeing* something, the verb would have taken the accusative. But the genitive is derogative, shows condemnation. Socrates, it is charged, made them *look down on, scorn,* or *despise* the laws. It is this exactness of the Greek that made

it the most precise language ever developed, the perfect instrument through which God could reveal his will to men."

Embarrassed and with flushed face "Woodie" wanted to
throw her book at him. She rushed from Greek to piano
and banged the keys with such fury that the instructor
finally changed her piano lessons to a period preceding
Greek.

What a beginning for romance! But who can predict the
ways of love? One thing only seems essential—you have to
see before you can love. When Armstrong entered the college three years before, he had noticed Harding's "little
girl," then thirteen, but to him she was only a child. Now
in a group of six dour masculine faces even a blind man
could see the laughter and mischief and youth of a sixteen-
year-old girl. Striking too was the combination of almost
childlike loveliness with an intelligence that could hold its
own with the maturest of the men. He loved to tease her,
but his admiration grew each day. She was completely different from the girl with the beautiful blond hair who
could never be induced to read simple English, and to whom
Greek would have been as impossible as a leap to the
moon.

Being the only instructor for the class, he too was not
hard to see. But the sight was not always favorable. She
had not wanted him to take her father's class, and his
teasing when she missed her grammar was infuriating. Still
he knew his work and was a wonderful teacher. Her father
perhaps could not have been better. But he was nothing
but a teacher.

Then circumstances took a hand. Woodson and the three
girls who roomed at her father's home wanted to attend a
meeting at the Ryman Auditorium. Her father was too busy
to go, but he suggested that they ask Armstrong to accompany them. He was unencumbered with many duties
and was thoroughly dependable; he could be trusted with
the girls anywhere. Perhaps since she was the President's
daughter, the lot fell to Woodie to ask, and he gladly
agreed to go. Since she was the only one in his class, and

since it would be humiliating to make him tag along behind like a watchdog, she found herself from courtesy walking with him. To her surprise she found him very interesting, kind and attentive.

The chaperoning continued at intervals for a year or more. Then suddenly their eyes were opened. They were returning from a meeting on a night magical with stars and moonlight. As she looked up at the sky she suddenly said, "You have a birthday on January 6."

He smiled quickly. "I know someone else who has a birthday on January 6. I wonder how much difference there is between them." Then they counted the difference—exactly nine years.

"But that doesn't matter," he said. "There is ten years between my father and mother."

The words were out before he could catch them. He could bite off his tongue, but that would never bring them back. The little member which no man can tame had suddenly lighted a great fire. It startled them both with what had been secretly building up in his heart, what he had never admitted even to himself. In confusion and embarrassment he spoke hardly a word more, and whether he even saw the stars any longer is doubtful, for between them a new star had arisen, to him so bright he could not face it, to her so incongruous she could not believe it.

Rushing into the house, she cried, "Girls, I had a proposal tonight!" and burst into hysterical laughter. As she told the others, they all laughed with her. For days after, when they saw the tall, slightly stooped professor cross the campus or met him coming out of a classroom, they could hardly suppress the smiles.

But the Greek continued. The instructor showed the faintest trace of embarrassment as her eyes twinkled up at him, and he never referred again to "Miss Woodson's grammar." He even seemed at times a little reluctant to pass a question to the "next," as he had so easily done before.

The chaperoning continued. Only now she took a strange new interest in that "mother" who had married a man ten years older. What kind of woman was she? What kind of man was that father? And what had their son been doing all those years before he came to teach her Greek? There were so many things to learn, and so many things to tell. And all of it so interesting and new.

> Let me not to the marriage of true minds
> Admit impediments

wrote one who knew the ways of love better than all his countrymen. The Nashville school certainly proved his faith. In spite of every barrier love found a way. At the Nashville Bible School the boys and girls were never alone together. The girls could have company three times a year—on Thanksgiving, Christmas, and the last day of school—but always with chaperons. They could talk with the men a few minutes after the Sunday and Monday night meetings. But Armstrong was away preaching on Sundays and the field was wide open for all his rivals.

And these were many. One, when he saw the trend of things, told her bluntly, "I'd rather see you in your grave than married to Armstrong!" Consigning her to the grave did not suggest to Woodie a deep concern for her happiness.

Another, who was furiously jealous when she talked with any one else, always had someone watch her when he was away. When he saw she was interested in the young professor, he ridiculed the stoop of his shoulders inherited from his father.

"He looks just like a blackbird roosting on a rail!" he declared. But his jealousy kindled her interest even more.

When his friend, Abraham Foster, began showing an interest also, Armstrong called him aside and said, "Look here, Brother Foster, if you mean business by paying attention to Miss Woodie, all right. But if you don't, I want you to quit."

Perhaps "Brother Foster," being a good friend, withdrew for friendship's sake, or perhaps he had little hope of success. At any rate he dropped out of the race, if he was

really ever in. There was now one down and four to go.
But one of these was a constant irritation. He was quite
tall, and when the Monday night meeting closed he quickly
stepped over the rows of chairs to get to Woodson first,
while the young professor had to move with dignity down
the aisle and found himself cut out. He could only walk on
with a heavy heart, and he found it hard to muster a smile
next day in Greek. He tried in vain to get her to avoid the
persistent chair-vaulter. "Just step aside and ignore him,"
he urged.

"You step a little faster yourself if you want to talk to
me," she retorted.

But love overcomes its difficulties. Woodson's close friend,
Clara Benedict, lived just off the campus, and Woodie could
visit her freely. Since Dr. Bryan, another of the young professors, was paying attention to Clara, he and Armstrong became great cronies. It was easy for the two teachers to call
at the Benedict home and let Mrs. Benedict play the chaper-
on for a change.

Two accounts have come down of the engagement. Woodson, years later, declared that she accepted him on one condition. She knew that if she married a teacher in a Christian
school she would have a life of sacrifice ahead. This she did
not fear; she had always known sacrifice, often extreme. But
for the past five years her father and mother had kept
college girls in their home. This she did not want.

"I want my own home," she said. "I don't want to spend
the rest of my life in a dormitory."

Armstrong, however, declared there was no such stipula-
tion; she surrendered unconditionally. At any rate, he declared, he had never asked her to live in a dormitory; he
had merely hinted, and she herself had suggested it. But if
love "hopeth all things," it also "endureth all things," and
never fails. So they were married, and spent forty very happy
years together keeping girls' dormitories.

After the engagement Armstrong was permitted to visit
her once a week in the home, but the chaperoning stopped.
Big brothers are often critical of younger sisters, and Leon

Harding had riddled all Woodson's suitors till now. But he had a genuine respect and affection for Armstrong, who had often helped him master his Latin lesson in a matter of minutes. Her father had said, "All right, my dear, if you want Armstrong, go to it. He is droll sometimes, but he is every inch a man."

Only Lipscomb was doubtful. He loved both of them but he was uneasy about Armstrong's health. "He is the most outstanding young man we have," he protested to her father, "but he will die of tuberculosis before they have been married any time."

To Woodson, once the momentous decision was made, a new problem arose. What should she call the man she was going to marry? After a custom now completely outdated, young men at the Nashville Bible School always used "Miss" in speaking of girls, girls used "Brother" in speaking of the young men, and wives used the dignified title of "Mr." in speaking to or about their husbands. Woodson had always called her teacher "Brother Armstrong," but now a change had come.

"What are you going to call me when we are married?" he asked her one evening, when she had continued to use the "brotherly" title.

"Well, I suppose I'll call you Mr. Armstrong as my mother and my grandmothers have always done," she replied.

"No, you don't," he said emphatically. "I don't intend to be a stranger in my own home."

"What shall I call you then?" she asked, puzzled.

"My people have always called me Nelse," he replied. "Would that be all right?"

"Nelse? I could never call you Nelse," she said.

"Why? It's short for Nelson."

"When I was a child I knew an old man named Nelson who simply scared me to death. In the morning his beard might be six inches long; in the afternoon it reached down to his waist. I knew only a wizard or someone supernatural could grow a beard that fast, and when I met him I ran as fast as my heels could carry me. I didn't know till years later that he often stuffed his beard under his vest to keep it from blowing around. But "Nelse" would remind me of him, and I don't mean to be afraid of my husband."

"Well, what about John? My name is John Nelson, you know."

"Anything but John! Half the old men around here are called John. I think I'll just say Jack," she teased.

"Oh, no," he protested. "That's a nickname, and I never liked nicknames."

Even the dignified grandmother took a hand later. "Jack!" she sniffed. "Humph, sounds like you're calling your dog."

She was only teasing, but Jack it became. Through the long summer at Scottsboro she addressed him in a daily letter, "Dear Jack." He replied, "With love, Nelse," or "John," till the final letter which, in resignation, closed "With love, Jack." To his surprise he found, like many another, that love had made a new man of him!

The wedding came in June, immediately after Woodson's graduation. She was now nineteen. The groom wore his first tailored suit, selected with her assistance. The bride and her four child attendants were in white. Only a few close friends were supposed to come, but Harding, whose generosity knew no bounds, the day before the great event, without the knowledge of the family, had invited everybody on the campus and in the neighborhood. The house was filled to overflowing.

Woodson had insisted that her father perform the ceremony, but he was too emotional to trust himself. He merely promised to think about it, and either he or his father, J. W. Harding, would do it. J. W. Harding of Winchester, Kentucky, had the reputation of having married more couples than any other man in the state. He had a courtly, gracious manner and always followed the custom of kissing or "saluting" the bride.

Woodson did not know till she stepped into the room who was to perform the ceremony, but she had declared that if her grandfather performed it, she was not going to let him kiss her; she would give her first kiss to her husband. But she was reckoning without the skill of the venerable "saluter." As the ceremony closed, before she had time to move, her grandfather stepped forward gracefully, in perfect time with the music, put his arm around her, gave her his courtly kiss, and stepped back without missing a beat.

The couple left immediately for Gadsden. Their friend, Charley Dorris, had been married a few days earlier, and a group of boys had given him and his bride a rousing shivaree, making the night hideous with discordant whistles, beatings on pans and drums, and blood-curdling warwhoops. One of the boys asked Woodson what she thought of it.

"Disgusting! It's the crudest thing I ever heard of!" she declared.

"O ho! O ho!" he laughed. "Just watch out! We'll give you a better one yet."

But by shivaree time they were far on their way to Memphis. As the train chugged to a stop at Gadsden, the crowd loafing around the depot was larger than usual, for it had been rumored that Nelse was bringing home his city bride. Men left off whittling and stared down from the porches in front of the stores. Unused to the unpaved streets with their ruts and rocks, Woodson stumbled and nearly fell.

"My God, he's married a crippled woman!" rumbled a voice in the crowd.

Nelse was anxious for his people to love his young wife and for her to love them. But he also understood the gulf that lay between them. For years she had hardly been out of the city; they had never been in one. She frankly preferred flagstone and concrete walks to the dust and mud of country roads. For several years she had known little but Latin, Greek, logic, and the rest of the college courses; they hardly knew such subjects existed. Added to this, Nelse's mother had never wanted the children to marry, and always felt that no girl was good enough for her boys. She had found fault with all the girls they had liked. It was a delicate situation, but his joy at being home again, and his love which embraced them all, were so contagious that the gulf was temporarily bridged, and the visit was a happy one.

Ed, the younger brother, who had been in Nashville and had seen the bride, met them with a team of handsome, high-stepping horses, and helped to make the visit easy. Even the weather cooperated. Strawberries should have long been gone, but late rains and cool days had brought a second crop. They gathered heaping gallons and served them with cream and sugar and hot buttered biscuits. Nelse outdistanced all his brothers by eating thirteen bowls. What marvelous power love and good strawberries can give!

The young bride had much to learn of country ways. On the meager income of even as great and successful a preacher as her father, they had to watch carefully in the city to make ends meet. But here where money was even more scarce, Mother Armstrong cooked berries down to a pulp, poured off the delicious juice for the pigs to drink, and continued to cook the pulp into a thick waxy jam, which, spread on buttered biscuits, was food for the gods. When the city bride remonstrated, "Mother Armstrong, let me take this juice home with me; we can use it at home," she merely replied, "Tut, tut, child; it isn't worth anything. Let the hogs have it."

Then when Mother Armstrong set out a great stewer of potatoes to peel, the economical bride again protested.

"But, Mother Armstrong, we can't eat all these potatoes."

"Let's peel them anyway. If we don't eat them, the pigs will," she replied. And the bride peeled, still wondering why people cooked for pigs what many in the city found it hard or impossible to buy.

Armstrong was anxious for the family to love his wife, and nearly every summer, until they moved West, they spent some time at Gadsden, Woodson often remaining there while he was away in meetings. His father, who was naturally friendly and loveable, was instantly won, as were the other children. But it was several years before Woodson felt that Mother Armstrong accepted her fully. When Nelse's older brother James David died leaving four children, Mother Armstrong took Tolbert and the youngest child, a little daughter Rosebud. Nelse and Woodson took two boys, Early and J. D., to rear with their own daughter Pattie Hathaway. Woodson was an accomplished designer and seamstress, and could take old garments or inexpensive materials and convert them into attractive new dresses for her little girl. When she offered to make Rosebud a dress each time she made one for Pattie Hathaway, Mother Armstrong was finally won.

The visits to Gadsden, with its luscious strawberries, were enjoyable brief vacations. One year, because Armstrong was continually bothered by sore throat, the doctor suggested that he let his beard grow to shield him from the wind and cold. Woodson urged him to shave it off before he went home, but he wanted to surprise his mother. He had sent Woodson and Pattie Hathaway on ahead until he could close a meeting; then with the luxurious growth of black beard and long mustache, he knocked at his mother's door, and in sepulchural tones, "Could you give a poor old man a bite to eat, and a place to spend the night?" he asked.

His mother, almost afraid of the bushy stranger yet wanting to be courteous, stood blocking the doorway.

"No, I'm sorry," she said. "My son's family is here; the house is full, and we are expecting him back some time today." She started to close the door, but his quick laugh made her turn.

"Why, Ma, don't you know me?" he asked.

Ma did, and she was furious. She broke into a torrent of tears at the trick he had played on her, and the glorious beard came off that night, never to reappear.

Chapter 5

EXPANDING HORIZONS

TO J. N. ARMSTRONG the seven years following his marriage were a time of rapid growth. In addition to fulltime teaching he now combined increasing evangelistic work, further advanced studies toward the master's degree, and writing as an associate editor of *The Way,* a new journal edited by President Harding.

As a full-time professor with a new wife to support his salary was $16.66 a month, but house rent took $10 of this. Harding suggested that they board Leon Harding and another boy, and the bride who did not want to keep a dormitory readily agreed. Leon paid $10 a month for his board, but unhappily the other boy paid nothing. They later served meals to a few other boys. All teachers had similar salaries except President Harding, who, since he now taught only Bible, took no salary from the school. But there were no complaints. To them the college was an unselfish missionary service and they gave their lives to it with joy.

Needless to say, the salaries at Nashville had to be supplemented by preaching on Sundays and by evangelistic work through the summers. The summer meetings especially gave

Armstrong increasing power, and the range of his activities extended from Tennessee to all the states around. Most of the meetings contained no incidents of unusual interest, but a few illustrate difficulties an evangelist in those days had to endure and the resourcefulness required in unexpected emergencies.

For instance, illustrative of the increasing skill with which he could adapt his preaching to local conditions, Armstrong found that in one congregation one of the elders had become a virtual dictator instead of a shepherd of the flock. One morning he had become so furiously angry that he locked the church door, forcing the congregation to meet in a grove outside. When Armstrong was called for a meeting and learned of the condition, he preached each morning on the qualifications and work of the elders, trying to show both elders that they were not qualified for their work. It was done so tactfully and yet so forcefully, that finally the tyrannical one interrupted the sermon.

"Brother Armstrong," he said, "I know I'm not qualified to be an elder, but I've been appointed, and how can I get out of it?"

"Brother Haynes, that's exactly what I've been wanting you to see," Armstrong replied. "You don't have to get out; you've never really been in, because you have never been qualified."

When he relinquished his position of authority, the congregation made rapid progress.

At another place a young girl from a prominent family had trusted her lover too far and had become an unmarried mother. She was deeply penitent, made a public confession, and did all she could to overcome the injury to the church. But it was the kind of sin about which all tongues wagged, and the leading elder, who announced her confession, felt the heavy condemnation of the group. Yet he knew what the Master had said and he could not reject her.

"Well, Jenny," he sighed, "I guess we'll have to forgive you, but it ain't going to be easy."

And it was not. Jenny came to every service, but no one spoke to her. The pew where she and her mother sat was deserted, and the two were left in frozen isolation. When Armstrong learned about it, he preached a series of sermons on what forgiveness means, how far we all fall from perfection, and how hopeless and lost we would be if the Omnipotent treated us as we treat each other. The ice was melted, and the group took Jenny into their hearts again.

Like all preachers he sometimes ran into unexpected complications which required resolution and courage. In one meeting he was staying in the home of a leader who had a forty-year-old widowed daughter. Many years before, because of a Capulet-Montague feud between the two families, the father had broken up her plans to marry a childhood sweetheart. The young man had never married. He was an excellent man, and a preacher, but feuds in Tennessee as well as Verona can be unreasonable and bitter. The young woman had married, but after her husband's death her former sweetheart asked her again to marry him. At the close of the meeting one evening he explained the situation and asked Armstrong if he would marry them.

"Where is the bride?" Armstrong asked.

"She's hiding in the shadow of the trees yonder," the man replied.

The two were mature people, long separated by the hatred of others, but now determined to live their own lives, and his sympathy went out to them.

"Will we need a light?" the man asked. "I think I can find one."

He had seen the glow of a light through the trees, but when he went for it, he found it attached to a buggy.

"Can't you do it just as well in the dark?" he asked, anxiously.

By that time the father had discovered what was going on and was running through the trees bellowing at the top of his voice for his daughter. Fleeter of foot and in the darkness, she was able to escape, but it was some time before the groom and the preacher could find her. In the meantime they had grabbed two sympathetic witnesses, the "knot" was quickly tied, and the couple whipped the horses and sped away in the night.

Armstrong returned to his room and to bed, but his host paced the floor all night. The next morning he ate his breakfast in stony silence, and at the morning service he tried to stop the meeting. But with baptisms occurring nearly every night the enthusiasm of the church was too great. He was ignored, and by the following Sunday his anger was replaced by penitence, and he made a public confession of wrong. For this maturer Romeo and Juliet the outcome was happy.

One of Armstrong's early appointments was at Fosterville, Tennessee, and on February 13, 1899, in spite of the pleas of his wife he went to the appointment as usual. One of the marks of faithfulness, of one's ability to endure hardships as a good soldier, was never to miss an appointment no matter what the weather might be. The Saturday had brought heavy snow, sleet, and ice with the thermometer dropping to twenty-seven below zero, the coldest night in fifty years. Woodson was almost right in arguing that no one would come to church at Fosterville that morning. Only one man and his boy braved the storm and struggled through the snow to the church. Since an evening service was out of the question, Armstrong returned to Nashville by the afternoon train instead of the next morning. Coaches in those days were loosely constructed, and the wind whistled in around the windows and doors. When a woman complained to the conductor that she was cold, he threw up his hands in exasperation.

"Look at that stove down yonder," he pointed to the end of the coach where the pot-bellied cast iron heater was red hot from the pipe to the grate. "Do you think you can get that any hotter without melting it down? Better put on some clothes next time."

Not expecting him home till morning, Mrs. Armstrong had gone to her mother's to spend the night, and when he returned in the evening Mrs. Harding insisted that they both stay. They were expecting the baby in another month, and there was danger in facing the wind and snow. But he wrapped her, head and foot, in a blanket and carried her like a baby across the street and into the house. There the fire had burned out in the fireplace, and the eggs they had placed on the hearth had frozen and burst. A bushel of sweet potatoes they could not afford to lose was also frozen, had to be cooked, and furnished a monotonous diet for days.

The baby was born, March 27, and was named Pattie Hathaway after the two grandmothers. But such a name was too large a mouthful for Truman Ward, her little playmate, and he condensed it unintentionally to Pataway, and Pataway it has remained. It was a difficult birth, and medical science lacked something of our modern skill. But Armstrong managed to postpone for two years the bitter disappointment to his wife of knowing she could never have another child.

The Good Book says that the rewards of the faithful Christian are great. For no one leaves houses or lands or fathers or mothers or brothers or sisters for the Lord's sake and the gospel's that he does not receive a hundred times more in this present world, even with added persecutions. Every faithful preacher has found this true, for hundreds of homes are opened to him and give him the best they have, service which he could not expect from his own family. Sometimes this best in the nineties was not like accommodations at the Waldorf Astoria, but a faithful preacher adapts himself with sincere appreciation to the accommodations his people can give. So Armstrong did. Food in Tennessee and Kentucky is unexcelled anywhere, and the difficulty most preachers face is resisting the temptations set before them. But even there, in out-of-the-way corners, Armstrong sometimes found food problems. Few places had screens and someone protected the table by waving a cloth or a leafy branch above it. Once he was expecting a slice of delicious chocolate cake until the woman waved the branch and the flight of flies left it white.

At another place his bed was so infested with bugs that he could get no sleep for feeding their insatiable appetites. He finally tricked them by sleeping on the floor. How they fared when their free meals disappeared he never knew. At another place his kind hosts, in burning summer heat, gave him the family feather bed. Not to hurt their feelings he removed it secretly each night and slept on the straw mattress, replacing it carefully in the morning as he made up the bed, a practice he always followed and always taught his students. But the good woman somehow found out.

"Why, we took that off our own bed just for you," she said, with disappointment.

"I'm terribly sorry," he replied, "and I appreciate it very much, but you see I'm not used to feather beds and I can really sleep better on the mattress." So the feather bed was returned to its customary place and everybody slept better.

The generosity of people, even in the poorest homes, knew no bounds, and they gladly shared anything they had. At one home where he and Mrs. Armstrong were invited for dinner, pigs were rooting around and under the house, a large log served as a high step to the front door, and the floors inside sagged so steeply they had to watch their step to avoid falling. The family had invited the whole church for dinner. In the combination dining room-bedroom they had to use everything from rocking chairs to boxes, benches, and the bed to seat the guests. For coffee they had only one spoon, which they passed around for each to stir and taste his coffee.

Although generous with guests and with friends, many churches in those days had never been taught to give. At one place where farmers were making comfortable livings, buying more land, and accumulating substantial bank accounts, the Sunday contribution, which was his pay, covered little more than his railroad fare. He resolved to teach them how to give. He really took off his gloves and told them what it meant for Christians to give with purpose, with liberality, and with cheerfulness. They were awakened by the shock and insisted on giving him more, but he refused. From that time on, however, the church became interested in missionary work and grew liberal in contributions.

At one meeting a sawmill man drove in five miles from the woods for each morning service. He listened carefully and made notes of the scriptures used but often could not locate them in his Bible when he returned home. He asked Armstrong to hold a meeting the next summer near his home in a brush arbor he built in a cedar grove. But it rained nearly every day and the meeting was moved to his house with small groups, often only his family, present. He had a good barn and good livestock, but a miserable house, almost bare of furniture, and with broken window panes replaced with paper. Armstrong preached on the home and the parents' responsibility to their children. After the meeting the man began improving his house, putting in window panes, and getting some comfortable chairs. He understood that cows and horses need good housing and good care, but he had never thought about his wife and children.

Near Hopkinsville, Kentucky, a single Christian family wanted Armstrong to come for a meeting where no church existed. It was an outright missionary effort and he accepted it gladly. He never scheduled meetings years in advance. He arranged them in January or February for each following summer. There were always far more calls than he could fill, but he accepted all he could in the order, first, of where he felt he could do the most good, and second, of which calls were received first. This time he knew the meeting was needed, and his heart went out to a family trying to build a church where no church was.

Toward the close of the meeting, however, the family handed him a fund made up from the people in the community, with a list of all the donors and the amounts. He carefully sorted out the sums and returned them to those who gave.

"I appreciate what you good people have done," he said. "But I came here for you, not for your money. I wanted to give you the meeting. If you want to pay the railroad fare, that will be all right, but the meeting is my gift to you."

At another place which had recently completed their church building at considerable sacrifice, he left a good portion of their contribution on the mantel where the people with whom he stayed found it after he was gone. He was afraid they would refuse to accept it if he offered it directly.

With such liberality it is not surprising that the Armstrongs lived often on the verge of want, but strangely enough—or should we say "providentially"—each actual want was supplied. On one trip to Celtic, Texas, the meeting he had just left continued over Friday night. After he bought his ticket he had only fifty cents left and unexpectedly had to stay overnight at Howe. He prayed that he might find a clean place to sleep. It was past eleven at night when he arrived at Howe and the only light he saw was in a drug store.

"Where can I find a hotel?" he asked the druggist.

"There's no hotel here," the druggist replied. "You might stay with an old couple who live down the street. I'll show you their house," and he went to the door to point it out.

He awoke the couple and they took him in. The next morning they asked who he was and why he was there. Finding that he was a preacher and on his way to a meeting, the old woman said, "I usually charge fifty cents for keeping people, but I never charge preachers but thirty-five cents." That left him fifteen cents for a sandwich, and he was ready to preach the morning sermon when he arrived at Celtic.

As a student at West Tennessee Christian College, Armstrong had first learned of the trouble caused by forcing instrumental music into the worship of the church. Now he was to learn more vividly the methods often used by its advocates in proselytizing, and even causing division in churches. He was informed that the Missionary Society of the Christian Church, with its high salaried head, had not established a single new congregation in the Hopkinsville area in ten years. When some Christians started a new congregation at Pilot Point, the head evangelist wrote that if the little group would supply seventy dollars a month, the Society would give thirty and would send a minister to them

regularly once a month. Without their permission the preacher suddenly appeared and attempted to impose himself on
them. He deposed the elders and appointed new ones in
their place. But the members resisted the effort to take them
over and got rid of the preacher. Many small churches,
however, yielded to such pressure, accepted the monthly
evangelist, soon quit meeting except when he came, and
gradually died. The practice of taking over existing congregations instead of establishing new ones created much bitterness everywhere.

When Armstrong was called to a meeting in Obion, Tennessee, the church there had been divided because a few had
introduced the organ into the worship. Those who opposed
it offered to purchase the house or sell to the others, but
could get no agreement. Finally a compromise was reached
to use the organ only in Sunday school, but not in the
regular service. Then the man who owned the organ took it
out and the two groups met together again, but still with
opposing views. Armstrong preached kindly but forcibly on
the issues involved, and apparently there was no further
trouble at Obion.

Mrs. Armstrong rarely accompanied her husband in his
meetings, especially after Pataway was born because she was
afraid to be a burden to the people. One time when they
went with him, the baby nearly broke up the meeting by
slipping away from her mother and playing peekaboo at
another child from around and between her father's legs
till her mother snatched her up again. Armstrong was so
deeply interested in what he was saying, however, that he
did not know the child was occupying the pulpit with him,
and was puzzled at the laughter of the audience.

Shortly after his marriage Armstrong took his wife and his
sister Ora with him to a meeting at a country church in
West Tennessee. He had warned them both in advance what
to expect.

"Just eat whatever is set before you asking no questions,"
he had paraphrased Paul's instructions.

But some things you must see to believe. Even with his warning they were unprepared for what they found. The house they stayed in was large but old. The second floor, a single enormous room or loft, had four double beds with no screens or curtains around them. Other visitors came and all beds were filled. At bedtime someone gave the signal.

"Well, ladies, it's time for bed," and the women went up first, undressed and went to bed. The men followed, undressing in the dark. The next morning the procedure was reversed; the men arose first and dressed in the dark. The women followed.

The combination kitchen-dining room was large, and black overhead with soot from years, perhaps generations, of cooking. Above the table the bare, murky beams were covered with cobwebs, and their host cautioned them kindly, "Keep a sharp lookout above; they's spiders up thar, and sometimes they draps in our vittles."

But spiders were not all. The table was left "dormant" all day long, as Chaucer expressed it, containing cups of molasses, jams, and jellies, and these had become seasoned with a rich mixture of small black ants. Just what flavor they gave the molasses and jams has not been reported, but obviously they produced a more balanced diet by adding proteins to the carbohydrates. The men ate heartily, "asking no questions," but the women found their appetites waning in the midst of plenty.

The situation demanded action. Three meetings were to be held on Sunday with dinner on the ground. The family would be away all day. The young bride and her sister-in-law, pleading a special task, stayed home from the afternoon meeting and cleaned the kitchen and dining room. Cobwebs, the ancestral home of generations of spiders, were ruthlessly destroyed, pots and pans were given a luster they had forgotten they ever possessed, dishes, table, and floor were scrubbed to a healthy glow. They were thoroughly happy with the miracle of transformation and looked forward with youthful eagerness to the praise of a delighted hostess.

She returned in the evening, built up a fire and got ready the evening meal, but apparently never noticed a thing amiss. The girls were mystified. Had she actually seen no change? Or was she deeply insulted and giving them the old silent treatment? But her manner was just as friendly as before.

Perhaps there was an easier explanation, had the girls only guessed. Her eyes evidently were not of the best. Sufficient proof was the fact that she had already had five husbands, and her present husband had also had four wives. Unlike the Samaritan woman, she believed in marriage. But her marital life was a tangled maze of experiences. She was a great talker, but often forgot whom she was talking about.

"That was my third husband," she would say, "or was it my second, or fourth. I get 'em kinda mixed up, it's been so long ago."

Events she could remember, but not in the administration of which husband they occurred. Mrs. Armstrong, being quite a young bride and inexperienced, marvelled how love could change so quickly and embrace so many. She wondered if it had now found a final resting place.

"Mrs. Jones," she asked one day, "if your present husband were to die, do you think you would ever want to marry again?"

"La, child, yes," she cackled. "They's too many nice men in the world for me to live alone by myself the rest of my natural life. If the Lord takes one man away from me, they's always plenty more."

Such instances of rustic hospitality, however, convinced the young bride that she should follow the Apostle Paul's admonition to be a "keeper at home" and let her husband endure the hardships of evangelization "as a good soldier." She could bear his burdens better by keeping a well-managed home for him to return to.

Chapter 6

WESTWARD PIONEERS

BREAKING LONG-ESTABLISHED ties is always painful. When Mr. and Mrs. C. C. Potter insisted that James A. Harding accept the presidency of the college they planned to build at Bowling Green, Kentucky, in memory of their son, Harding agreed with great reluctance. Not wishing to injure the school at Nashville which he and David Lipscomb had founded ten years before and which he dearly loved, he arranged with Lipscomb and the faculty for a suitable successor and refused to take any of the faculty with him except Armstrong.

Armstrong had been with the school eight years and had become, next to Harding, the most popular instructor in the faculty. Lipscomb wanted to keep him and urged him strongly to stay.

"I love the school," Armstrong said, "I love every teacher in it, and had I not believed I could do more good in my new field, I would gladly have remained."

The years he had spent in Nashville had been rich in experience and growth. Besides his teaching, he had preached nearly every Sunday, sometimes three times on a Sunday, but during those years he had received from preaching not more than enough to pay the house rent—ten or twelve dollars a month. Through 1901, for instance, he preached every Sunday but received the contribution on only one Sunday each month—seven or eight dollars above expense of the trip. Mrs. Armstrong cut up her wedding dress to make clothes for the baby, but they felt they were engaged in a great service.

"Our living has been close," he wrote, "but not as close as Paul's and Christ's, I am sure; so we are satisfied. These years have been the happiest years of my life."

It is difficult in the materialistic age created by our affluent society to understand the joy with which men of great ability like Armstrong, the Hardings, and a score of others offered themselves as living sacrifices for a cause they loved. Even in those days such men were exceptions, mar-velled at and often condemned as impractical. Armstrong says of his contemporaries. "Possibly there is not another practice surrounded with so much danger to Christians as that of seeking and using money. So great is the fascination that thousands are giving their lives wholly to it. So com-pletely are they captivated by it that they measure every man's success by his possessions. To be sure, if God has given me the ability to make money and I do not use it, I am as guilty as the unprofitable servant in the parable of the talents who was cast into outer darkness. How then may a child of God use his ability to make money and be pleas-ing to God in its use? It is a matter of motive, and the right motive is to use it for the Lord." The danger was in being blinded by the glitter of wealth and losing sight of the end and purpose of life.

"A young doctor," he related, "said to me that the world is living too fast for a man to choose his profession, make a success of it, and at the same time be a Christian. The same kind of statement was made to me recently by a very successful farmer of Kentucky. If Paul had made tent-making a separate enterprise from serving God, as most people seem to consider their businesses, and had sought to make it an ostentatious success, it would have taken all his time. He would have had the 'evil eye,' and been thus separated from God."

But if ever men had the "single eye" which Jesus commends, it was these early teachers in the Christian schools. Speaking of Jesus' demand that his disciples "deny" themselves, Armstrong said, "Our Lord means, if anyone desires to follow him, he must lose sight of, or disregard himself, in seeking the interest, comfort, and blessings of others. One might imagine that this life of self-denial is an unhappy life, but it is far from it, for it is the only truly happy life open to men. The only way to seek one's true interest and welfare is to live for others, losing sight of oneself as nearly as possible for one to do. There is pleasure in living for self, but happiness is wanting. Pleasure is found in gratifying the flesh; happiness, in gratifying the desires and longings of the soul."

The thing that made these years the happiest of his life was this singleness of view, the spirit of selflessness that filled the school and all its teachers. He said later, "The Nashville Bible School would long since have been a worldly institution and perverted from the true intention of its founders, had those who love it sought to make it a successful school from a worldly view point."

Leaving the many friends he had made at Nashville, however, brought sadness. He mentions especially John E. Dunn, who had double dated with him. As he visited Woodson, Dunn visited Essie Odom, one of Woodson's closest friends, who stayed in the Harding home.

"Those were good days," Armstrong said years later. "College friendships are abiding. There are no dearer times." One of the outstanding qualities of Armstrong to the end of his life was loyalty to friends. He might rebuke them sharply if he felt they were wrong, but he loved them and supported them courageously and unselfishly in any emergency.

The opening at Bowling Green was delayed till October 8 to finish the building. Armstrong had visited the campus earlier in the summer, located about two miles from town on the main highway from Louisville to Nashville in a rich bluegrass section. The building going up was a three-story brick, trimmed in stone. It would give the new college much better facilities than Nashville could offer for a number of years, and he was enthusiastic about it.

"It is going to be very handsome," he wrote, "and I believe one of the most convenient buildings for its purposes in the whole country. From the ground up nothing shoddy has been permitted to go into it, either in material or in workmanship. The second and third floors are to be 'deadened.' The stairways are so arranged as to require the least possible walking in the halls." This was because the upper floors were to be rooms for students, while the ground floor contained the chapel and classrooms.

In addition to erecting an excellent college building, the Potters turned over to the new institution their spacious two-story brick home as a dormitory for girls, and a hundred-forty-acre farm to serve as endowment. In recognition of their generosity the school was named the Potter Bible College.

The opening was auspicious, and every room was filled. Later another home was built to be used for either boys or girls as the need demanded, and still later a separate chapel was constructed.

Armstrong was head of the Greek department, but also taught Latin and Bible. Even with his heavy load he continued his advanced studies, taking Hebrew under M. C. Kurfees, who came down regularly from Louisville for the class. He received the Master of Arts degree. But since that was in the day before colleges were accredited, he later had the degree validated by further work at the University of Oklahoma.

As at Nashville rigid economy was necessary. Teachers got rooms and groceries, but other expenses had to come from preaching or other activities. The Robinson House, with its beautiful lawn and stately trees, furnished rooms for boys on the second floor while the Armstrongs and the

R. C. Bells had apartments across the hall from each other on the first floor. Since there was a barn, Armstrong bought a beautiful black horse and a buggy to drive the two miles to town and to appointments. They also raised a garden and chickens. The Brown Leghorns made contributions of eggs but roosted too high in the trees to catch. The White Plymouth Rocks, however, furnished some delicious meals and a small income. But when Armstrong found the first "sackful" he carried to market smothered and stone dead on arrival, he learned that chickens live on inexpensive air as well as on more expensive grain.

Since no one apparently was supposed to be hungry on Sunday nights and the college served no supper, Mrs. Armstrong and Mrs. Bell decided to supplement their husbands' meager incomes by giving the students Sunday evening meals. For a small sum they served all the fried chicken, hot biscuits, preserves, and jam the young people could eat. These meals became so popular they added homemade candy and other delicacies. The results were not phenomenal, but there was money enough for a few presents and for a roll-top desk and swivel chair for each husband. Armstrong's desk served him faithfully for more than thirty years, and the chair continued until it finally collapsed years after his death. To the family its demise was like parting from an old friend who had supported them through countless hardships.

When Mrs. Armstrong finally learned that there could be no more children, she and her husband were anxious to adopt a child as a companion for Pataway. Every child, they felt, needed a brother or sister to give opportunity for love and sharing with others of like age. They were thinking strongly of a little boy in town whose parents had died and left him largely running the streets. But Mrs. Harding pleaded with them, almost in tears, not to take him. His parents were not of the best repute. The child was considerably older than Pataway and had already formed some bad habits. Disappointed in this attempt, they visited an orphanage in Louisville, and with Brother Kurfees' help found a lovely little girl two years younger than Pataway.

They were about to arrange for adoption when word came that Armstrong's older brother James David was at the point of death from pneumonia, and before Nelse could reach him he had died.

His second wife, a mere girl, wanted to keep the children together, but found it impossible. By Christmas she agreed to let them go. The Armstrongs took Early, thirteen, and J. D., four, just eleven months younger than Pataway. This solved the family problem. J. D. and Pataway grew up together with the close affection of brother and sister, and each would have fought for the other. In school Pataway was always a conscientious student, but J. D. was somewhat less concerned. More than once he rushed home calling out, "Mamma, guess what grade sister got in arithmetic! An *A*!"

"Well, that's fine, J. D.," his mother would say. "And what grade did you get?"

"Aw, I got a *B*." But he was prouder of his sister's grade than if it had been his.

To the Armstrongs he and Early became their children, and they tried to make no distinction between them and Pataway in their affection and in the advantages they gave them. They actually bought more shoes and clothes for the boys than for the little girl, partly because the boys were harder on clothes, and partly because Pataway worried more about the expense. Often she would say, "Mamma, J. D. needs a new pair of shoes."

"Yes, and I think you do too."

"But, Mamma, I can wear these a little longer, can't I, Mamma? We don't have money enough for us both." Even as a child she was aware of how careful they had to be about expenses.

Early had a large share of his grandfather Robert Armstrong's sense of humor. He loved to tease and joke, and could tell whoppers with a perfectly straight face to see if people would swallow them. Once when Pataway was worrying about the expense, he suddenly declared,

"Stop worrying, I can write you a check for a thousand dollars."

"You can't do it," Pataway retorted. "You know you can't write a check for a thousand dollars."

"I can too," he insisted. "Can't I, Uncle Nelse, write a check for a thousand dollars?"

"Yes," Armstrong said. "You certainly can." Pataway was furious at his taking sides against her. But he explained that Early's check, of course, would be worthless.

There was something hard to explain, however, about the family's finances. The income which could barely cover the needs of three suddenly had to take care of five. But looking back years later, Armstrong could not remember that they were any more strained with five than they had been before. Paul had once said to the Philippians, "My God shall supply every need of yours according to his riches in glory in Christ Jesus." Perhaps the Philippians were not the only ones whose needs were supplied as they increased.

Their only robbery in a' lifetime took place in Bowling Green. The family was spending some weeks at Gadsden while Armstrong was in meetings and had left the house vacant. Someone must have spent several days in the house, leaving unwashed pots, pans, and dishes everywhere. Some clothes and some wedding presents were missing, but the occupant was honest enough to leave his name, "Slippery Dan, June 15-20" written in large letters on a sheet of paper. But he left no address, and the date was wrong, for the family had been at home then. He also left a woman's dress, which cast some unpleasant suspicions on "Slippery Dan."

In those years, before the accreditation of colleges became a requirement, when any group of competent teachers willing to make the necessary sacrifices could establish a new institution, Armstrong was dreaming of a Christian school somewhere west of the Mississippi. He and Woodson Harding talked it during their courtship. At Bowling Green they took R. C. Bell, B. F. Rhodes, and R. N. Gardner into their plans. The four men constituted an extremely able nucleus for the faculty of any college, and their deepening friendship developed into a love that held them close together for a lifetime. R. C. Bell, tall, slender, and straight as an arrow, a great lover of Emerson, possessed a poetic imagination which gave his sermons distinct literary quality and made him a great teacher of both English and Bible. But he possessed a gentleness of nature which shrank from discipline and which later made his responsibilities as president of Thorp Springs Christian College difficult. B. F. Rhodes had a brilliant mind, a flashing, often ironic wit, was widely read, and had a memory stored with knowledge of nearly every conceivable subject. R. N. Gardner, well built and with a fiery temperament, was a speaker of great force and an inspirational teacher. All these, however, looked to Armstrong for leadership. He was only a little older, but had longer experience in the Christian school, a far-sighted soundness of judgment that all respected, and a decision of character that did not shrink from responsibilities and difficulties.

When in 1904 the four friends were looking for a suitable location for the new school, Gardner's brother, A. D. Gardner, who had been county clerk at Paragould, Arkansas, for a number of years and had accumulated some money and land, offered a forty-acre farm two miles from Paragould if they would locate the college there. Armstrong spent two or three days at Paragould looking it over. The farm had a good two-story house, a barn, some outbuildings, and a good orchard. Though the raising of money for college buildings and dormitories would be a formidable task, the group agreed to Gardner's offer. Armstrong announced on August 23 that "In September A. D. Gardner, R. C. Bell, B. F. Rhodes, R. N. Gardner, and I will open a new school at Paragould, Arkansas. For about six years some of us have proposed to establish, in a new field, another Bible school, and it now seems that God is giving us the desire of our hearts."

But the plan was soon changed. Armstrong went from

Paragould to Odessa, Missouri, for a meeting. There a Mr. Foster said:

"Brother Armstrong, we have a nice school building here that is idle. It was built a few years ago for a college which was not successful. It has a two-acre campus with beautiful maples on Main Street just a half mile from the business center of town. I believe the town would donate it to you if you would bring the college here."

Armstrong looked it over. The building was a two-story brick, with an auditorium on the second floor that would seat three hundred fifty. There were seven classrooms, a library with about two hundred fifty books, and a laboratory modestly equipped. The building with its six tall chimneys was surrounded by large old maples and a thick bluegrass lawn. The city readily agreed to deed the property to the new school.

Armstrong immediately notified the others, and Rhodes and the Gardners came up. All agreed that Odessa, with its population of two thousand, forty miles from Kansas City, was the best location for the college.

For Armstrong, Bell, Rhodes, and Gardner all to leave Bowling Green at once would take the heart out of the faculty there. To one of less faith than Harding possessed it would have been a crushing blow. Much as he regretted their leaving, he was so interested in extending Christian education to new areas that he gave the new school his fullest support. True to his expectation, Potter Bible College had doubled the number of young people receiving a Christian education; the new school should triple the number.

The Western Bible and Literary College could not open, however, until September 1905. They first needed a dormitory, and R. N. Gardner stepped out at Bowling Green to give full time to raising the money, and Armstrong published appeals through the papers. A. D. Gardner advanced $3,000 for the purchase of a nine-acre tract across the street from the college building to be used for dormitories, and teachers' homes and gardens. Money as usual came in slowly and in small amounts. A school boy gave five dollars and had to do his own laundry all year as a consequence. A girl gave her Christmas present of ten dollars. But the dormitory went up—a three-story frame building with a large reception room, dining room, kitchen, and family apartments on the first floor, rooms for girls on second, and for boys on third. As with nearly all dormitories in those days, there were no bathrooms or water inside. Students and teachers ran shivering around the north side of the building, braving the winter wind and snow, to bring water from the well.

In the campaign for funds Armstrong made one of his characteristically strong statements that for years was quoted to condemn him.

"The starting of this work," he wrote, "does not depend on your gift, for God's hand is not shortened. Your salvation may depend on it, but the school does not. If you have means in your hand and are a servant of God, it is God's means; and to be a faithful servant, you must use his means in the place where you believe it will do the most toward building the kingdom of God."

It seems strange now that anyone would condemn a Christian school. But when the Potters started the college at Bowling Green and asked Harding to become its president, Daniel Sommer, editor of the *Octographic Review,* a widely read religious journal, started a bitter crusade against Christian colleges. Armstrong's statement was interpreted by Sommer and his friends as a threat that anyone who would not contribute to the college would be damned. Twenty years later a woman wrote Armstrong to ask if this was what he meant. He replied that the statement had been misunderstood and interpreted in many ways, but after twenty years, "I like it pretty well yet." It was not a threat, he explained, but many Christians who believe in Christian schools never help to bear the burden of them.

"They prefer to put their money in pigs, calves, lands, and businesses, with the hope of gain. They have never learned to use money except to gain money. They are giving dimes and dollars to worthy causes, whereas they should be giving their hundreds of dollars. To them it may be possible that their salvation depends upon their giving to some cause. If they keep on using their money as they do, it may prove in the end condemnation to them. I am not their judge, neither is it my business to decide how or where they shall use their money. But it is my duty to show Christians the crying needs of this school effort and the great good that can be done through it. That a Christian can sit by and see the worldly environment now surrounding school children in this country and not be stirred to a holy desire to offer them a cleaner one is a reflection on his Christianity."

Slowly the money came in and the building went up. By June of 1905 the group of teachers themselves had given $2,361.01, and gifts from hundreds of donors in many states totaled $1,873.58. A. D. Gardner was finally repaid, but to finish the work Brother Thornton of Blackwater, Missouri, made a loan of $3,000.

The college opened in September, 1905, with one hundred students, which grew to one hundred sixty-five before the year closed. A large group had followed the teachers from Bowling Green, but Bowling Green and Nashville were still as full as their facilities allowed. The faculty included Armstrong, as President and Professor of Bible, Greek, and Hebrew, R. N. Gardner, Vice-President and Professor of Mathematics, Bell, Professor of English and Philosophy, Rhodes, Professor of Bible and History, A. D. Gardner, Professor of Business and business manager of the college, F. M. Dinsmore, in science, Mrs. Armstrong, in expression, and Clara Sullivan, in music.

It was a competent and extremely unselfish faculty, but none of them had actually administered a college program, and the first year came near financial tragedy. At Nashville and at Bowling Green Harding had handled all the finances, but since A. D. Gardner had extensive training and experience in business, the financial management was left to him. The charge of sixty dollars a semester for board, room, tuition, and fees was in line with the charges of similar

colleges in those days, for education everywhere was regarded as an altruistic service. Armstrong had taken it for
granted that the kitchen and dining room would be managed
by Mrs. Armstrong and Mrs. Bell, as Mrs. Harding had
always directed it at Nashville and at Potter Bible College.
But like many strong men the Gardners did not want to
burden the women with such responsibilities; they saw no
reason why the men could not handle this program as well
as the rest.

They employed Will, a hotel chef, to manage the kitchen,
and one of the students to do the buying and keep the
accounts. At the opening of school to be perfectly safe they
collected the board money for the entire year. Will was a
marvel in planning and serving the meals. His hot biscuits
melted in one's mouth. His steaks and roasts were tender
and deliciously flavored. His pies and pastries made the
mouth water. Then one day calamity fell. Mrs. Bell had
gone out to the garbage cans to throw away some scraps.
She hurried back to the dormitory.

"Miss Woodson," she panted. "Come with me; I want to
show you something."

Stealing cautiously around the building, they uncovered
the garbage cans and saw with dismay great lumps of dough
and large chunks of perfectly good roast, which had been
discarded because Will believed in serving only fresh stuff,
never leftovers. That night they found a large lump of dough
still unconsumed in the stove. This had gone on for months.
A member of the board had been fattening his hogs on the
rich refuse but seemed not to realize what was happening.
The women told their husbands, and they called the Gardners into hasty consultation. The books were examined, and
they found that Will, in about three months, had used
practically all the board money for the year.

The men immediately begged Mrs. Armstrong and Mrs.
Bell to take over the management of the kitchen and dining
room, but the women refused because they saw no way to
serve meals without money. As it happened however,
Missouri had an abundant apple crop that year. When

people learned of the situation they brought wagon loads of apples and filled the basement. Boxes piled high were placed in all the halls, and students ate apples raw, baked, fried, in pies, in sauce. Friends contributed turnips, turnip greens, and other vegetables, and sometimes even money. Students took the reduced fare in good humor and everybody was happy. The next year Mrs. Armstrong managed the kitchen and Mrs. Bell the dining room, and the meals were just as tasty, if not as rich, as Will's had been, but they kept within the budget.

Before the school opened at Odessa, however, one of the strongest preachers in the Midwest wrote Armstrong, "If the lines are ever drawn against you, you will have to go back to Tennessee or Kentucky for preaching." He was referring to Sommer's fight against the Christian colleges.

"I have never known the time in history," Armstrong replied, "when the faithful teacher of the word could not find a schoolhouse, a cave, or at least a portion of God's blue dome under which to teach God's message. The opposition to us in the Midwest cannot be stronger than the opposition in the New Testament times by the Roman Empire, and we have come to stay." But they soon found the "lines" through the Midwest drawn as hard as the opposition could make them.

"Some of the preachers," Armstrong wrote later, "buried their convictions and slaughtered their consciences because they were afraid. Others walked the fence and played 'shut mouth' because they feared they might lose their places in the synagogue."

For Missouri was in Daniel Sommer's vast empire. Sommer, who for many years had edited and published the *Octographic Review* in Indianapolis, Indiana, was a man of great force, a power in the pulpit, a prolific writer, whose word to many churches was absolute law. He was a champion of many great truths, but for some reason had become bitterly opposed to Christian schools. After unsuccessfully trying to arrange a debate with him, Harding had ignored his repeated attacks, and Sommer had said, "Brother Harding is the only man connected with the *Advocate* who has treated me fairly." Sommer was bitter in his attacks against the *Gospel Advocate,* and finally became so unfair, Lipscomb felt, that he ordered his name never to appear in the *Advocate* again. He charged that Sommer would never meet an argument fairly, but always resorted to abuse. When E. A. Elam, an editor of the *Advocate,* once suggested that Jesus rode into Jerusalem on an untrained ass, Sommer was sure that he straddled or rode on both asses at the same time. When Lipscomb criticized Sommer's position on marriage, Sommer ignored the argument and came back with an attack on the *Advocate's* Sunday school literature.

As soon as the college started at Odessa, Armstrong said, "The guns were turned upon us." Congregations withdrew fellowship from those who patronized Christian schools, and isolated those who were sympathetic. One family refused to enter the college building at Odessa because the college taught music and the building was "polluted." Little financial support could be expected in Missouri except from the Thorntons.

Desperate efforts were made by friends to have a full and fair discussion of the right or wrong of supporting Christian schools, but their pleas were ignored. Then Sommer charged that the college men were unwilling to affirm their practice because they knew it was unscriptural. With characteristic courage Armstrong decided to meet this opposition head on, and after considerable correspondence reached agreement with Sommer for three debates, two of them oral to be held with B. F. Rhodes at Odessa and repeated at Hale, Missouri, the third to be written between himself and Sommer.

Pitting Rhodes against Sommer was a David-Goliath affair. Sommer, over six feet tall, broad shouldered, a veteran of many battles, had been a preacher for thirty-seven years and was a master of sarcasm. Rhodes, slight, little more than five feet tall, and with a boyish face, was only thirty-seven years old and had never debated except with college friends. But he was a master of logic and wit, and not only held his own, but soon took the lead. Sommer had said in October,

1906, that all he had ever said against the Christian schools could be classed under two heads—the use of the "Bible" and "Christian" in their names and the use of "the Lord's money" to support them. But in the first debate, at Odessa, he avoided both issues, though pressed repeatedly by Rhodes, and excused himself by saying he would attend to them in the next debate at Hale. When pressed again at Hale, he excused himself by saying he would get to those issues in the written debate.

As Lipscomb had already found, Sommer spent nearly all his time ridiculing the qualifications of the faculty and the use of such titles as "Bachelor of Arts" and "Master of Arts" as pompous affectations. He condemned the entertainments at the school with their music and readings, and the literature required in English courses. "I would rather my child would be carried through a course of reading in ungodly fiction under an infidel or skeptic than under a devoted Christian," he declared. Rhodes answered effectively such criticism, but when he pressed Sommer for a definition of "the Lord's money," Sommer replied that a man had to pay taxes and support the needs of his family, and the rest should be given to the Lord. When Rhodes replied that "the family's needs" included education, Sommer did not reply, but he supplemented his definition by saying that all money contributed to the church on Sunday was "the Lord's money." To this Rhodes replied that the school would never accept a penny from any church contribution if that would satisfy him. To this Sommer replied, "You school men have been so mean already that I have lost all confidence in you, and I do not know whether you could do anything to reinstate yourselves in my confidence."

Once in the debate, answering Sommer's criticism that the college mixed secular subjects with the religious and then asked people to support a religio-secular institution with the Lord's money, Rhodes held up a huge open volume of Sommer's paper before him and cited passage after passage of secular material side by side with religious articles to show that Sommer himself was publishing a religio-secular journal

and urging people to support it with money above taxes and
family needs, and therefore "the Lord's money," according
to Sommer's definition. As Rhodes held the enormous volume before him—large as an outspread newspaper—with only
his knees visible below and his head bobbing up and down
above, the whole audience broke into uncontrollable laughter.

For months the *Octographic Review* had offered *Uncle
Tom's Cabin* along with the *White House Cook Book* as
prizes for sending in subscriptions. When Sommer denounced
the college for including novels in English courses, Rhodes
reminded him of his advertising *Uncle Tom*. Sommer explained, "There is a lady there in Indianapolis who presides
over the *Review* office, and has for nearly twenty years, and
she esteemed that book so highly that she put it in . . . and
when I saw it I protested against it, and told her she ought
to leave it out, and in the course of time it went out."
The "lady" was his wife.

To this apology Rhodes replied, "I thought he (Sommer)
was not an ordinary man, but I find he is. He is a genuine
son of old Adam,—'the woman thou has given me to be
with me, she gave me of the tree and I did eat.' I tell you
Brother Sommer has hard work making these people believe
that he is under any woman's thumb."

When Sommer was squirming under Rhodes' comparison
of the college organization with the similar organization of
the *Octographic Review,* Rhodes said, "I don't blame him
for feeling hot on the chair. It is hurting and I know it.
You put a live coal of fire on a turtle's back and he will
stick his head out every time." At the burst of laughter the
chairman rapped sharply for order and suggested less levity
in the discussion. But Rhodes's logic, quick repartee and
keen wit, and Sommer's failure to meet the real issues
opened the eyes of many.

Though Sommer furnished the stenographer to take down
the debates, it is customary for each debater to edit the
stenographer's transcription of his speeches before they go
to press. Rhodes spoke quite rapidly at times, and it would
have been difficult for any stenographer to catch every word.

On March 25 Rhodes wrote Sommer asking permission to edit the transcriptions of his speeches, but his request was ignored. He wrote again on April 15: "I am informed that your stenographer reports that he has had difficulty in transcribing my speeches. Both custom and common justice sanction my request and I am astonished that you have not given your assent to the request ere this . . . In view of the confessed difficulty of the stenographer in transcribing, unless my request is granted, there will be strong presumptive evidence of an intention on your part to act unfairly. This I do not wish to believe and so shall not attribute any such unworthy motive to you until I am compelled to do so."

To this letter Sommer replied on April 17: " . . . We don't get a proof until the type is set, and then we cannot allow changes from the M. S. [*sic*]. This indicates that you should have the M. S. of your part of the discussion if there is any need of it by reason of the reporter's inaccuracy. But I do not feel like trusting you with that M. S. Brother W. G. Roberts trusted an innovator with a M. S. and could never get it back . . . "

Sommer's refusal to let Rhodes see the transcriptions of his speeches before the book was published speaks for itself. But even with the advantage of editing his own speeches and leaving Rhodes' in the rough, Sommer was not content to let the debate speak for itself. He added a twenty-six page appendix of extra material without giving Rhodes an opportunity to see or reply to it. But such was Sommer's way of dealing with opponents.

Debates in those days were often rough and tumble affairs, but the written discussion between Sommer and Armstrong, the third in the series agreed on, is, in some ways, a curiosity among debates. James A. Harding had found it impossible to reach an agreement with Sommer on an acceptable proposition, and Armstrong found the same difficulty. The only propositions Sommer was willing to debate no one could accept:

1. It is scriptural to use a part of the Lord's money to establish schools that are three-fourths secular, and

*largely ungodly, in order to afford certain preachers an
opportunity to teach pupils in certain parts of the Bible.*

2. It is scriptural to use the word "Bible" in naming
   schools that are three-fourths secular, and *largely ungodly,* and *to use fallacies in advocating them,* and
   then, refuse to consider what is said against them, and
   divide the church of God in contending for them.

When Armstrong saw it was hopeless to arrive at a fair
statement, he suggested that they discuss their differences
without a set proposition.

To this Sommer agreed. Since Armstrong had to affirm
the right of Christians to maintain schools, he naturally
assumed that he would lead with the affirmative argument.
But Sommer, contrary to all normal procedure, insisted
in taking the lead with the negative. This arrangement would
allow him to wander as far from the issues as he pleased
and would supposedly compel Armstrong to follow, con-
fining himself to such argument as Sommer introduced. The
debate was to cover two propositions:

1. The unscripturalness of establishing religio-secular schools
   with the Lord's money, and
2. The unscripturalness of *applying sacred names* to things
   of human origin.

In the *Octographic Review* of August 20, 1905, Sommer
had approved, with W. W. Otey, the following principles:

"1. Christians may band themselves together to teach
    secular knowledge.
 2. They may teach the Bible a part, or all the time.
 3. They may do this to make a living or as an act of
    charity."

In 1901, when the Potters were planning to build the college at Bowling Green, Sommer wrote them:

I write you with reference to your new enterprise. As
you have decided to expend means left in your hands
by your dear dead for the purpose of education, I have
no criticism to offer.

In the discussion with Armstrong he also approved Alexander Campbell's Buffalo Seminary as being perfectly scrip-

tural. All these admissions made it impossible logically to oppose Christian schools, and Armstrong relentlessly blocked every attempt to evade the issue and exposed every inconsistency. Each writer was to contribute eight essays to the first proposition. But when Sommer's first three essays, more than a third of the debate, merely republished out-dated material from the *Octographic Review,* Armstrong became convinced that his opponent meant to ignore the issues as he had in his debates with Rhodes. He then reminded Sommer that he had boasted that college men "would not discuss the questions, that they were lacking in sincerity, candor, and courage to a greater degree than the 'digressives,' Roman Catholics, Mormons, or even infidels."

"It is a sin and a shame that Sommer himself now ignores everything placed before him," Armstrong said. "He has 'puffed,' 'blown,' and does his bragging behind his Chinese wall with barred gates. [For Sommer never permitted an opponent to reply in the columns of his *Octographic Review.*] Truly his courage is great when the enemy is far off.

"A dog behind a strong fence often shows great bravery so long as the fence is between him and the traveler, but when the open gate is reached he loses his bristles, sobers down, wags his tail, and barks very deliberately."

Stung with the rebuke, from this time on Sommer filled his essays with abuse, sarcasm, ridicule, and misrepresentation such as children might use in quarrels. He accused Armstrong of "calling him a dog," charged him with "unmitigated falsehood," called him a "slanderer," and Rhodes an "unscrupulous witness." When Armstrong, in irony, referred to Sommer's charge that he and others are liars and wicked "college advocates," Sommer accused him of admitting his wickedness because he accidentally omitted quotation marks around "liars" and "wicked"!

"He has applied both of those words [wicked and liar] to himself and to certain other college advocates," Sommer exclaimed. "I suppose he knows the real character of himself, also of his associates." And again: "Is it any wonder that he confesses himself to be a 'liar' and 'wicked'? . . .

No wonder that Prof. A. applies to himself the word 'liar' and 'wicked' . . . My slanderous opponent, who confesses that he is 'wicked' and a 'liar,' . . . I did not suppose that their chief advocate would confess that he and his colleagues are 'liars' and 'wicked'". . . "I have only been skirmishing with men whose chief defender says they are 'wicked' and 'liars'. . . A man who confesses that he is 'wicked' and a 'liar' cannot be fully exposed."

Thus went the abuse through essay after essay on the childish pretext of an omitted quotation mark! Toward the end Sommer abandoned all attempts at argument and spent his time ridiculing the English in Armstrong's and Harding's catalogs. When Armstrong showed that Rigdon, Reed and Kellog, and other grammars justified the uses he had criticized, Sommer repudiated such authorities.

"I have examined Rigdon's *Grammar*," he said, "and when the proper time comes, I calculate to expose it."

Despite the abuse and misrepresentation Armstrong, with masterly skill, kept the real issues before the reader and showed that Sommer's admissions logically surrendered his whole fight. Actually Sommer's deepseated antagonism seemed to be against J. A. Harding, J. N. Armstrong, and the men who ran the colleges, rather than against the schools themselves.

To get everybody to read the debate Armstrong offered free copies to all who requested them. Sommer sold his for fifty cents a copy. But when Armstrong ran out and sent to him for additional copies, Sommer generously made no charges for them.

The debates marked the decline of the opposition to Christian schools. But it is hard for strong men to give in. Sommer and others continued the bitter fight for twenty-eight more years with an intensity that divided friends, created enemies, built up "anti-college" churches that refused to fellowship anyone who approved a Christian school. He and W. G. Roberts accused the college of dividing the church at Odessa, and mentioned a "Mr. Sharp" as opposing the school. There was no "Sharp" at Odessa, and Mr.

Sparks, who was possibly meant, approved the college fully and had two sons in it.

Unknown to Armstrong, however, Sommer was finally beginning to see his mistake. Whether the three debates had any influence in his change of views or not, or whether it was the mellowing of age, in 1933 he made a visit to David Lipscomb College, one of the schools he had fought so tenaciously, and to Freed-Hardeman, to explain his change of attitude. He was courteously received and spoke two or three times in the Lipscomb chapel, attended Bible classes, and taught one or two.

Despite the bitterness of Sommer's attacks, Armstrong's attitude remained kind. "I am sorry that a man of his ability." he said, "has wasted so much energy in waging a fight against a work so manifestly right. Though he has been severe beyond measure in criticism of his brethren, I am ready to cast over him tonight a mantle of charity and leave him in the hands of a gracious Father who always does right."

In his *Apostolic Review* (successor to the *Octographic Review*) he said, "To take a position and hold it requires courage, but it requires more courage to recede from a position and acknowledge we were wrong." It was a straightforward confession which must have taken much courage, but he had come to regard Christian schools in the light of Romans 14, a matter of personal judgment which should not cause division. But his feeling toward Armstrong had not fully changed.

"Professor Armstrong," the *Review* said, "went into the school business head over heels on his own hook, but he now gives the churches to understand that the debt is theirs. And when the mortgage is cleared, the Professor assures us, that action gives the brotherhood one free four-year college." It charged, however, that Armstrong was trying to "filch" the money from the churches. Brother Srygley, in the *Advocate,* reproached the *Review* for such misrepresentation.

But when the author of this biography met Sommer in Chicago in 1934 Sommer inquired kindly about Armstrong and Rhodes, and then said, "I used to be quite dogmatic about a number of things, but I have learned more in these later years."

In May, 1938, Armstrong saw Sommer at the "Unity Meeting" in Detroit where Armstrong spoke. It was their first meeting since the debates thirty-two years before, and the old enmity had vanished.

"We met like old friends," Armstrong wrote, "and no one was kinder to me than this veteran of the cross. He was not on the regular program, but several times he put himself on during the meeting, and that ninety-year-old disciple was a marvel in clear thinking and expression. He fairly bounded up and into the pulpit several times during the meeting. The night of my lecture he, my severest critic thirty years before, was sitting on the front seat. When I finished he was about the first one to congratulate me. Yes, he has modified his attitude toward those with whom he differed in the years gone by. There never was a time when Brother Sommer was making his most intense effort to teach brethren that our schools were wrong, that he would not have been a welcome speaker on our programs right in our college halls had he been willing to treat us as brethren. That he disagreed with us would have made no difference. No, it is not our differences that hurt, but our manner of differing. But we all rejoice that Brother Sommer saw his mistake and that his course has established his repentence of his wrong treatment of brethren."

Just before writing this tribute to a former "enemy" now a friend, Armstrong had learned from W. W. Otey that Sommer had been blind since June of 1939. Though Otey had also disagreed with Sommer, he spoke of him with affection and said he expected to see him in heaven.

"Brother Otey breathed into this paragraph the breath of heaven," Armstrong commented. But before Armstrong's tribute could be published, Sommer died, February 19, 1940.

Chapter 7

A VACATION OF A LIFETIME

THE BATTLE BETWEEN "David and Goliath" was now over. The college at Odessa could look forward to a better understanding among the churches and to somewhat better support. But in the spring of 1907 Armstrong found with deep regret that he must give up his work in Missouri. For several years he had been troubled frequently with acute sore throat. Mrs. Armstrong once said he could not stump his toe without getting a sore throat. Often the childhood remedy of swabbing with coal oil controlled it, but he had to close a meeting in 1898 and again in 1903 when he became so hoarse he could not speak. In the summer of 1906 he helped nurse his brother Ed and had seen him slowly die of starvation when tuberculosis of the throat prevented swallowing.

"I could eat a cow if I could only swallow," Ed once whispered to his mother. The doctor tried forced feeding through the rectum, the only method then used. But when he told the mother it would not relieve Ed's hunger and would only prolong his life a few days, she had them discontinue it.

For Nelse, who felt closer to Ed than to any other of his brothers, it was a painful experience. That winter at Odessa the weather was wet and cold, and his throat was sore continually. Finally Mrs. Armstrong insisted that he see a doctor.

"You will be dead in five years," Dr. Mackey told him, "unless you go to a dry climate. You have no trouble yet, but you have all the soil for it." Years later when he met Armstrong again, Dr. Mackey said, "Armstrong, I gave five other men the same advice I gave you. They ignored it, and all five are dead."

Harding urged him immediately to return to Bowling Green. "You could preach every Sunday and rest the balance of the time. You could teach Hebrew and one or two classes in Greek—not enough to weary you." But the climate at Bowling Green was not dry.

To Armstrong the doctor's advice seemed a tragic blow. He loved his work, with all its sacrifices. Neither he nor the other five men who formed the heart of the faculty had received a cent of income from the college above bare room and board. They had applied everything on the debt and had made their living from preaching, though churches then paid little, and often nothing.

"When I left Kentucky and Tennessee," Armstrong said, "I did it with an aching heart. I hated to leave brethren and churches that I loved," But the school at Odessa was the work he had set his heart on. It was like giving up an only child.

"I am sorry to leave, for I should like to live and die here," he said. He felt keenly the obligations he had led others to take. "I helped them start. Some had at great sacrifice given liberally to the work, and that, too, because I was connected with it. I felt my obligation to these and I felt at first that I could not leave for their sakes."

The school needed $4,000 to pay the mortgage on the dormitory and about $900 for other obligations. Armstrong's appeal through the papers brought in $3,416.25 by November. He later visited the school and helped further in raising the money. At one meeting, so stirring was his appeal, and people were responding so enthusiastically, that when one young married student jumped up to make a gift, R. N. Gardner waved him down.

"Sit down! Sit down!" he cried. "You have no money to give. You have a wife and a child to support." But the young man could not be discouraged.

The college at Odessa continued its good work until it closed in 1916. Its enrollment was never more than one hundred sixty-five. It never applied for accreditation, for accreditation was hardly thought of in those days. When it closed, the material in the dormitory was converted into an apartment house, and the college building reverted to the town. It was never used for school purposes again. Dow Merritt, who visited it twenty years later, wrote, "Through the broken windows of the old school house one could see bales of hay and straw. The campus was a ruin. In a sense the school was 'Dead.' But in reality, not dead, for from it continued a strong stream of influence."

Immediately after its close, students transferred to Cordell Christian College, Cordell, Oklahoma, where Armstrong had by that time become president and where other teachers from Odessa were in the faculty. So Cordell had actually become the successor of Odessa, and Harper College and later Harding College carried on this stream of succession. This was recognized even by the court. Amanda Couchman of Bowling Green, Kentucky, who knew and loved the Armstrongs, had made a will leaving a thousand dollars to the Western Bible and Literary College of Odessa, Missouri, when Armstrong was president, but she died and her will was probated after the college closed. In 1936, however, Harding College, then at Searcy, Arkansas, was legally recognized as the lineal descendent of the Odessa school, and the bequest was granted to it. At that time sixty-five people connected with Harding College, from its president to assistants in various fields, had been former presidents, teachers, or students of the Odessa college, or children of those teachers and students.

From Odessa also came a host of leaders in the church around the world—the Dow Merritts, George M. Scotts,

Leslie Browns, A. B. Reeses, and others in Africa, the Orville Bixlers and E. A. Rhodeses in Japan, Don Carlos Janes, who probably did more than any other man of his time to encourage support of missionaries, and a long list of preachers, teachers, and devoted church leaders. So the influence of the school flows on. But the time came when parents demanded accredited institutions, and it was impossible, as President Gardner stated, to find men with advanced degrees willing to teach at the extreme sacrifice necessary. All honor and gratitude, however, should go to those heroes whose devotion kept the school running through eleven long and difficult years. It closed with all debts paid and all obligations met.

Armstrong's sudden leaving was a blow both to the school and to him. R. N. Gardner, who took over the presidency, said, "It is with sorrow that we see him leave. He will remain president of the school and will work for it in the field. All the other regular members of the faculty will remain." Armstrong had already been catalogued as "president," and this could not be changed, but he gave up all responsibilities.

"I know of only a few men," Gardner continued, "who have sacrificed as he has to do good. He looked not on his own things but to the things of others. During the darkest days, financially, of the Nashville Bible School he taught there, scarcely knowing one day where he would get provisions for the next. Thinking it was his duty to help in the new school at Bowling Green, he went there and taught, receiving scarcely enough to live on. Then he came to Odessa, and his sacrifice has been no less here. During all this time he accumulated no earthly goods, for he could not and do the work he did."

Some years before, E. A. Elam of the *Gospel Advocate* had asserted his faith that God provides for his people, but had criticized those who seemed to believe that "God will send down bread from heaven, give houses ready built and furnished, and do more for the preacher than for the wife and children at home." Elam reduced faith to a practical basis and argued that the farmer in tilling the soil trusts God for a living, because God has ordained planting and reaping as the way to receive it; and likewise God has ordained that they that proclaim the gospel should live of the gospel.

Armstrong loved and admired Elam, but he felt that his criticism misrepresented many who trust in God and might even encourage a wrong course. Efficient farming was not necessarily "trusting in God," for an atheist might be an excellent farmer and grow rich without any faith in God. A man's faith might be only in soil and seed, and in his own labor and skill. No intelligent farmer would till a rocky, sterile piece of ground when he could find rich fertile soil. So Elam's idea might encourage preachers who expect "to live of the gospel" to choose only the wealthy churches, "the rich soil," where preaching would pay. But both farmers and preachers, Armstrong felt, ought to trust in God, not in farms nor in men. If they fulfill the condition of "seeking first the kingdom of God," even if this requires work in poor communities or labor with one's hands, as it did with Paul, God would supply the living. There should be no fear.

This was the kind of faith that had sustained him through the years at Nashville and Bowling Green. But leaving Odessa required an increase of faith. His summer was filled with meetings, but he had no promise of anything beyond. Then unexpectedly came an invitation from Brother Lander Barker of Las Vegas, New Mexico. Barker lived on a ranch in the mountains, but he had a house in town where his daughter and two sons lived and went to school in the winter. Omar Barker, one of the sons, later contributed interesting short stories and poems to the *Saturday Evening Post*. In the house was a separate small apartment which Barker offered Armstrong rent free if he would preach for the little church of twelve members. The church met Sunday mornings in a rented building and Wednesday evenings in a private home. It could pay nothing, but Barker's arrangement at least supplied housing.

Before leaving for New Mexico in October Armstrong bought a money order for seventy-five dollars. On the train in Kansas a preacher asked how he expected to live out there. "I'm going to 'seek first the kingdom of God'," he replied, and the preacher laughed. Like many, the preacher doubted if it would work. Armstrong arrived in Las Vegas with his seventy-five dollars, deposited it in the bank, and looked around for something to do to supplement his small reserve. Brother Turner, a son-in-law of Barker, who owned a meat market in town, happened to mention that he could not find workers to pick a field of pinto beans out on his ranch.

"I'll pick them for you," Armstrong volunteered.

"You will? I'll give you half of all you pick," Turner said. Day after day, Armstrong picked, and his share lasted all winter long with beans a daily diet.

"They were the best beans I ever ate," he reported. But one day as he picked Turner rode out, and said, "Armstrong, the bank closed today."

"No, Brother Turner, they can't do that," Armstrong protested. "I have all my money there." But they did. The bank issued small amounts of script which was accepted by merchants in town, but Armstrong asked for little or none, and when he left Las Vegas the next August the bank paid him his deposit in cash.

The beans were supplemented occasionally by some farm products and by milk, churned almost to butter by the long trip from Barker's ranch, and once by a supply of bear meat, which furnished tough chewing for several days. Once when he went to the meat market, Turner asked, "Brother Armstrong, got any money?"

"Yes, I've got some money," Armstrong replied.

"How much? A nickel?"

"No, I've got more than a nickel."

"Here, take this," Turner ordered, and pushed a five dollar bill into his pocket. He bought from Turner whatever meat was necessary, and Turner always marked the bill paid at the end of the month.

As Christmas drew near, there was no money for presents. Mrs. Armstrong made a doll dress for Pataway and something for J. D. and Early and there was a plate of homemade candy Christmas morning. But they used their last coal on Christmas day and had no money to buy more. They could have borrowed from Turner or Barker, but Armstrong was ashamed to mention the need. Instead he and Mrs. Armstrong prayed earnestly about it. On Christmas afternoon the Turners took them all out to the ranch for a big Christmas dinner and to spend the night. The joy of Christmas, however, was impaired by thoughts of the cold house they must return to the next morning. East Las Vegas was a railroad town, but Armstrong knew nothing about railroading. He had milked on the farm, and thought he might apply at a dairy. But on returning home from Turners the next morning they found two letters in the mailbox. One was from his old schoolmate R. C. White, then of Chattanooga, with a check for twenty dollars as "a Christmas present he thought he might use."

White was a good man with a big heart. He loved his wife devotedly and never left the house without kissing her. But he frequently forgot to fill the woodbox before he left for an appointment, and Armstrong had often chopped the wood and filled the box for her. Perhaps the twenty was a belated recognition of this kindness!

The other letter was from the church at Little River near Hopkinsville, Kentucky, where Armstrong had preached. In it was a check for fifty dollars. They were now rich! They could warm the house again and replenish the pantry. The climate at Las Vegas, however, was so delightful that even in January they needed fire only in the morning and evening, and in summer the nights were so cool they needed two or three blankets.

For a week in the summer Barker invited them out to the ranch. His cabin was in a deep, narrow valley between two mountains. Along one side ran a swift stream filled with speckled trout. Before daybreak, while others slept, Barker stole out with his fishing tackle. On the breakfast table each morning would be a great, heaped-up platter of delicious mountain trout, fried to a golden brown so skillfully that even the bones, as Pataway remembers, crumbled in one's mouth.

"That summer," Armstrong said years later, "was the only vacation in my life, and it was a good one. It was the only year we ever lived when we did as we pleased, ate when we pleased, and slept when we pleased."

They climbed the mountains, pulled up the steep places by holding on to burros' tails. They rolled down deep drifts of snow in the brilliant summer sun. With the high altitude and crisp mountain air they could walk miles and never grow tired. The trouble with his throat cleared up never to bother him seriously again. He grew to believe the New Mexico climate could cure almost any pulmonary illness and add years to one's life.

But many who came were not so fortunate. Las Vegas was a health resort for tubercular patients. Outside the city proper was another city of tents, with wooden floors high off the ground, with windows to admit as much sunshine as possible, and stoves to protect against the chilly nights. These were filled with patients, many of them half dead when they arrived. They had waited too long to come.

Although the vacation and rest were what Armstrong needed, he was unwilling to spend a year doing nothing. He was finishing the written debate with Sommer, to be sure, but he now planned to teach Mexican children English as an opportunity to reach them with the Bible. In the spring, however, he arranged for Dr. L. K. Harding to lead singing for him in some meetings. Leon Harding was one of the outstanding singers of the time, leading in meetings for his father and for T. B. Larimore. He brought his own song books and at Las Vegas drilled the little congregation in many of the great hymns they had seldom heard.

He also helped his sister out of a little embarrassment. Mrs. Armstrong was a teacher of speech and grew up using the "general American" pronunciation now common on all television and radio circuits, but she found some marked dialectal variations at Las Vegas. Being a stranger, she had avoided mentioning the differences, but two of the young women were continually correcting her.

"I don't want to be rude to them," she told Leon, "but I thought you might show them their own pronunciations could be improved." And he did. When they used an odd pronunciation, Leon would cut his big eyes around, and with a quizzical smile, mimick them. "Did I hear you say 'I jes

wander'?" he asked. "I thought it was 'I just wonder'."
Or "Did you say 'wan die'? Don't you mean 'one day'?"
He soon had the girls almost afraid to open their mouths,
but he was so tall and handsome, and made his corrections
in such a good-natured way, they could not be angry.

But even Leon was whipped in Estancia Valley, where he
went next with Armstrong for a meeting. He left his books
in his room because they told him they had books at the
church. Their book, however, was the old *Gospel Gleaner*,
a collection of the racy, dancing church songs common in
many places in those days and similar to those being used
today in certain avant-garde fashionable city churches. Leon
explained to Brother Tuttle that he was unacquainted with
these songs and could not lead. When Tuttle led, however,
he sang the bass. After church Tuttle said, "Brother Armstrong, I expect we'd better use Brother Harding's books.
He said he couldn't lead these songs."

"Leon can lead any song that was ever written," Armstrong said.

But the next two nights Leon tried leading with his own
book. Only one voice piped up, a Baptist preacher's daughter. They sang duets for two straight nights, with the rest of
the audience silent listeners. Finally Leon gave up, and on
the third night he said, "Brother Tuttle, I believe we'd
better use your book." The first song he started he raced
through like a whirlwind, and the audience nearly lifted the
roof. They simply yelled the songs out, and everybody was
happy. It was a great meeting with a number of additions.
Leon had to leave early, and he said with genuine regret,
"Armstrong, I hate to leave you out here in this kind of
place."

The most difficult meeting was at Tucson, a university
town of twenty thousand population. Brother Grant had
tried to establish a congregation there the year before, but
an evangelist of the Christian Church had torn the group
up. Only one man and five women were left. The man, however, would not take the lead, and because he felt it would
be wrong for the women to lead with him present, he did
not attend services. As the time approached for the meeting,
Armstrong had no money for a ticket and hesitated to bor-

row, but the day before he was to leave he received a check for twenty-three dollars from the women, with the note, "We thought you might need this. It is the contributions for three Sundays."

The women obtained a tent, which unfortunately they erected downtown in the business section, instead of in a residential area of the city. Aside from the women the attendance through the four Sundays never averaged more than nine or ten. The people in Tucson had never heard of undenominational Christians.

"They stood and looked bewildered when we knocked and told them what we were," Armstrong said. "They thought we must be Mormons or something worse. Spiritually the town is a wreck. It cares no more for God and the Bible than it cares for Confucious and his philosophy. In fact, it knows nothing about either. The people are not opposed to our teaching, for they know nothing about it. They are merely irretrievably indifferent to spiritual matters. They don't go to church anywhere."

The husband of the woman in whose home he stayed was always courteous but never attended a service. His wife said she would never ask him for a cent to give to the church; she took in sewing and earned her contributions with her own labor.

Before the summer closed a new door opened that was to bring, along with persecution, one of the happiest and most fruitful periods of his life. Shortly after Southwest Oklahoma was opened to white settlers, Jim Harrel, a real estate broker at Cordell, Oklahoma, became interested in establishing a Christian school. He and others hauled timber in wagons from El Reno and built a three-room school, called Cordell Academy. On Sundays the building was used for church services. It was the first school in that area, and almost the first building in town. Though the enrollment its last year reached one hundred thirty, Cordell was too new to support an institution of that kind, and the school soon closed.

About 1905, however, O. H. McGavock and J. D. Tant discussed the possibility of establishing a Christian college in Southwestern Oklahoma. McGavock had six children whom he wanted to give a Christian education. He lived to realize this ambition, making provision before his death for the continued education of the children who were not yet through. W. D. Hockaday, owner of a prosperous merchantile business at Granite, Oklahoma, promised his full support. At McGavock's invitation representatives from all the churches in the area met at Hobart. Enthusiasm was high. The delegation from Cordell comprised real estate men who were able to offer greater inducements than others. So Cordell was chosen as the location for the college.

From Jim Harrel the promoters purchased one hundred sixty acres on the north edge of town, reserved ten acres for the school, and divided the rest into lots. Announcements were published widely. A day was set for auctioning the lots, and people came from long distances to buy. They gladly paid more than the lots were worth because the money would go into the college. Many bought who never intended to move and later sold to others. With the proceeds of the sale they started what G. A. W. Fleming glowingly described as a "towering, magnificient brick building." For its time it was a good building, two stories with a half basement. It had twelve classrooms and an auditorium that would seat three hundred. The second year they were to build a three-story dormitory with half basement.

J. H. Lawson, a good man and an able preacher, was chosen president and given a five-year contract. The school opened in temporary quarters in September, 1907. Unfortunately, however, friction soon developed between Lawson and Jim Harrel, a member of the board, and Fleming, a member of the faculty, and Lawson resigned before the year closed.

In the spring Fleming and some members of the board visited Odessa and offered the presidency to both Rhodes and R. C. Bell. Both declined. Bell, however, mentioned Armstrong as the man who could head such an institution, but he immediately wrote Armstrong, warning him about the trouble at Cordell. When Armstrong returned from the Estancia meeting, he found a letter from the board urging him to visit Cordell and talk with them about taking the presidency. Cordell was in the dry climate which had greatly improved his health. As a Christian college it offered him the kind of work he loved.

On his visit to Cordell he preached for the church, and the people were delighted. He also was impressed with the vision and good judgement of the board, and especially with W. D. Hockaday, whose rugged features and blunt frankness inspired confidence. He returned to talk with Mrs. Armstrong, however, and before giving final acceptance he wrote the secretary of the board for an understanding on two points. The college had not required all students to study the Bible.

"If I come," he wrote, "I want every student to carry at least one Bible class daily."

He also supposed the college was incorporated, and he was doubtful about the measure of authority the board would expect to exercise. When he and his associates had started the work at Odessa, the former institution had been incorporated and chartered by the state. The group paid the state fifty dollars to dissolve the charter that they might be free to direct the college as they felt best.

"If I accept the presidency," he wrote, "I am willing to be subject to the board in my work as president, and as a teacher of Greek, Hebrew, English, and so forth, but when I teach the Bible in your school I will be subject to no board or other authority save Christ and his church."

As a matter of fact the college was not formally incorporated until April 2, 1909. Though one or two doubted the wisdom of requiring a Bible class of every student, Hockaday stood strongly for it, and the board readily agreed to both stipulations.

So in August, 1908, Armstrong gave up the vacation of a lifetime, in a climate where every day was a delight, to return to what he supposed would be the joys of a Christian school, only to find himself embroiled in the most unpleasant situation he had ever faced.

Chapter 8

MY BELOVED WEST

"PAPA, THERE'S a fire in the kitchen! Papa, wake up, Papa! They say there's a fire in the kitchen."

Armstrong, suddenly awake, saw the child by the bedside shaking him. Instantly he smelled the smoke, which was already filling the hall outside. He leaped to his feet, calling, "Woodson, wake up; there's a fire!"

"Go, wake up J. D.," he told the little girl, as he began gathering clothes together.

On their way from Las Vegas the trains were late and they missed every connection. To pass the time in Amarillo he had taken the children to a movie, something he had never done before. Charlie Chaplin was on the screen in a silent slapstick comedy. Pataway especially was greatly impressed at the way he eluded the police, hiding in masses of shoe boxes, changing his appearance, making himself long and slender, sliding down drain pipes, teetering on the edge of skyscrapers high above the street till she felt like grasping her seat and holding on in terror.

Between Amarillo and Clinton their train was delayed by a wreck, and they had to spend the night in Clinton. The small hotel near the depot looked pitiful, but Clinton had no good hotels and the hour was late. Armstrong examined the beds and found them clean. But he thought it strange that the man and woman at the desk were unwilling to take his money. The hotel was being sold, and the two involved in the transaction seemed not to know who owned it at the moment. So they went to their rooms without paying. Fortunately, as it turned out, there was no room with enough beds for all four. They took adjoining rooms and left the doors open into the hall to hear the children if they called. Had all been in a single room with the door closed, no one would have heard of the fire till too late to escape.

Pataway must have been uneasy in the strange place and away from her parents. She was suddenly awakened by voices in the kitchen below. The voices were low, as if the speakers did not want to awaken anyone, but she caught the word "fire" and began to smell smoke. No fire alarm was ever given; no attempt was made to awaken the sleepers. One other occupant of the hotel was later helped through a window to safety, but no one was killed.

Expecting to reach Cordell that day, the Armstrongs had worn their best clothes and had spread them out carefully on different chairs. But with the smoke billowing in there was no time to dress. Armstrong crammed the suitcases with everything he could find. Pataway could not wake her brother, even by spanking. Her mother spanked and he still slept on. Finally his father's spanking got results. By now Pataway was crying. "That's the third spanking he's got tonight," she wailed.

Grabbing the suitcases, Armstrong urged them out. "Come on, Woodson, come on, Woodson, hurry!" he pleaded. Leading J. D., still half asleep, he and Pataway rushed down the narrow stairway. But when he turned, Mrs. Armstrong was not with them. She had lost her way in the smoke and headed back toward the fire, which was now flaming up through the kitchen ceiling. Armstrong called again, and she followed his voice down the stairs to safety.

On the street Pataway suddenly remembered her doll and began screaming. To the child it was like the burning of a living baby. Her father started back into the building, but someone caught him and held him back. A moment later the upper floor collapsed and the flames shot high into the air.

They had to dress on the street. Mrs. Armstrong had lost her best waist, escaping only with the collar, cuffs, and belt. J. D.'s shoes were behind in the fire. Luckily Armstrong had grabbed up from beneath his pillow the sock with his money in it, but the other sock was gone. In his childhood a neighbor woman had spent the night in their home, and had forgotten a bag of gold—eight hundred dollars—under her pillow. She was planning to buy a small farm with it. Of course, they easily restored her money, but the incident impressed Nelse indelibly with the importance of some device that would keep him from forgetting his money on a trip. He had decided Hambone's plan might be a good one. Hambone had said, "If'n ah had a dollah, ah'd keep it in mah sock, if'n ah had a good sock." A man surely would never dress and leave a hotel without his socks on. This time in the hurry of departure he remembered his money sock but could never locate the other.

The entrance into Cordell of the new president of the college the next day was acutely embarrassing. Clothes were all rumpled, the boy had no shoes, the president himself had one sock on and one sock off, and all hats were back in the fire. People in those days simply never went without hats. The only hat Mrs. Armstrong could find for the little girl in Cordell was a cheap, fly-specked panama, which could never be worn without cleaning. Washing it, however, softened the straw. So with the artistry Mrs. Armstrong had with clothes, she dyed it a dark cream, reshaped it, added ribbons, and transformed it into a very attractive model. It was days before the trunks arrived with their other clothes. Added to all this, they had come from the cool mountains of New Mexico to the blazing heat of an Oklahoma August, when winds sometime almost blistered the face.

Living arrangements at first were also discouraging. Not a house could be rented. Armstrong had arranged with a contractor to build him a house across the street from one corner of the campus, but it was far from finished. For two months they lived in a large bare classroom on the second floor of the college building. There was no closet for clothes, and no bath in the building. They cooked on a three-legged "monkey stove," had to carry water from the yard up two stories, and carry the waste water back down two stories.

The room was on the southwest corner of the building, the direction from which all "cyclones" came. Nobody in Oklahoma ever called them tornadoes in those days. Armstrong had never known the fury of an Oklahoma storm. In Tennessee and Kentucky rains usually came with little wind. But rains in Oklahoma were often heralded by boiling, black clouds, lightning and crashes of thunder, and accompanied by winds that bent the trees and drove the rain in horizontal sheets. The strangeness of these storms kept him watching at the windows many nights with the lightning apparently playing about his head. After they moved to their home and had a telephone installed, he always called A. H. Symcox, who owned a strange new instrument called a barometer, and Symcox became his weather predictor.

The move to their home came much sooner than they expected. The teacher in the primary room, which was down the hall next door to their temporary living quarters, found Pataway with high fever, and sent her to her room.

"Diptheria," the doctor said. "Get her out of here immediately so we can fumigate the building, or we'll have to close the school."

Their house still had no doors and most of the windows were not yet in. It was late October and a cold rain was falling. Don Hockaday, J. E. Blansett, and Lemon Carpenter, mature students, hastily moved the "monkey stove" and nailed quilts and blankets over doors and windows. They crammed clothes into any container at hand, mixing books and bacon, eggs and shirts. Mrs. Armstrong later dug out one of her best dresses from a potato basket. They bundled Pataway in blankets against the rain and carried her down. With such emergency measures they kept warm until the carpenter could get the windows and doors in.

But there was much to do in finishing the house. Some young people, children of two of the board members, had been hired to apply the prime coat of outside paint. They got into a playful fight and spattered gobs of paint over the walls. Armstrong attempted to apply the second coat, but the paint simply would not smooth out. Like Ralph Waldo Emerson, he was a scholar, thinker, and teacher, not a painter or carpenter. He could hardly drive a nail without bending it. Emerson once could not get a young cow into the barn lot. He pulled, but she would not come; he got behind and pushed, but she would not go. Their maid saw the difficulty and said, "Mr. Emerson, let me try." She filled a bucket with feed, held it under the cow's nose, and led her straight in. Armstrong knew cows better than Emerson, but he did not know painting or carpentry. Mrs. Armstrong finally applied the last two coats of paint herself. She also, with his help in pasting, papered the entire interior.

One of the first additions in the spring was a storm cellar. Early, J. D.'s older brother, had rejoined the family from Turner's meat market in New Mexico. He and Armstrong dug the cellar. Mrs. Armstrong measured the boards to go across the top, and Armstrong sawed where she marked. They covered the boards with tar paper, and coated this with a heavy layer of hot tar before heaping the dirt above it. The kitchen of the house was too small for both a coal and a gasoline stove, so the latter was put in a narrow pantry opening on one side. On this they heated the tar. But the tar suddenly caught fire and flames leaped to the ceiling. Armstrong forgot the gasoline and began trying to jerk the stove out of the room, but the door was too narrow. Grabbing the flaming pot of tar with his bare hands, he threw it out the window. Luckily the last drop of gasoline in the stove had just burned out and there was no explosion, but soot from the flaming tar covered the walls and hung in ropes from the ceiling.

Cementing the walls of the cellar completely baffled him. Try as he might he could not get the plaster to stick. Finally Mrs. Armstrong tried. The plaster clung as it was supposed to do, and she troweled it down to a smooth surface. There is always magic in a woman's touch!

All these inconveniences were overcome readily and with

good humor, but more serious trouble started almost from the first. The responsibility of a board of trustees is to determine the purposes of a college, establish the broad outline of its policies, and choose the administrative head. It is the responsibility of the administrator—president or chancellor—to translate the purposes and policies into a detailed, concrete program and to carry it out in harmony with the will of the trustees. The president in turn regards his faculty as a legislative body to help him determine the specific details of the program. It is understood that the president is free to choose his faculty with the approval of the board. It is also understood that the board retains the veto power over any appointment or over any specific policy of the administration which it regards as conflicting with the established purposes and broad policies of the institution. Unless there is such conflict, however, the board should not interfere with the internal operation of the school. Certainly no one member of the board should interfere, but whatever direction the board chooses to give should be the action of the entire board.

The preceding year President Lawson had resigned before the year closed because these lines of responsibility were not observed and friction developed between him and G. A. W. Fleming of the faculty and Jim Harrel of the board. Armstrong had now the same faculty and the same board. They were all new to him and he to them. Nevertheless, with these two exceptions there was perfect harmony and cooperation all year long. Fleming, head of the business department and business manager of the college, was a very friendly, likeable young man, intelligent, energetic, and aggressive. He and Harrel were largely responsible for locating the college at Cordell. Harrel had started the earlier Cordell Academy. The new board purchased from him the land for the new college, and he and Fleming had organized the sale of lots. When Lawson resigned, Fleming had carried on the administrative functions, and had made the trip to Odessa to find a new president.

It is easy for those so deeply involved to feel such a personal attachment to an institution as, perhaps subconsciously, to resist relinquishing authority. An insignificant incident illustrates the difficulty. The catalog had set the opening assembly for the new year at 9:00 a.m., and announcements were so made. The county superintendent Hubbard, Senator Massingale, and Mr. S. C. Burnett were all present to speak, and a full audience had assembled, when Fleming informed Armstrong that he had told friends in town the assembly would be at 10:00. Armstrong said nothing, and he and the speakers and audience, with various degrees of impatience, waited the hour for Fleming's friends to arrive.

A more troublesome problem arose over discipline. Fleming, supported by Harrel, favored regulating the activities of all students alike, those in their own homes as well as those in the dormitory, and to require certain study hours even in the homes. The faculty disagreed. Armstrong felt that enforcement of such a policy would require a spy system and would be taking over responsibilities that properly belonged to parents. He always favored as few rules as possible, appealing to students to "do right." The best results in building character and establishing right principles in young people, he believed, was to treat them as you would your own children, with firmness, but with love and confidence. Through his thirty years as president of a college this was the attitude he always had. He loved the students, and instinctively they responded to his love. One girl wrote long afterward, "I did not mind cheating in _____'s class, but I would never cheat in Brother Armstrong's. He trusted us."

At Searcy years later a boy from Virginia stole his roommate's best suit and was on his way home before it was discovered. Armstrong promptly telephoned the police. Luckily they located the trunk at the station before it left, arrested the boy, and held him at the city jail. Armstrong telephoned his father about what had happened and promised to do all he could to release the boy and start him on his way home. But when he offered to go the boy's bail, Mrs. Armstrong remonstrated.

"Jack, you know that boy is a thief. He's no account. Don't obligate yourself for him."

"Woodson," he said, "I talked with that boy's father,

and I know how concerned he is. I promised him I would do anything in the world I could to help his boy. If that were your boy, in jail a thousand miles from home, wouldn't you want some one to help him?"

Mrs. Armstrong had no more to say, for her heart was as generous as his. Naturally there were cases of discipline, and students occasionally had to be sent home, but the cases were few. Armstrong's stirring chapel speeches on "Liberty Is Found in Doing Right" are remembered by thousands. They moved students to correct wrongs and established in them a sound basis of moral values.

It is sometimes hard, also, for one who handles the money of an institution not to feel a sense of power. There was never any serious trouble, but enough unpleasantness existed that in the spring Armstrong handed the Board his resignation. This came as a shock. Because of Lawson's resignation the previous year, the confidence of the people in the school was at a low ebb when Armstrong took charge in the fall. Through the year he had won the confidence of the town, and the future again looked bright. Until his sudden resignation most of the board were unaware of any unpleasantness. But they had lost one president, and they were not about to lose Armstrong. They refused to accept the resignation. Even Harrel enthusiastically urged him to stay. Armstrong, however, explained that he was trying to avoid unpleasantness but that a college does not need two heads.

"The only condition on which I will stay at all is that Brother Fleming give up the business management," he said.

This was agreeable with Fleming, provided the few hundred dollars which he had contributed in starting the college were repaid him. Armstrong immediately made out a note for the amount he indicated. A member of the board signed it with him, but Armstrong paid it himself. This settled all difficulties with Fleming, and they remained friends. Armstrong always spoke of him with kindness, and when Armstrong started publication of the *Gospel Herald* and needed a cylinder press, Fleming ran an advertisement in it from April to June, offering to donate to the press a third of all commissions made on loans through him by June 1.

But Fleming's stepping out brought a bitter fight from Brother Harrel, a fight in which Fleming himself seems not to have been involved. Harrel was secretary of the board. He and Fleming were business friends, and he apparently wished to control the college through Fleming. He now accused Armstrong of lying, and called in Hockaday and other members of the board to hear his charges. Armstrong felt keenly the injustice of such an accusation. From a child he had hated falsehood, and was honest even to his own hurt. Harrel was a native of Cordell, a leader in the church, and a member of the board from the beginning of the school. Armstrong was a newcomer with less than a year of association with the board and with the people of Cordell. He asked Brother Bell, a merchant in town, and Brother O'Neal, both good men and leaders in the church, to talk with Harrel, but they could get nowhere with him. They suggested that Armstrong see him again, and this he did, but Harrel was obdurate. A. E. Freeman, a member of the board and a well-loved minister, also tried to settle the trouble. Finally the elders, with members of the board, spent two days investigating the charges. Brother Tomlinson, a member of the board, said, "Brother Armstrong, I wouldn't take a hundred dollars for the revelations that have come out of this meeting today." All the elders were agreed that Harrel was wrong and should make the wrong right.

A special meeting was held, in which Harrel read a long paper. He offered no apology and gave no indication of righting any wrong.

"Does Brother Harrel mean by this paper that he is ending his fight against me, and that the matter is settled between us?" Armstrong asked. But Harrel refused to reply. "Brethren, I don't call this any settlement," Armstrong said. All agreed.

The elders finally felt there was only one thing left to do. Brother Grogan, one of the elders, then took charge. To the whole church assembled he read the scriptures regarding the withdrawal of fellowship. He explained the situation and the judgment of the elders, that since they had done everything possible to persuade Brother Harrel to right the wrong, the church should withdraw its fellowship from him. Only Brother Young had dissented. He agreed that Harrel had done wrong and must make it right, but he hated to disfellowship him. As the congregation stood in approval of the action of the elders, only one row of seats, about twelve or thirteen people, remained seated.

Since the withdrawal automatically made Harrel ineligible to serve on the board of trustees, W. D. Hockaday, who had become chairman of the board, called a meeting to fill his place. The board was composed of able men of good character and independent judgment. A. E. Freeman, Henry E. Warlick, and J. W. Ballard were outstanding preachers. W. E. Tomlinson and W. D. Hockaday were successful business men. Brother Harrel was present as usual, and no one spoke up.

"Brother Freeman, take this chair," Hockaday said, and he stepped aside to give Freeman his place. "I make a motion that we exclude Brother Harrel from the board of trustees," Hockaday said. The motion was seconded, and carried, apparently with only Brother Harrel not voting.

But Harrel was a tenacious fighter. He immediately tried to bring a lawsuit against the board, and asked a lawyer to examine the books, hoping to find some mismanagement of funds or some illegal technicality, but the lawyer could find nothing on which to base a suit. Hockaday came over from Granite and met Harrel on the street.

"Jim," he said, "I told my wife I was coming over here to go to the poorhouse with you."

Hockaday, whose daughter Sallie Ellis became the wife of George S. Benson, later President of Harding College in Searcy, Arkansas, was a man of courage and conviction. He was the leader in the church in Granite and held the respect and good will of all who knew him, but he did not shrink from a fight when it was necessary, even if it took his last cent. From this time till the college closed he and the board gave Armstrong and the administration unqualified support. Hockaday believed that after a board had employed a president in whom they had complete confidence, they should let him run the school without interference from board members or others. Armstrong said of him later, "He was a man of safe judgment and excellent foresight. He has been the greatest giver to the school in cash. We shrink to think what would have been the condition of the school today, if it had not been for W. D. Hockaday." Certainly had it not been for Hockaday's support Armstrong would have left at the end of the first year.

"It was a terrible time," he said. "I never want to go through with anything like it again." Once during the trouble Brother Harrel said, "Armstrong simply outgenerals us every time." Actually he was not outgeneraling anyone. He was only trying to do the right thing, the fair thing. There was no reason for the trouble ever to have arisen. By the close of the spring semester it was settled, and all was clamness and peace.

In 1910 the small group which drew apart with Brother Harrel were restored to fellowship. Elders from a number of churches met with the elders of the two congragations in Cordell and union and good fellowship were reestablished. "Tears of joy," it is related, "were in every eye." A. E. Freeman was engaged to preach for the united group for a period of time to help cement the fellowship. He was followed by John Harrel, the brother of Jim, and later by others. Following this trouble Armstrong wrote of the Cordell church, "In some respects I have never seen a better church. We live at peace among ourselves. For nearly four years now we have had hardly a jar among us. Most of these years we have been truly of one heart and one soul."

In spite of the fact that the elders of the church with much forbearance tried to settle the trouble and only as a last resort used the scriptural method of discipline, opponents of Armstrong tried for years to find something wrong in his actions at the time, but with no success. For instance, Daniel Sommer, with whom he was just finishing his written debate, rushed down to Cordell and hurried back to Indianapolis to write it up in his *Octographic Review*.

"We grieve like a child over the trouble and division that took place at Cordell over the college that was built there," he wrote.

"From the laying of the first cornerstone of Cordell

Christian College until this very hour," Armstrong wrote in reply, "There has been no trouble or division, over the college question among brethren in Cordell, in the sense in which the college question has been discussed in the *Review*. In fact, the trouble here arose, raged, and reached white heat, and the question of the righteousness of having such schools was involved in the matter no more than the righteousness of Christians building and establishing homes was involved."

Thirty years later E. R. Harper, during his fight to oust Armstrong from the faculty of Harding College, visited Cordell in vain to see what he could find against him. But Armstrong's record was clear.

With all the unpleasantness finally past the school entered upon a period of growth and enriched service.

"Those ten years were the happiest of my life," Armstrong said, many years later. "I had the best school I have ever had because it was small and easily leavened. We never had a more loyal group of students, because the fight had brought the loyal support of every student."

The second year B. F. Rhodes and R. C. Bell joined him from Odessa, and the third year S. A. Bell and W. T. Vaughan.

He and Rhodes had fought the battle for Christian education against Sommer, the giant of the North, and Armstrong had a great admiration and love for him. He said more than once, "I know of no man his equal in his peculiar field. It was said of Daniel Webster once that he was a living lie because no one could be as great as he looked. So Rhodes is deceptive. He is a prince, but no one would think so to look at him. Of him R. L. Whiteside said, after seeing him at work: 'He is a cheat.' He was far greater than, at first glance, he might appear to be. All his life he has been a great teacher."

To his deep regret, however, Rhodes and Bell remained only one year. Thorp Springs College offered Rhodes a place and he accepted. On finding that Thorp Springs needed a president also, Rhodes made a special trip to persuade Bell to accept the presidency. He feared the blow it would be to

Armstrong and suggested that they not mention it to him until arrangements were definite at Thorp Springs. Though the presidency of a college seemed at the time a greater service than he could give at Cordell, Bell still felt he must talk with Armstrong before making final commitment. Losing two of his best men at once was a stunning blow. But Armstrong never tried to hold teachers against their will.

"If we had not been pressed financially," he said, "I should have tried hard to keep him (Rhodes), but it might have been selfish. Then later, even at the close of the year, when R. C. Bell's name and picture were in our catalog for another year, he too was asked to come to Thorp Springs. I didn't think we could give him up. I told him I didn't want him to go, but left him free to decide it. He went, and I have never felt any loss in this school worse than I felt the loss of his going. But he went away loved and loving. I have never loved him more than now, and I believe he reciprocates my love."

Bell's attitude is well indicated by his sending Armstrong the material for the next Thorp Springs catalog to be printed on the *Gospel Herald* press. Armstrong comments in the next issue of the *Herald*: "Brothers Bell and Rhodes are known to be consecrated men that will make a thing go when others are hunting salaried positions. Their wives are full partners with them in carrying the burdens. If it were not for the devotion of such hearts to the cause of our Master, not a school in the brotherhood would open next year. There is hardly an occupation in which the teachers in our schools could not double their present salaries."

The ties that bound these three friends together were very close. Although opportunities at times seemed better elsewhere, Bell returned to the college at Harper and at Morrilton for other periods of association, and Rhodes returned to Cordell and Harper, and after a short period at Abilene, returned to spend his last years with Armstrong. Whenever, after an absence elsewhere, he or Sister Rhodes wrote to ask if there might be an opening again, Armstrong was always overjoyed to have them back "at home."

With the trouble ended the only difficulty Armstrong faced

was the Oklahoma storms. During a class once in his first year the wind arose, the sun dimmed out, and the sky grew dark, but there was no lightning or thunder.

"We must have a storm on us," he said. "Do you think we had better dismiss school?" But the class laughed.

"No, Brother Armstrong. It's just a dust storm." In a little while the dust cloud passed and the sun shone again with its ancient glory.

The second year he had a storm cellar dug between the college building and the dormitory, large enough to accommodate all dormitory students in an emergency. And the emergency came when the unfinished steps down into it were only a slide of red clay. Two small twisters had struck near Cordell in the afternoon, demolishing some farm homes. Then as darkness settled down black clouds boiled up from the southwest, the path of tornadoes. Some one called up the dormitory steps, "A cyclone's coming; get down to the cellar at once."

The boys rushed from the second and third floors two steps at a time. The rain was pouring. Blansett was holding back the cellar door, but as the last boy plunged down, the wind whipped the door out of Blansett's hands, giving the boy a resounding crack on the head as he went down. Blansett hurried in and held the door tight with the rope attached to the underside.

Suddenly the wind stopped and there was a great silence. "It's here," some one said, "let's pray." The prayer began, but it was hard to listen. For the ceiling suddenly seemed to heave up and down with the suction of the wind, and all wondered if the earth above would fall in and bury them.

In a moment the storm was past, and some one said, "It's safe to leave now." But the incline was now soaked with the rain and slippery as glass. The students made it easily, but the piano teacher, a stately, dignified woman, who had returned from town in her best clothes and had taken no time to change, slipped and slid back down the muddy incline. Blansett reached down from above to help her.

"Now, Miss Hille, just take it easy," he soothed. "I'll

help you up; just take it easy." Carpenter pushed from below as Blansett pulled from above. But again she slipped
and slid, red clay covering her clothes. It took the third
attempt before they "soothed" her out. Down below, Pataway and Gussie Teague were so convulsed they stuffed hand-
kerchiefs in their mouths to keep from laughing outright.

The rain was still pouring, but students and teachers went
out to search for the injured and the dying. The cyclone
missed the campus by three hundred yards but cut a path
through the northwest side of town, killing five people and
injuring others. The Symcoxes, whose faithful barometer had
foretold the storm, had all gone to their cellar. When the
storm passed and they opened the door, the place where
their house had stood was empty space. Morning revealed
the first story torn to splinters, the cast iron kitchen range
rolled into a ball. But the second story had been lifted very
carefully and set down gently in a neighboring field, with
everything undisturbed. An alarm clock on a study table was
ticking away as if nothing had happened. A farmer on the
edge of town had shut his two mules up for the night. The
barn was blown to pieces, and the mules were picked up and
carried through the air nearly a quarter of a mile and deposited none too gently in a wheat field. The farmer found
their landing site and traced their tracks through the mud
back to where the barn had stood.

But the next morning the sun was bright and the day as
serene and beautiful as if five people had not died in the
night.

Through the ten years at Cordell Armstrong spent nights
watching the storm clouds but felt a sense of security in
Symcox's barometer and the storm cellar. Later at Harper,
Morrilton and Searcy, where there were no storm cellars,
he relaxed.

"I'll just trust the Lord to take care of us," he said, and
this burden was happily lifted.

Armstrong's meetings through the summers at Cordell
were more and more confined to the West, but when he did
get away for a meeting in Tennessee, Alabama, or Florida,
he invariably longed to get back to his "beloved West."

From a visit to his mother in Tennessee he wrote home,

"I love the broad expanse of the western prairies and the level acres of corn, cotton, and wheat; I love the 'home of alfalfa'; I love the high, dry climate and the ozone of that invigorating breeze with which the West is so enriched; but above all I enjoy the Lord's work there."

Wherever his work was, there he was supremely happy.

Chapter 9

MAKING A COLLEGE CHRISTIAN

WITH THE year's trouble ended Armstrong could set about building the kind of college he had long envisioned. He had a clear concept of what a Christian school should be, but what means should be used to make and keep an institution really Christian?

"To guide a mind to think truly and wisely," he wrote, "to judge properly, reason correctly, is a masterful work. Were this the greatest work to be done in the rearing of a child, it would be enough to engage the undivided thinking and planning of fathers and mothers. But in this mind, even in the lowest type of man, is something still more beautiful and wonderful. By some it is called conscience, and by others the moral sense. Call it what we may, it separates man from all other animals and fixes his destiny eternally different. Robbed of this power, man is no longer man. Through its abuse he gradually sinks so low that language reels to tell the story. The real and lasting advancement of every community, nation, and people lies in the consciences of its people. So in our work our chief aim is to send every boy and girl home at night with a tenderer conscience, a greater respect for right and duty. To teach a boy how to live a hundred years and train him to be an intellectual giant without this conscience culture is to curse the world and him."

Even with this ideal, however, students differ widely in ability, and the object of every teacher, he believed, should be the highest attainable perfection in the material he receives.

"Don't cry out that perfection is impossible," he said. "We have been attempting perfect spelling, perfect writing. We shall not make any worse mistake in attempting perfect men and women. What kind of man or woman ought we to try to train our child to be? One whose body is sound, the ready servant of his will, doing with ease and pleasure all the work it is capable of; one whose intellect is a clear, logical force, dependable for thinking and expressing; one whose memory is stored with a reasonable amount of the great and fundamental truths of Nature and the laws of her operation, of the important accomplishments of mankind; one who is alert, lively, cheerful, hopeful, with passions trained to heel; one who is the servant of a tender conscience, who has learned to love beauty, whether of Nature or of art, to hate all vileness, to respect, to assist, and to work with his fellowman—this is the sort of product we teachers are expected to work for."

In attaining this ideal, however, Armstrong was generations ahead of many educators of his time in recognizing the importance of individual differences. He quoted a report from the United States Commissioner of Education in 1911 that only seven students out of every hundred who finish the grades go on to high school, and of high school graduates only five of a hundred go on to college.

"As long as a school system disregards individual differences," he declared, "as long as the boy with the quick mind must plod along in the same groove with the slow, we can expect ninety-three failures out of a hundred. Teachers should study the child himself—his individual needs. They should quit working for grades and completion of courses, and work for boys and girls."

In the college at Cordell teachers gave the individual attention which was needed. One Monday morning, in a blizzard driving straight from the North Pole across the Oklahoma plains, there was a knock at Armstrong's door. When the stranger entered and removed his overcoat, beneath his regular coat he had a heavy red woolen shirt. It was S. T. Tipton, forty years old, who had come to enroll in school. He was a successful farmer, owner of a number of rich farms around Tipton, Oklahoma, but he had almost no education, and he wanted to be able to teach effectively in Sunday school and be a leader in the church. On examining his ability in reading and arithmetic Armstrong thought he might begin with the third grade, but he doubted if a man of that age would stay.

"Brother Tipton," he said, "you need not sit in the room with the children. You can stay in the study hall, and see the teacher at the times she tells you." He wanted to remove all embarrassment.

"No, Brother Armstrong," Tipton said, "I might miss something that way. I'll stay in the room with the children."

He did, and the children loved him. But he soon outstripped the third grade, went on through the other grades and through high school, and in a short time was able to make public talks, teach Sunday school classes, and become a leader in his home church. He later established the Tipton Orphans Home and endowed it with money and lands. It was this type of individual assistance which the school at Cordell was constantly giving.

But perfection in education requires more than individual attention. This was why only the Christian school, Armstrong believed, could give an ideal education.

"The very idea that a school from which the eternal wisdom of God is purposely, legally, persistently ruled out of its course of study can train any child for complete living, or make the best possible boy out of what he is, should be an insult to every believer in God," he said.

He was deeply interested in the determined fight of the women of Oklahoma City in 1914 to require daily reading of the Bible without comment in every classroom. Opposition arose immediately from Rabbi Blatt of Oklahoma City and from the Knights of Columbus. R. C. Ottinger of the American Secular Union and Free Thought Federation of Chicago threatened a propaganda campaign in Oklahoma City to "expose the real character of the Christian fetish book," which he claimed had "in a thousand ways and for a thousand years hindered the civilization of men." The Union letter listed nine radical demands which it was seeking to enforce on the entire nation. Among these was abrogation of all laws looking to the enforcement of "Christian morality," and replacing these with "a natural morality." These demands were fifty years before the "new morality" which is now so widely hailed even by some church leaders.

"That the Bible has hindered civilization for a thousand years," Armstrong wrote in reply, "depends on what a man calls civilization. If Mr. Ottinger thinks of civilization as following the 'natural morality' which his Federation advocates, the morality of the beasts of the field and the birds of the air, the Bible has hindered that. This is the kind of natural morality reported by Seneca in Rome when women reckoned the years by the number of husbands they had. Juvenal speaks of those who are divorced before their marital garlands are faded, and whose chief distinction it was to have had eight husbands in five autumns; while Martial founds one of his epigrams on the almost incredible story of one who married within a month her tenth husband, a woman whom Martial, in spite of his own licentiousness, called 'an upright adultress under cover of law.' Against such civilization the Bible has been a hindrance. But what shall we say to these demands? What do they mean to the future of our boasted civilization? 'Rome was not built in a day;' niether did she fall in a day. No individual, no family, no nation can purposely oppose God without paying the cost. Sooner or later the account must be squared."

He challenged the Union to select the best man they could find and debate with him two propositions concerning the Christ and his claim to be the Son of God. Each would write six articles of two thousand words on each of the propositions. The challenge was ignored.

"But keeping the Bible out of the public schools," Armstrong pointed out, "is not the work of the corrupt, or wicked, or non-religious. Were there no Catholics, Jews, or agnostics, or irreligious, it would still be excluded. It is the 'Amen Corner' members of the sectarian churches of this country! The Clergy, the Bishops, and the Presiding Elders! The Reverend and Right Reverend."

After much pressure from the Women's Bible Club of Oklahoma City, a special committee of the school board agreed that if the major religious sects, Hebrew, Catholic, and Protestant, would make a list of selections from the Bible which all would approve, they would have it published and place a copy on each teacher's desk and recommend a daily reading without comment. But no such publication developed.

Although he sympathized with the effort of the women, Armstrong recognized that it was hopeless. The book which, he felt, above all others could shape and form the character and refine the qualities of men had to be left out.

"We have long been trying to *reform* men," he said. "Only in very recent years have we learned that our real business is *formation* and not *reformation*. The practical and scientific way is to emphasize constructive plans for building manhood and womanhood. For instance, the boy must be taught that money-making is not to be compared with man-making; that there is something infinitely better than a millionaire of money, and that is a millionaire of character. The millstone about the neck of the republic is the man with the materialistic, sordid, selfish interests. To save the republic we must produce the boy with the nobler ideals, with spiritual vision, and with the power to see and to grasp the higher values of life."

He had great sympathy for teachers in the public schools who were trying to do an ideal job under impossible handicaps. Deprived of the influence of the Bible, how could they give students the moral and spiritual training they should have? A prominent superintendent had recently talked to Armstrong about a girl who was giving him much trouble.

"I shall be glad for you to try her in your school," he

said. "Nothing but the religion of Jesus Christ will ever do her any good. And you know we can't teach it here as you can." The superintendent was not a member of the church of Christ, but he recognized the need of a spiritual influence he could not give in his school.

The failure of Christian parents to recognize such need grieved Armstrong deeply. Citing the alarming increase in crime—two and a half times the increase in population—he asked;

"Where is the fault? It lies in the training of children. If we do not change our methods, the stream of crime, in the next fifty years, will overflow its banks beyond control, and our country will be verily drenched with crime. Wait, brethren, till your children come home full of worldliness, indifferent to, if not despising, the church, and then weep and say, 'We sent to the wrong school.' Hold to your money; hug it to your heart, and send your children where the religion of our Lord is scoffed at and worldliness runs rife. Put your money into hogs, cattle, alfalfa, and more land, and let your children grow up in an environment that can but curse them eternally. Let your daughters marry the 'toughs' of that environment because of your inexcusable mistake in putting money into hogs instead of your children. Go on, but know thou that for all these things God will bring thee into judgment!"

Since this prediction we have seen the increase of crime and violence even beyond his fears, with organized mobs defying city and state authority and threatening civil war.

He wanted the college at Cordell to be, not superficially, but genuinely Christian. When he attended the Baptist University he had found a pronounced "preacher class" among the students. Preachers received free tuition and special favors. Other students shunned and maligned them. When he came to Cordell a similar condition was growing. "Preachers" received free tuition, and non-preachers were excused from Bible. He quickly changed this.

"I would quit the school tomorrow," he said, "if we were not allowed to teach every student daily the word of God. Did our Lord say 'preachers are the salt of the earth and the light of the world?' Every Christian is to be a preacher to the extent of his ability. The school that makes a distinction prepares a special class that will demand special privileges. Like the lawyer, they will have invested in a profession; their training will have been a costly investment, and they will therefore demand more for their work and refuse opportunities that cannot pay well. How then will the 'poor have the gospel preached to them?'"

To make the school Christian, then, Armstrong believed that every student should be well informed about any question affecting the Christian faith. In addition to Bible classes every one attended a Monday night meeting where living issues of many kinds were discussed. On controversial questions he invited outstanding speakers to present their different views, and meetings often grew exciting. But he was never afraid of fair discussion. It was the means of sifting truth from error and bringing a sound basis of unity.

Dr. W. H. Freeman, a retired physician who moved to the college about 1912, had heard that the faculty taught some kind of "illusion" about God's "special providence," a question which was causing much concern in Oklahoma and Texas. He asked Armstrong if he might discuss it with him, and the arrangement was made for the next Monday night. Armstrong suggested that he define "special providence" as he understood it, and that Dr. Freeman then follow.

In opening the discussion Armstrong said there was really nothing "special" about God's providence, or care, for those who were obedient to him, but God had promised many blessings to the obedient which he had not promised to the disobedient and rebellious. One of these was that he would answer the prayers of the faithful, and he quoted Paul's exhortation: "In nothing be anxious; but in everything by prayer and supplication with thanksgiving let your requests be made known unto God. And the peace of God, which passeth all understanding, shall guard your hearts and your thoughts in Christ Jesus . . . And my God shall supply every need of yours according to his riches in glory in Christ Jesus." With other passages he illustrated promises made to the obedient which are not made to the rebellious.

As Dr. Freeman arose to speak, he said, "Brethren, I

really have no speech. I have evidently been misinformed about the meaning of 'special providence.' I believe as firmly as Brother Armstrong does that God answers the Christian's prayers. If this is 'special Providence,' then I also believe in it."

Often in such meetings those who thought they were a world apart found unity when they examined the issues honestly and sincerely.

Through that spring Dr. Freeman gave a series of chapel talks which were to influence the good health of a number who heard him as long as they lived. But his greatest blessing to the Armstrongs was in saving the life of their daughter. Pataway had one attack of diphtheria in 1908. In 1916, a friend whom she was visiting unthoughtedly arranged a pallet for the two of them with blankets used with a child who had recently died of diphtheria in the home. Pataway immediately contracted it a second time. The family doctor said there was nc antitoxin in town, but at her age he thought he could handle the case by swabbing. But she grew steadily worse. The deadly membrane was covering the throat, fever was running high, and finally she was becoming delirious. It was summer and Armstrong was away in a meeting. In desperation Mrs. Armstrong called Dr. Freeman. He took one look, and said, "We must get antitoxin at once."

"But the doctor said there was none in town," Mrs. Armstrong exclaimed.

"Surely that cannot be," Dr. Freeman said. "I'll see." In a few minutes he was back with all the antitoxin needed, and he took over the treatment at once. The drug store informed him that they always had antitoxin, but the Armstrongs' doctor refused to buy from them, and the other store had been out.

The family doctor never called at the home again, nor telephoned to see how the patient was doing. Some weeks later he sent a bill. When Pataway's brother carried him a check, he seemed greatly relieved that she had fully recovered.

"I was afraid the uvula might sluff off," he said. Such a

result would have impaired her speech forever, but without Dr. Freeman's timely help the result would have been still more tragic.

The Armstrongs never forgot the kindness. In 1944 a month before his death, Armstrong had seen a letter from Dr. Freeman in the *Firm Foundation*, and he wrote him at once.

"It warmed our hearts and caused us to live again those good years we spent together at Cordell. We could never forget them! I can never forget your great and good service to us and to the college."

Dr. Freeman replied immediately, the letter reaching Armstrong two weeks before his death.

"Nothing could have given us more happiness," he wrote, "except your presence, which perhaps we will never enjoy again until we meet 'over there,' where, as you suggest in your letter, 'We will talk it all over,'" Dr. Freeman was then eighty-nine and Mrs. Freeman eighty-two. Armstrong's affection for old friends and his loyalty to them knew no bounds. He counted them a rich heritage.

In his desire that students hear all sides of any question Armstrong dismissed the Monday night meeting once in 1914 so that the whole school could hear a Mr. Bundy of the Charles T. Russell persuasion speak on "Who Created Hell." The "Bible Doctrine of Eternal Punishment" had been discussed at the college the preceding week, and this was an opportunity for students to hear a different view.

The auditorium of the courthouse was filled. Mr. Bundy defined the word *hell*, from Anglo-Saxon *helan* "to cover," as merely a "covered place, a grave," and asserted that men were responsible for filling it with terror. There was no such place as Milton had pictured except in the imaginations of men. With much shrewdness he attempted to explain away Bible references to hell and eternal fire. His misrepresentations were glaring but so plausibly put that Armstrong felt the lecture should be answered. At the close he pressed to the front and asked permission to make an announcement, but Bundy would permit none. The meeting was his and he wanted nothing to impair the impression he had made. Armstrong waited till the audience was dismissed, then rapped for attention.

"I had asked to make an announcement," he said, "which Mr. Bundy would not permit. Now that he has dismissed the audience, and it is no longer his, I want to announce that tomorrow night in this same auditorium I will reply to Mr. Bundy's lecture to all who may care to attend."

The next night, in spite of a howling blizzard, the courthouse was packed, with people standing in all available space. With perfect courtesy toward Mr. Bundy, and granting the sincerity of his views, Armstrong gave a masterly and convincing exposition of the scriptural teaching on hell and eternal punishment. The two speeches stirred the entire city and produced more Bible reading in Cordell than had been done for many years.

Along with Bible classes, chapel, and Monday night meetings, the annual Thanksgiving lectures were also highlights in helping to make the college intelligently Christian. Speakers of outstanding ability like James A. Harding, R. H. Boll, Joe S. Warlick, and many others gave inspirational talks, but sometimes the program covered controversial issues. It was such a meeting in 1915 that, surprisingly, called down the criticism of the caustic T. R. Burnett and the saintly John T. Poe. Burnett called it a "preachers' convention," and declared if it "was called by the church, it was wholly unscriptural," but if by the college, it discussed "ecclesiastical questions." "Will somebody arise and tell us the nature of this hybrid production that has sprung up in Oklahoma soil within recent years?"

Armstrong replied that the meeting was not a "preachers' convention." It was called neither by the church nor by the college, but by a group of Christians interested in teaching young people truth on many important questions and that most of those who attended were not preachers.

Poe asked if the purpose was to advertise the college, and, if so, was that not prostituting religion to a worldly enterprise? Armstrong replied that making the college better known was certainly a secondary consideration, which rightly added to the value of the meeting. "But absolutely no effort was made to *show* the school. One of the preachers was asked when he got home how the school was progressing, and he replied, 'I did not see any school.'"

The purpose of the meeting, Armstrong declared, was to try to heal the divisions and factions among the disciples and to create a more brotherly feeling. "We hoped for unity, for harmony; we hoped for a more brotherly spirit in our differences. The spirit throughout the meeting was of the very best. Brethren who have heretofore been regarded as radical showed a real anxiety to find union ground and manifested a willingness to surrender preferences and choices that they might agree with brethren. Perhaps nobody was converted by the discussions but he at least discovered that there were two sides to a question and saw the possibilities of his being wrong."

The truth is, had the program of 1915, like the earlier Thanksgiving lectures, avoided controversial subjects, there would have been no objection. A similar meeting was held in Ardmore, Oklahoma, the year before, and one of the "fighting" subjects was "Special Providence." T. B. Clark of Whitewright, Texas, reported, "We all looked forward with anxious hearts to the discussion of 'Special Providence.' Well, that godly man, whom everybody loves, J. N. Armstrong, was the first speaker, and a more appreciated talk was not made during the entire meeting. I believe Brother Armstrong's talk was endorsed by all . . . To say the truth Brother Armstrong's speech was a fitting one to close a feast of good things like this meeting was."

If Armstrong's speech on such a controversial subject "was endorsed by all," it is a glowing tribute to the uncanny wisdom which seemed invariably to guide him in time of crisis.

But the criticisms were a humorously pathetic commentary on how difficult it is for even good men to face up to honest differences and seek to resolve them by a frank exchange of views. On such criticism R. L. Whiteside, commented.

"I have known J. N. Armstrong a long time," he wrote. "He is a scholarly Christian gentleman, and is incapable of a

mean thing. Yes, Brother Critic, he errs in judgment; everybody does but you. I put Cordell Christian College on the
list among the best . . . Christian colleges have their enemies and knockers. Cordell has them. But someone has
said: 'Every knock is a boost.' 'Abuse is a pledge that you
are felt,' says Emerson. A live man or institution will meet
opposition, and will also make friends and supporters.
Everybody shuns a grinning skeleton, but nobody abuses it.
The Christian colleges are evidently alive."

This effort of Armstrong to lead Christians to a more
profound unity of faith, to respect honest differences that
in no way hinder complete obedience to the will of God,
was the beginning of a lifelong struggle that was in later
years to bring searing persecution that only a man of great
soul could have endured without bitterness. But to students
the sincere search for truth was a constant inspiration.
Among the young teachers at Cordell no one was more
popular than Webb Freeman, son of A. E. Freeman, a
prominent preacher and member of the board. Webb was
slender, handsome, intelligent, an interesting speaker, a
perfect penman, and a superior teacher.

"No better work in Latin is being done in the Southwest
than he is doing in his classes," Armstrong wrote. "He
is a faithful gospel preacher of much ability; and if the
university doesn't spoil him, we have a right to expect great
things of him."

After receiving his degree from Cordell, Webb went on to
the Southern Baptist Seminary at Louisville, where he received the Doctor of Theology *summa cum laude.* At Yale
he received a Masters with the same high distinction, and
had completed all work for the Doctor of Philosophy except finishing his thesis and taking the final. When he
dropped out because of his sister's illness, Abilene Christian
College immediately offered him a position. Armstrong had
been uneasy about Webb's graduate work, but he was re-
assured by the sincerity of his faith. He realized that his
scholarship might arouse the suspicion of some, and that a
new and different way of expressing his views might raise
questions, but he was grieved that Abilene did not keep him.
With a little patience, a little time for adjustment, he felt

that Webb might have given years of superb scholarship to the Christian schools. In his "love letter" to Dr. Freeman in 1944 Armstrong mentions a letter he had just received from Webb. "A very good letter indeed. Most of all I enjoyed his expressions of faith in the Lord and in his Book. Webb has always been good."

Webb had heard of Armstrong's illness, and his letter was a beautiful tribute to his old teacher.

> I suppose I am more of an Armstrongite than anybody else, so far as my way of thinking is concerned. My inspiration from James A. Harding gave me more independence of thought than has been best for me as a co-worker with conservative brethren. Your plea for "Undenominational Christianity" set me out in a religious life as a great adventure—always learning a little more, always open to new truth from any source, always respectful of the other believer's conscience, always seeking to retest my ideas by the writers of the Bible, and never willing to be bound by any human interpretation.

Armstrong might not have agreed with Webb on some things, just as he differed with others, but the fact that both recognized the supreme authority of Christ and the Scriptures and were obedient to them constituted a bond of unity overshadowing such differences.

Important as were Bible classes, chapel, and Monday night meetings in helping to make the college Christian, even more vital were the lives of Christian teachers. Men like R. C. and S. A. Bell, B. F. Rhodes, J. E. Boyd, Webb Freeman, W. T. Vaughn, R. A. Zahn, and women like Mrs. Armstrong, Mary Shepherd, and Marie Hille, inspired a loyalty to the Master, which in turn made students loyal to everything good in the school. Above all, students felt the influence of J. N. Armstrong. *Educere* means "to lead out," not "to drive, force, or beat out," and Armstrong and the faculty were "leaders" who moved students by example rather than command.

No one at Cordell ever dreamed that childish yells were needed to create mature "college spirit," or that winning teams were necessary to build loyalty to an institution. Armstrong was never opposed to reasonable athletics. He defended the school against attacks by Daniel Sommer for having athletics.

"Does the *Octographic Review*," he asked, "teach that it is a sin to play ball? It is natural for young men to want to play, and to oppose it is to oppose nature. But many schools carry it to the extreme. A team that plays once a week often loses three days of actual study, and often the conduct of teams on trips is rough. A hotel manager recently told me he had refused to accept one team because of their previous conduct. But at Cordell students play for fun. There is no coach, no admission fee, and no games are played outside town."

Students organized their own baseball and basketball teams and played with enthusiasm. There was no football. At Hobart, just south of Cordell, the son of the county judge was killed in a football game and the town arose in sorrow and indignation and abolished football.

"One of the wonders of this age," Armstrong wrote, "is that any sane management approves and encourages the football game. Now that one boy has been killed at Hobart that town has eliminated the game. Why could it not have been done before? Will Hobart's experience be useful to her neighbors? Or must a poor boy be sacrificed on the altar of football in every town before the country can be delivered from the horrible consequences of the game?"

The college boys had earlier made an abortive attempt to introduce football, and Armstrong had made no objection, perhaps because he knew that without a paid coach to drive the men it would be quite harmless. A fairly large group gathered on the field. Two teams were lined up with instructions about plays and tackling. At the kickoff Don Hockaday, the bulkiest man in the line, caught the ball and started down field. He was slow but ponderous and carried the puny tacklers along with the ball till practically the whole team finally brought him down. When he was able to scramble from under the pile, the skin was peeled from his nose and his face was bloody. That ended football at Cordell forever! A game that could hurt a boy like Don whom everybody loved was simply out!

But loyalty and school spirit? Cordell was full of it! It was not built on yells and sports but on things far more enduring, and it was expressed in many ways. The first year, for lack of money, the half basement of the college building was left unfinished, and there were no walks. The second year Armstrong announced that he would like to finish the basement and lay walks. As usual he led the work. He and Rhodes, Bell and other teachers donned overalls. All the boys and most of the girls turned out in work clothes. The men mixed cement, trundled wheelbarrows, poured concrete, and trowled it down to a smooth finish, and the girls brought water, cakes, and encouragement. Teachers and students worked together—without pay—for love of a college that belonged to them all.

Following the basement they laid walks; G. W. Kieffer, a student with experience in masonry, worked far into the night to give the finishing touches. Following the walks, at Dr. Freeman's suggestion and with his aid, students planted one hundred fifty trees to beautify the perfectly bare campus. But trees, even with persistent watering, grew like snails in the hot, dry climate, and years later when the college closed, one almost needed a microscope to see them. But students were doing their best for a school they loved.

In those days final examinations were finished on the last Wednesday of the school year, and the commencement exercises came the next morning at 10:00. But the final program of the year always came that night at 8:00—usually a play, sometimes written as well as directed by Mrs. Armstrong. With all classes finished the day before, all but the graduates could have left for home Wednesday evening, but no student or teacher ever left till after the Thursday night play.

The final program my first year at Cordell (1909) was "The Merry Milkmaids," an operetta in which Mrs. Armstrong with her rich alto and Willie Klingman with his beautiful high tenor took the leading roles. Rather than miss the performance I paid John Tomlinson to drive me across the country to Dill after the program to catch a train. To a fifteen-year old country boy it was a startling event, and Mrs. Armstrong a vision of grace and beauty.

When I reached home and described the program to my older sister, she asked about the Armstrongs and whether they had any children.

"Yes, they have one daughter," I said, "and a nephew whom they are rearing as their son."

"Why don't you marry the daughter?" my sister asked.

"Why, she's just a child," I replied. At fifteen a ten-year-old seemed too young even to notice. I had seen her the first day I was on the campus, when, with dark-tanned face and pigtails flying in the wind, she had raced down hill on a little wagon, running me off the sidewalk in front of her father's house. But six years later, cast together in a play, I really saw her for the first time. What a miraculous change six years can bring!

Aside from the positiveness of his teaching Armstrong's personality, in an indefinable way, permeated the whole institution. His kindness, courtesy, generosity, fairness, faith, and deep convictions were contageous. As Mary Shepherd once said, if students were having a party, when Armstrong entered, every face lighted up. He brought confidence and happiness wherever he went.

Both he and Mrs. Armstrong treated the students as their children. How far-reaching their generosity went one can never know. But the second year I was at Cordell I was surprised one cold day before Christmas, when Armstrong called me in.

"Here is an overcoat," he said "that my wife wants to give you. She has been watching you come from town without a coat and is afraid you'll be sick." He held up a beautiful, warm coat, and insisted that I put it on. I was speechless. My father had died in the spring, and I was determined to defy the blizzards and shiver the winter through without a coat. But this one lasted me for years, and I have never loved another quite as much.

Armstrong's childhood Christmases were always scant—a few sticks of peppermint candy, an orange—but he always loved gifts that brought happiness.

"May a holy benediction rest upon the thoughtful and considerate," he once wrote, "upon those who think of others and are considerate of their pleasures, ease, and happiness; even upon those who feel it their mission to make others glad, and whose chiefest joy is found in lightening the burdens and sweetening the cup of other hearts." But he encouraged giving chiefly to those in need. "Find out who is poor and what they are poor in, and fill up the measure of their wants," he would say.

His personal force was contageous. He wanted students to live vigorously and to do every job right. "Whatsoever thy hands find to do, do it with thy might" was a favorite quotation, and he told of the king's pitiful failure when Elisha told him to smite the earth, and the king smote it thrice. Elisha turned on him with indignation, "Thou shouldst have smitten five or six times; then hadst thou smitten Syria till thou hadst consumed it; whereas now thou shalt smite Syria but thrice." The king's failure was in the very weakness of his character. He often quoted his old teacher, McDonald, "Don't make irongray marks on the blackboard. Bear down so that everybody can read what you write." And he spoke with such disgust of hands that felt like spongy slabs of sidemeat when you tried to shake them that Lemon Carpenter went to the other extreme and crushed the bones of those courageous enough to shake with him. He urged students to prepare in advance for emergencies, not wait till the battle was on, for right preparation acts spontaneously.

"A trainman once told me," he said, "that many people are hurt in wrecks because they jump from their seats and are thrown about. 'If you are ever in a wreck,' he said, 'keep a tight grip on your seat and hold on.' I never forgot his advice, and whenever I took my seat in a coach, I always took a firm grip on the arms of my seat before I began reading or fell asleep. Once on a trip to St. Louis I was asleep in my chair when the train left the tracks. I awoke to the screaming of people, who were filling the aisle and swaying from side to side of the coach, but I found myself grasping the arms of my chair with all the strength I had."

As a disciplinarian Armstrong was never harsh, but always firm. Dow Merritt, who gave so many years of dedicated service to Africa, relates that he once moved out of the

dormitory to the home of Brother Tomlinson, a member of
the board at Cordell. Armstrong called him in immediately.

"Dow," he said, "I understand that you have moved out
of the dormitory. Did you have your father's permission to
do this?"

"No, sir," Dow replied.

"I think then you had better move back," Armstrong
said, kindly.

"Do I have to, Brother Armstrong?" Dow asked.

"Well," Armstrong said, slowly, "you'll have to move
back, or go home."

Dow moved back. He was not upset or offended, for
Armstrong had been kind. But when parents held the school
responsible for the conduct and welfare of their children, he
could assume that grave trust only if they were in the dormitory where experienced teachers could give wise oversight.

Years later when Dow's older brother Clyde came with
him to see Armstrong, Clyde said, "Brother Armstrong, this
is Peck's Bad Boy I sent you at Cordell."

"Dow never gave us any trouble," Armstrong replied. And
Dow was taken aback, remembering what Armstrong had
long forgotten.

His usual method was to call in a student and talk with
him personally before a situation got out of hand. Mrs.
Earl Smith tells of his calling in Earl's brother Virgil. "He
manifested such love and concern that Virgil was soon in
tears. He told Earl he had rather take a good whipping than
to meet Brother Armstrong for a talk of correction." Mrs.
Smith remembers how effective his chapel talks were:

"We never heard a man speak that equalled him in moving
students to want to do right. I remember how my own heart
was touched and moved to do what I believed to be right
if the whole world turned against me. I could never understand how anyone could ever deviate from the right after
being in his classes and hearing his chapel talks."

Those were the days before student sit-ins and rebellions,
but once when a group of the boys became obstreperous
over the strictness of rules, Armstrong laid them out in a
chapel speech.

"This school has few rules," he said, "and those we have

are for the good of us all. If you don't like some regulation, we shall be glad at any time to talk with you about it, but until it is changed in a reasonable way, we will respect it. We love every one of you, and we'd hate to see you leave; but if you can't respect the policies of this school, the trains still run, and I'll personally help you pack your trunk." To my surprise at the close of the speech the boys who were causing trouble rose to their feet and led the audience in prolonged applause. No one ever packed his trunk.

Even the children, who sat in the front rows at chapel, felt his appeal. One day Mary Shepherd, the primary teacher, saw two of her boys fighting on the grounds. When they all came in, Jim Bills' hand went up.

"Yes, Jim," Mary said. Jim went over to Joseph Rutherford and held out his hand. "Joe, I started that fight," he said. "I'm sorry, Joe." All was quiet as death in the room as the children watched the two boys solemnly shake hands, and tears stood in Mary's eyes. Another time Jim had taken a banana from an arrangement being painted in the art class—a temptation just too hard for any child—but his conscience wouldn't let him rest and he told Armstrong what he had done.

Unlike blind worshippers of rules, however, Armstrong believed there could be justifiable exceptions to man-made regulations. They were not like the laws of the Medes and Persians, but, as Jesus put it, rules were made for men and not men for rules. There was a dormitory regulation that all lights must be out by eleven o'clock. In reemphasizing it in chapel Armstrong would say, "No lights are needed after eleven, because all decent people, with one exception, should be in bed by eleven." He never identified the "exception," but his eyes would twinkle across the chapel at Mary Shepherd. "Miss Mary," the daughter of J. W. Shepherd, was the primary teacher and one of the loveliest of women. Because she needed to study later than eleven, she had bought a kerosene lamp to use after lights were out.

Even about smoking Armstrong hated to lay down hard and fast rules but sought rather to persuade boys to give up the habit.

"In a hundred years," he would say, "a preacher who

uses tobacco will be rejected from the fellowship of the church, just as a man now is who uses whiskey. The use of a thing so deadly in its results and so far-reaching in its effects, must be stamped out by the on-rushing army of our God. For the sake of the unborn, every Christian must quit to remain Christian. In a hundred years no Christian can sell the stuff, being forbidden by his conscience."

Instead of absolute prohibition, Armstrong established the "Unclean Grounds," a space back of the outdoor privy, where students who simply had to smoke could do it apart from the "clean" and perhaps with an appropriate measure of embarrassment. They were also supposed to attend the "Unclean Class" weekly for a lecture on the dangers of smoking.

Girls, of course, in those days did not smoke at all. Many years later, after girls began smoking, the daughter of an old schoolmate of his entered college and felt she just could not break the habit.

"When you feel that you simply have to smoke," he told her, "and there is no way to avoid it, come to our apartment and smoke there, but don't smoke in your room or among the other girls." She took advantage of the arrangement only a few times, and then apparently the smoking stopped as he had hoped.

He emphasized continually in classes and in chapel talks that it is not rules or laws, but principles, that make men.

"A girl or boy is not what he is in broad daylight with guards standing around, but what he is in the dark with no one to see him but God. Great men and women have been great because, like Daniel, they had principles they could not violate." He loved to tell of Mr. Long, a friend of the school, who had advertised a herd of cattle for sale. A long distance telephone call came in.

"Mr. Long, I have read your ad that you have a hundred seven head of cattle for sale. Would a hundred five dollars a head interest you?" That was five dollars a head more than Long had just accepted for them.

"Yes," Long replied, "it would, but they are already sold, just a few minutes ago."

"Are they still in your lot?" came the insistent voice.

"Yes, they are still here."

"Has the buyer put up any money on them yet?" asked the voice.

"No," Long replied, "but my word is up on them."

Long was in striking contrast to another cattleman Armstrong also used to cite, who made a practice of salting the feed heavily the morning he was to sell so that the cattle would drink huge quantities of water. A buyer who suspected the trick rushed over before daylight, found him salting the feed, and immediately called off the deal. He had no intention of paying twenty-five cents a pound for water.

"All great civilizations," Armstrong used to say, "are built upon trust. We have to trust the physician, the mechanic who repairs our car, the man who delivers our coal or oil. We use the trust plan with you students just as far as you will allow us. This morning you have a perfect record. Not a blot on the page. If it is ever blotted, you must do it yourself. But if you want to do wrong, insist on doing wrong, no one on earth can prevent you. But we will do our best to get you to want to do right."

He loved to trust people, for he believed that most people are innately good and want to do right. At a railroad station one day he saw two boys who seemed in deep trouble.

"Boys, what seems to be the trouble?" he asked. "Can I help you?"

"We thought we had enough money to buy our tickets home," the older boy replied. "But we lack eighty-five cents."

"Well," Armstrong said, "maybe I can help," and he began searching his pocket. "Yes, here you are," and he handed the boy a dollar.

The younger boy quickly reached into his pocket, drew out a dirty, thumbed copy of the New Testament, and held it out.

"I read this book every day," the boy said, "and we'll send the money back to you."

A bystander, who had been looking on with an amused smile, remarked to Armstrong, "You'll never see that money again."

"Oh, yes, I think so," Armstrong replied. "I'll trust any boy who reads his New Testament." In a few days the money came in.

Armstrong's constant effort was to help students develop the personal convictions and integrity that would make outward restraints unnecessary. G. W. Kieffer, who later taught with us many years at Harper and Morrilton and was a member of the board at Searcy, tells how effective that effort was.

"Of all the great men I have been associated with, Brother Armstrong's influence was the greatest in inspiring me to devote my life to faithful Christian service. Like the Apostle Paul he did not rely upon 'excellency of speech,' but spoke with his heart to our hearts, and our hearts responded. He manifested by his life that he 'had been with Jesus.' He tried to represent in his life the same Jesus whom he preached from the scriptures. He did not feel that he must 'put on a big front' because he was president of the school, but he sometimes wore collars till they were frayed, and he made a practice, rain or shine, of walking the mile and back to prayer meetings with the students."

In discipline committee meetings Armstrong often said, "If we make a mistake in the disposition of this case, let it be on the side of mercy rather than severity." Kieffer tells of one boy who had been called before the committee several times and had pleaded that he had never been in a place before where the rules were so strict. When school closed and he had to return home, he was found sitting alone on the curb at the depot crying. He had fallen in love even with the rules.

The secret of Armstrong's relations with students was that he loved them, and they instinctively responded to his love. He was always ready to do anything possible for them. In Monday night meetings when students were making first efforts at public speaking, he listened intently. "I try to hold them up with my eyes," he said. Kieffer tells that he taught a Greek class one whole year just for him alone. That may sound strange today, but it was nothing unusual for him.

Serious as was his purpose to fill the school with the spirit of the Christ, he was never sanctimonious, but always easy, informal, and friendly. His sense of humor was often delightfully unexpected. When Mary Shepherd was at home one summer, a mouse ate a hole through her old winter coat, left in the dresser drawer at school. To her surprise, instead of lamenting her loss, Armstrong commented with a smile, "Miss Mary, I think the Lord wants you to have a new coat." Whether that was the Lord's intention or not, the mouse provided a good reason for a purchase she would not otherwise have made.

People, he felt, often looked at things more seriously than they ought. Ed Grindley relates that at his first meeting with Armstrong he said, "Brother Armstrong, I don't know whether I have done right or not. A friend and I went into the drug store the other day to get a cold drink, and he said, 'Ed, let's flip a coin to see who'll buy the drinks.' And we flipped a coin."

"Well," Armstrong said with an amused smile, "Who won?"

His sense of humor was often combined with a homely wisdom and shrewd good judgment. Having to leave for an appointment one day when the family was also gone, he was troubled about what to do with a sum of money collected from student fees. There was no safe at the college, and the family apartment had no locks on the doors. He called Mary Shepherd to see if she could keep it for him, but she was also going out.

"But I know what we can do," she said. "We can put it in my stove." Each room in the dormitory was heated by a small coal stove, and in the warm spring weather her stove had had no fire for weeks.

"Miss Mary, you're a genius," he exclaimed. "No one would dream of looking for money in a stove." And the stove became his bank for the day.

Many years later as Mary and her husband, Claude French, were driving him through Detroit to one of the city parks, dodging the fast traffic and frantic pedestrians, he suddenly asked, "Brother French, may I make an observation on your city?"

"Certainly, Brother Armstrong, what is it?" French replied.

"Well, it seems to me from this traffic that you have just

two kinds of people in Detroit—the quick and the dead!"

At the opening of school each year homesickness was often a desperate problem. Although Fleming had described the college as having a "towering, magnificent brick building," many students had come from local high schools with larger and better buildings, and dormitory rooms at first were minute cells. Such a shocking change from home was hard to bridge. One boy from Texas left the next day after he arrived, got ashamed and returned the following day, and left again for good the next. Armstrong always did his best to cheer up the students and get them over the epidemic.

"I'd be ashamed of you," he would say, "if you were not homesick. It would be a reflection on your father and mother. But I'd be even more ashamed of you if you didn't fight it out. Homesickness never killed anyone. My old teacher used to tell us of a boy who went away from home to work in a print shop. He got so homesick he felt he would die. He decided that if he could do something to actually get sick, he would have a good excuse for going home. So every day he dug out some of the dirt from the old stick and mud chimney and ate it. But to his surprise instead of getting sick, he got fat: And Benjamin Franklin had to stay with his job. We have better things to eat than dirt from stick chimneys, and we're not going to let you get sick, though you may get fat. So cheer up and get rid of your blues."

He sometimes combined the serious with the ludicrous in a surprising way. When the students had assembled in chapel one gloomy morning, he suddenly asked:

"Will everybody please stand?" Obediently all of us stood.

"Now look carefully on the seat beneath you," he ordered. Everybody turned and looked down.

"My wife lost a dozen eggs somewhere this morning and she asked me to help her find them," he explained. "Now you may be seated." In a suddenly lightened mood the chapel service began.

In many indefinable ways Armstrong and his faculty infused the grace and beauty of the Christian spirit into the school. It was his longing to give every boy and girl a Christian education. Once in a meeting when young people were being urged to give themselves to missionary work, Armstrong finally spoke.

"Men have different callings," he said. "I think it is wonderful when men like Dow Merritt go to the mission field, but when I travel through the countryside and see poor, dirty, uneducated children sitting on the doorstep of a shanty, my heart burns within me. I want to help them. I want a school for them. That's my calling."

He longed to make education free to every one had it been possible. He never turned away a student because he could not pay tuition. He always arranged work of some kind.

"I am ashamed of the boy who says he cannot go to school. Anybody that wants an education can get it, whether he has a penny or not. An education is not bought with money. The boy who sweeps for his tuition or board can get through if he only does his job right. But when I enter a room where a boy has swept and can write my name in the dust on the tables, I know what that boy will do; he will be a failure."

He always favored the small school of about two hundred. "Big things are hard to control, and big things grow wicked —proud and haughty." To be big, a school would have to appeal to the masses, the world, and so lose the very purpose of its existence. Writing from Harding College to Arthur B. Tenney, one of his old students, years after Cordell closed, he said: "Our school then was small, but I have never taught in a better one. It is not so easy to leaven a student body of five or six hundred. Besides schools are different now. They have turned into 'activities,' and it is difficult to do solid work and build students spiritually. Still we are doing a fine work here in spite of the difficulties and the problems of this modern age."

But it was with a degree of nostalgia that he looked back thirty years to the little school which had shared so much of the Christ spirit.

Chapter 10

A MARTYR TO CONVICTION

THE HEART OF an educator is in the development of his students, and he begrudges the time he must give to other matters. Before the twentieth century the president of a college was not expected to finance the institution. In fact, from the tuition and fees universally charged, colleges seemed little concerned about money. But times have changed, and today college presidents must give most of their time and skill to financial promotion rather than to scholastic excellence. Even at Cordell the trend was slowly beginning.

True, business leaders and promoters had sold lots to start the college, but once the buildings were up they expected the school to live on its tuition and fees or, like Shakespeare's chameleon, "eat the air promise crammed." When Armstrong accepted the presidency, the board had not yet finished the building. The basement was completely unfinished, the lighting system was incomplete, and the only heat was from coal stoves in the various rooms with pipes worming their way through walls to the central chimney. Yet on the unfinished plant there was a debt of $6,186.15. Theoretically the board was obligated for this debt; actually, however, the president of the school not only had to meet current running expenses, but also head the campaign to pay off the debt.

In recent years, both government and industry have realized the value of private institutions and have contributed billions to private colleges and universities. But when Cordell Christian· College started, neither business nor government felt any obligation to private education, and business even resented requests for donations. The conditions were especially unfavorable at Cordell. There were no millionaires known among those Christians seeking to be undenominational, and friends of the school had only meager incomes.

Looking back from these affluent times some have thought Armstrong must have been a poor financier. He would have denied being a financier at all; he was a teacher. He made no attempt to build endowments; he was building men. He had known R. L. Whiteside at Henderson and also at Nashville, where Mrs. Whiteside washed and ironed for people to help her husband through school. Whiteside had since become one of the most influential preachers and writers among the churches.

"Brother Whiteside," Armstrong once asked him, "are you a good financier?" Whiteside was always a thinker, and he pondered the question a moment before he replied.

"Yes, Brother Armstrong, I believe I am. I have always lived within my income, something a great many people never can do." From Whiteside's definition Armstrong was a "good financier," for he not only kept the college within its income, but eventually paid off all its debts.

Left by the board with the financial responsibility, he analysed the five major needs. First, the basement of the college building must be finished, a central heating system added, the lighting system completed, and plumbing installed. Second, the dormitory had to be completely remodeled. It had been designed largely by Mrs. Harrel to accommodate the maximum number of boys, but the rooms were tiny cells barely large enough for a bed, table, and two straight chairs. There were no closets and no baths. One year it had been left entirely vacant. Third, the debt had to be paid by 1915. Fourth, if the college was to be accredited laboratories must be equipped and the library enlarged. Fifth, teacher's salaries and current expenses had to be met.

Recognizing the need of some medium by which the college and its work could be presented favorably to Christian people everywhere, Armstrong, with a group of teachers and friends, started the *Gospel Herald*, a weekly journal. Through gifts and subscriptions such a journal would pay its own way, and in addition to acquainting people with the college and its work, would give the great Southwest an understanding of the spirit of the Christian faith which was greatly needed.

The campaign for funds to complete the college building was started in a great Thanksgiving meeting in 1909 in which Joe S. Warlick and James A. Harding spoke and in which Armstrong presented the need. This campaign provided the funds to complete the building, and even to lay some of the walks.

Mrs. Armstrong assumed the burden of remodeling the dormitory. With the help of an expert builder she moved partitions to enlarge rooms, made closets, and arranged baths. The cost even with some volunteer labor was over $1,600, and this she paid personally over several years from the tuition of her private students in speech. This seems a small sum now, but according to the Consumer Index it would be equivalent to $5,500 in 1967. But since Mrs. Armstrong's income was a fourth the average for that time, it was for her equivalent to a gift of $22,000 now.

Liquidating the large debt was the major problem. Students and teachers helped. Businessmen responded as liberally as could have been expected in those days. By May of 1915 only $1,250 more was needed. But 1913 to 1915 were years of extreme drouth. In 1913 seven colleges in Oklahoma closed, never to reopen. The Baptist State College with property worth $150,000 quit, and the property was sold under mortgage. Two Catholic schools closed.

"It has not been an easy thing to keep the heads of private schools above the water in this country during these hard years," Armstrong wrote.

Potter Bible College under George A. Klingman's presidency closed in 1913. The same year Sabinal Christian College in Texas pleaded pitifully for "at least a small" contribution to help buy the two frame dormitories, which were privately owned, but the school managed to struggle hopelessly on till 1917. In spite of the extreme self-sacrifice of its teachers Western Bible and Literary College closed in 1916. In 1914 Jesse P. Sewell was pleading in nearly every issue of the *Gospel Advocate* for help at Abilene Christian College. "They had property worth $20,000," he wrote, "and an enrollment of 170 to 207, and must have another building." In his last appeal, December 17, 1914, he said, "We are not compelled to have very much, only about six hundred fifty dollars; but this we must have or quit!"

The desperation of such an appeal involving such a paltry sum shows how hard it must have been in those drouth years for Armstrong to raise over six thousand dollars. Finally, as a last extreme the faculty agreed to sell forty student scholarships to apply on the debt. This in effect meant that the teachers themselves were making the final payment, for the money from tuition covered by the scholarships should have gone to payment of salaries. The scholarships sold at once, but because of a sudden slump in the world cotton markets at the outbreak of World War I seven scholarships were cancelled. S. A. Bell was sent into the field to sell seven more. By the fall of 1915 the debt was paid and the property was free. One teacher wrote, "The debt is raised. It looks as if it is almost a miracle."

Through all these years no college received warmer support and cooperation from the town and its business interests than did the college at Cordell. Armstrong had won the love and respect of its most prominent business and civic leaders. In 1914, when the Commencement exercises were held in the Princess Theater, all businesses in town closed so that people could attend. But even the warmest friendship in those days did not imply financial aid. The Lee Brothers, however, from whom Armstrong bought coal and building materials started the "Lee Brothers Scholarships," one covering tuition of the high school or college student making the highest grade for the year, and the other for the best student in the eighth grade. Armstrong relates that Lee Brothers were always most generous with him.

"Sometimes I had the money to pay for the coal I bought and sometimes I haven't had it. But John I. Lee was never the man to hesitate when I asked a favor. He never asked me to make a note at the end of the year. I usually wrote my own note, fixed the rate of interest and time of payment. It always suited him."

In preparation for accreditation Armstrong raised the money from students and friends to equip laboratories for home economics, manual arts, chemistry, and physics, and to increase the library. As further help to the library one year Armstrong, S. A. Bell, Homer Rutherford, and L. C. Sears gave their salaries for the entire year for the purchase of books. During this time they lived on the small incomes from their preaching.

By 1915, however, the college building had to be reroofed at considerable cost. Mrs. Armstrong again personally assumed this expense and paid for it by the proceeds from plays she directed.

Salaries of teachers and other operating expenses were a constant problem. Until Batsell Baxter came to be dean in 1916 no teacher received more than $35 a month, and for only nine months. Baxter, who had rejected an offer of $2,000 from a church, received $50 a month. Married teachers with salaries had to supplement their incomes by preaching on Sundays and holding meetings through the summer. A roommate of mine who worked in a bank once saw a check for $105 marked "salary," which Armstrong had written to W. T. Vaughn at the opening of the school year.

"You know, Armstrong has been lying about the salaries he pays the teachers," he declared. "I saw Vaughn's check, and he gets $105."

"There must be some mistake," I said. "I know Armstrong is no liar. I'll ask him about it." I went to him the next day.

"Yes," he said. "I gave Vaughn a check for $105 but that was salary for the last three months of last year. I was unable to pay all salaries at the close, and he said he could wait till school opened."

Armstrong was responsible for the finances, and when income from student tuition and fees was insufficient he took care of the deficit personally. Only once in eighteen years, however, did he turn aside to hold a meeting during the school year. Daniel Sommer immediately charged him with having a soft job, sitting at home with his wife and babies, figuring ways of extracting $5,000 from the churches while sacrificing preachers were enduring cold and hunger to preach the gospel. Armstrong immediately sent a reply, which Sommer refused to print, but which appeared in the *Gospel Herald* under title "Is It Right for Daniel Sommer to Do Right?" He explained that the pay teachers receive in Christian schools "could hardly be dignified by the term 'salary,'" that the two teachers who bore the heaviest load at Odessa gave all their salary to the school and the others received only enough to buy groceries, that he himself was receiving no personal salary and held meetings through the summers to pay the school expenses left at the close each spring. How soft was such a life?

Actually he carried a heartbreaking burden of work. Besides teaching a full schedule of classes, he was editor and publisher of the *Gospel Herald,* writing a large part of it himself, he preached somewhere every Sunday, and he had a heavy program of meetings during the summers. J. B. Nelson, who spent a week in lectures on the campus, says of the Armstrongs, "These two people are about the busiest couple I have met. They have duties upon duties that they perform daily. Brother Armstrong preaches about as much as the average preacher, teaches school five days a week, and looks after the college work in general, as he is the president. When it comes to work Sister Armstrong is not a whit behind him. She teaches expression, looks after the dormitory and her own private household, and many others." Among the "many others," she managed the kitchen and dining room for the school, planning meals, purchasing, and directing the service. Of the meals Nelson says, "I have never been in a dormitory where the boarders are as well and plentifully fed and as kindly cared for as in the dormitory at Cordell Christian College."

One thing lacking in that service, however, was coffee, which was never served in those days. Frequently when Armstrong in meetings was asked if he would like coffee. he would reply jokingly, "No, thank you. I have no bad habits." But he halfway meant it. When Bertha Belmar, a former student, brought her parents and her husband to visit the college in 1916, she brought coffee with her.

Under his burden of work, and with no secretary, it is no wonder that Armstrong could not keep up with his correspondence. W. C. West of Minco wrote him several times about a meeting and finally called him. In the next letter he says, "I have written you several times and had about made up my mind that J. N. Armstrong was a ghost and that there was no real man by that name. But now that I have talked with you, and I don't think ghosts ever talk, I know that you exist, and I hope to see you sometime and to hear you preach."

"Those who have written me," Armstrong said, "and failed to hear from me can get a little comfort out of the fact that I treat others as badly as I do them. I wish I could answer every letter that comes to me, but I just cannot do it."

D. H. Friend, in a letter to Brother Harding, said he had written Armstrong a love letter and would never have known he received it except that he had cashed the check he had sent for the *Gospel Herald*.

"I remember that 'love letter,'" Armstrong replied. "My failure to answer it was no sign of lack of love. I love him in the same old way. Some day I will tell him more about it; it may be I will not get time till we get to heaven, but then we shall be satisfied."

Friend had urged him to come for a meeting at Green's Chapel in Kentucky.

"I am homesick sometimes to meet old Kentucky friends," Armstrong replied. "But the work here presses heavier every year and holds me tighter, and when I go away I have to tear loose to go at all. This year a whole summer's work has been offered me in Tennessee and Kentucky, but two or three summers' work here." It was impossible to go.

His summer meetings were always strenuous. A rare break occurred in 1914, and he said, "I don't remember when I ever spent two weeks before in the summer time at home. It was a real luxury." At Douglas his meeting started with only seven present, one a child, but soon every seat was filled, standing room taken, and even the pulpit platform crowded. In 1915 he was home only five days during the summer, and this because Mrs. Armstrong had accidentally burned the manuscript for the new catalog when it was just ready for the printer.

"My wife and daughter are the guilty ones," he announced in the *Herald*. "When I received the news, I wrote that I was glad it was neither my wife nor my daughter, but my catalog that was burned." And he urged students to wait for the new one, which he promised would be better than the one burned.

Riding trains all night with no Pullman, preaching twice a day in each meeting, he was so tired when the last one began at Ardmore he felt he could hardly go through with it. But when he thought of the way people had treated him, giving him the best room, the best bed, chairs, food, overwhelming him with kindness, he felt "humiliated to the ground with my unworthiness."

In 1913, when many colleges were closing because of the drouth, there was a sudden flurry of enthusiasm for the building of a great "university" at Fort Worth. Early Arceneaux sent an urgent "Call for a University Mass Meeting," which Armstrong printed in the *Gospel Herald*. But he also printed an article from John E. Dunn opposing the "Southland University" idea. Dunn argued that Texas already had five Christian colleges, Tennessee four, and other states several more, all struggling for existence, and that the churches should give their support to these until they were financially strong. If a university is needed, one of these could then be so developed.

Armstrong endorsed Dunn's article warmly. He believed the churches were not yet ready for a "university," that qualified graduates from all the Christian schools were too few to justify it, that the most vital period in a child's education was the first twelve years, that talk of a "first class" university reflected on the present schools as inferior, and would lead parents to send their children elsewhere when these schools were actually giving superior work, and finally that the churches should rally to the support of the schools now running.

He rejoiced, however, that the talk of a university showed an awakening of people everywhere to the need of Christian education.

When the mass meeting was held, however, and G. H. P. Showalter was elected president of the new "university" but allowed to continue also as editor of the *Firm Foundation*, Armstrong wrote congratulating him.

"I know of no man that I would rather see at the head of the new school." His criticism, he explained, was in regard to the judgment of the brethren. "There are enough children in the homes of Christians in Fort Worth to give the new school patronage. Every one of these children should be in a Christian school. But I mildly suggest that where the brethren at Fort Worth have made their mistake is in allowing themselves to be deceived with their university idea."

There was no jealousy back of his criticism but rather an understanding of the condition of the church. All his life Armstrong was utterly free from jealousy of other schools or other preachers. When J. H. Lawson, after resigning the presidency at Cordell, wrote Armstrong in 1910 proposing to start a new school at Altus, only fifty miles from Cordell, Armstrong wrote back that he would be glad to help in any way possible to get it started. He cautioned him only about being sure of sufficient support and of finding a dedicated faculty who would sacrifice enough to make it succeed. Habitually when he appealed for support of Christian schools, he included all the schools, not merely his own; when he urged people to subscribe for religious journals, he mentioned all the journals, not just his own. But he did have shrewd practical judgment in financial affairs, and about the support a college could expect in those days. Neither Altus nor Southland University developed. The time was not yet.

From 1913 to 1918, however, in the struggle of several colleges for recognition, a rivalry developed which was not always wholesome. The publicity at times now seems amusing. C. R. Nichol, the new president of Thorp Springs, sent

Armstrong a glowing report of his proposed faculty with
W. F. Ledlow as "president of the faculty."

"We are persuaded we will have the strongest faculty ever
assembled in a school controlled by members of the church
of Christ," he wrote, but in his letter he expressed doubt
that Armstrong would publish the statement. Armstrong did,
and wrote a warm approval:

"I rejoice at the springing up of every school managed by
Christians. I rejoice at their success. Some have advantages
that others do not. I recommended to one young man that
he go to Nashville rather than come to us at Cordell, because of certain advantages at Nashville. But some of us are
skeptical respecting Brother Nichol's confidence in the Thorp
Springs faculty. When Brother Ledlow has had a little more
experience, he will find that, while B.S.'s and M.A.'s are
worthwhile, they do not make teachers. Teachers are born,
not made."

In the next issue of the *Herald,* Jesse P. Sewell announced
the faculty at Abilene:

"We concede to no school anywhere superiority to this
faculty from any viewpoint essential to a first-class Junior
Christian College."

A little amused at the rivalry, but anxious also to keep
it good humored, Armstrong commented on the relations
between the Nashville Bible School and Potter Bible College
of Bowling Green.

"More than ten years have come and gone," he said,
"and the two schools have been real sisters through these
years, and have lived seventy-five miles of each other. Some
of the dearest and best friends were fearful of the green
monster jealousy and the wicked spirit of rivalry. But I
remember with the sweetest pleasure that last Monday night
meeting in which we made love and farewell speeches,
pledging each other hearty support. Since that tearing apart
of hearts knit together, the two schools have worked beautifully, loyally, loving, and trustingly together."

For the most part, however, all the schools worked together harmoniously. All had the same problems with finances and with accreditation. It was not until around 1910

that accreditation became necessary. Armstrong was one of the first to recognize it and to make preparation by creating laboratories and improving the library and faculty. He urged superior students to obtain advanced degrees and return to the school, and he himself and S. A. Bell entered the university for advanced work.

In 1916, after R. C. Bell gave up the presidency at Thorp Springs, Rhodes returned to Cordell accompanied by Batsell Baxter as dean. Of Rhodes, Armstrong wrote, "He gives up his work at Thorp Springs and returns to us here. We feel that he belongs to us anyway, and rejoice that things have so turned that he sees his way clear to come back home." He was to leave once more for a year at Abilene Christian College but returned again in 1924 to spend the rest of his life with Armstrong and other old friends and fellow teachers at Harper College and at Harding College.

In Texas the State Department of Education set up standards for accreditation, and Abilene Christian College and Thorp Springs College were soon accredited as junior colleges offering two years of college work. This recognition was highly publicized, and people naturally got the impression that their work was now superior to that of the other colleges. In Oklahoma accreditation was left to the University, and at Armstrong's request Dr. Phelan of the University spent a day or more on the campus. In July Armstrong announced through the *Gospel Herald* that the University had granted the college three full years of credit for any student whose grades were satisfactory:

I do not mean that this splendid recognition by the University of Oklahoma makes our work superior to that of other schools conducted by faithful brethren. Others could doubtless have the very same arrangement we have, had they but chosen to do it. But any one who attempts to make the impression that our school has less recognition by its university than a junior college has, attempts to make a false impression. We Christians ought to rally to the support of all these schools. Any effort on the part of one school to draw patronage from another is like a sister's living on the life blood of another sister.

In the local Cordell *Beacon*, however, Armstrong allowed

himself the pleasure of a little fuller explanation of the significance of the recognition:

We have just received notice from the University of Oklahoma accrediting Cordell Christian College with ninety hours, or three full years, of college work. This is one full year more than any other Christian college has yet received. It gives Cordell the school with the most advanced standing; it places Cordell Christian College at the head of all our series of schools; and it rates her with the leading educational institutions of the state. With this standing students may complete three full years with us and enter the University as seniors taking their B.A. degrees in one year or their M.A. in two. This gives us an advantage of one year over the state normal schools that have only two years of accreditation.

With the debt cleared away, with the new recognition by the University, and with a growing enrollment the future of the college seemed assured. Even in the dark drouth years of 1913-15 Armstrong never became discouraged.

"We never think of Cordell Christian College's failing," he wrote, during the effort to liquidate the debt. "If God wills it so, it cannot fail. Should he will its failure, we will submit. Otherwise we count on no failure because of the debt hanging over it."

To meet the financial situation from the drouth and the collapse of the cotton market in 1914, he offered to take a bale of cotton to cover tuition and fees for any one who positively could not pay, but he warned that "anybody who could pay cash that takes advantage of this offer would make himself wicked!" But the enrollment was surprisingly good.

In 1915-16, he reported in the *Herald*, in spite of the late catalog the enrollment reached 216, "the largest body of students, I believe, in any of our schools except the Nashville Bible School. For the fall it is expected to be even larger, with students coming from as far away as Oregon, Iowa, Tennessee, New Mexico. Families moving have taken every available house. Such a condition has never before been known."

He later reported that the enrollment for 1916-17 had increased by a third over that of 1915-16. This would mean a total of 288. Several families had to be turned away because they could find no houses in Cordell, but two more houses were being constructed and were to have been available by November. Though such enrollments today seem trivial, they were larger than enrollments in comparable colleges. The Baptist University in Shawnee, a town of seventeen thousand, enrolled only 65 students in 1915-16, and Abilene Christian College only 147 in 1916-17.

It is ironic, however, that at the moment of highest prosperity, calamity was to strike. On June 28, 1914, the Archduke Franz Ferdinand of Austria was assassinated in Sarajevo, Serbia. The occurrence at first was scarcely noticed even in Europe, for bloody incidents in the Balkans were commonplace. Certainly no one could have dreamed that an event so far away would determine the destiny of a small college in Western Oklahoma. But the ambitious war lords in Germany had waited three years for an opportunity to strike, and on August 3, the Germany armies swept into Belgium and France, and all Europe burst into flames.

Most people in America were not unduly alarmed. President Wilson had been inaugurated in January, 1913, on a reform platform, a champion of the rights of man. His ideals were lofty. Furthermore, Wilson was a leader in the American Peace Party, which, along with many other organizations, was emphasizing peaceful negotiations in the settlement of international disputes. His Secretary of State, William Jennings Bryan, was an even stronger advocate of peace. The temper of America was strongly humanitarian and opposed to involvement in European wars. Ten days after the invasion of Belgium and France, Wilson issued his neutrality proclamation, urging that Americans be "impartial in thought as well as in action . . ." But even with this strongly antiwar feeling, Armstrong was fearful from the first that our country would be involved.

"Every Christian in the world," he wrote, "should pray to God respecting the European war. Daily we should pray that God may save the whole world from every evil consequence possible." He emphasized, as did Wilson, a neutral position, but his neutrality was based distinctly upon the Christian relationship.

"A child of God cannot be a partisan but a lover of men, all men. As to victory he must pray that God will work out the very victory that will be best for us, his children, both here and there."

Even after the *Lusitania* was sunk May 7, 1915, Wilson and Bryan tried hard to avoid war. Their first protest to Germany that the United States would not omit "any word or any act" to protect its rights, was strong and clear. This note Bryan signed with reluctance, but the second note his conscience would not permit him to sign and he resigned.

"Mr. Bryan's resignation last Tuesday," Armstrong wrote, "created an unparalleled sensation in government circles. Not only was Washington shocked, but the whole nation was surprized and distressed. To lose from the cabinet the staunchest advocate of peace is enough to put the nation in mourning."

But Armstrong's admiration of Wilson in the course he was forced to take was equally strong. Both Wilson and Bryan were caught in a crisis requiring action that violated long and deep convictions. Each had to respond in harmony with his highest sense of values.

"After all, we are persuaded the disagreement of these two great Americans is a matter of difference of judgment" Armstrong said. "Both the President and Mr. Bryan are ardent peacemakers . . . But their judgments differ as to how long the principles of Christianity should be applied, or rather as to when they should depart from the Prince of Peace.

"I ask Christians: How long must Christians follow the Prince of Peace? When may they depart from his method and use weapons? Under what conditions, in what emergency, may Christians adopt other means and methods than the Christ's in the settlement of trouble?"

These questions laid open a most radical change in the thinking of Armstrong himself.

"I used to hold very conscientiously that it was not only the right but the duty of every citizen to exercise suffrage. Especially did I believe that Christians should do so. In fact

I verily thought it was wrong for a Christian to fail to vote and do everything else that could be done in righteousness to put good men in office. I thought, if Christian men did not so perform this duty, that we might expect the wicked to rule and the government to be ruined with corruption. Now I am assured by a better knowledge of the Bible that the above position is wrong for the Christian, and that he is a foreigner to very civil government in the world; that he violates some most sacred principles of the Christ whenever he exercised political rights in any earthly government." This radical change of view came about from his acquaintance with David Lipscomb and James A. Harding. From these two men and from his study of the New Testament, Armstrong was convinced that the Christ had forbidden Christians to take vengeance, and had given this function to governments. The logical conclusion was that Christians, who are forbidden to take vengeance, could not be part of government whose responsibility is to take vengeance.

"Were I exercising political rights in this government and the country were to become involved in the terrible conflict now raging across the sea, I should hold myself ready to go to war at my country's call. Anything else would be cowardly of me . . . On the other hand, if one is a foreigner tonight, as I am, and his citizenship is in heaven, as mine is, he has no obligation to any human government save the duty of a foreigner, namely, faithful obedience to the powers that be."

But not from Lipscomb and Harding alone had come this growing concept of the teaching of the Christ. Through the great peace movements in which both Bryan and Wilson had participated, thousands had come to accept similar principles.

These views created no difficulty until April 6, 1917. Against a growing pressure by military leaders Wilson had continued to try for peace through negotiation. The French and Germans had lost 1,000,000 men at Verdun, England 400,000 on the Somme, Russia and Austria 2,200,000 in the Brusilov offensive, and Italy was at the breaking point. Germany concluded America would not fight and sank three American ships. Wilson at last delivered in person his famous war message to Congress on April 2, 1917.

"The world must be made safe for democracy," he declared. "Its peace must be planted upon the tested foundations of political liberty. We have no selfish ends to serve. We desire no conquests, no dominion. We seek no indemnities for ourselves, no material compensation for the sacrifices we shall freely make. We are but one of the champions of the rights of mankind. We shall be satisfied when these rights have been made as secure as the faith and freedom of nations can make them."

Causing the most comment was his statement that peace must be without victory: "Victory would mean peace forced upon the loser, a victor's terms imposed upon the vanquished. It would be accepted in humiliation, under duress, at an intolerable sacrifice, and would leave a sting, a resentment, a bitter memory upon which the terms of peace would rest, not permanently, but only as upon quicksand. Only a peace between equals can last."

Wilson's idealism instantly made him the moral leader of the world. Four days later Congress declared war. Immediately a war which all had opposed became a holy crusade, a war to end all wars, to make the world safe for democracy. The nation's opposition suddenly changed to a war frenzy. Local defense councils were set up in every county. Minutemen speakers were organized all over the nation. Mothers declared they only wished they had more sons to send to the battlefield. Girls patriotically met troop trains to kiss the boys going through. One boy, struggling to get free, threw a girl into a weed patch! But the whole country, as well as the girls, nearly lost its balance.

On May 18, A Selective Service Act was passed. But Wilson and other national leaders realized that the consciences of many people might be ruthlessly violated, and the act tried to make careful provision for those conscientiously opposed to war. So patriotic was the Selective Service board in Cordell, however, that they tried to send everyone into service, even men physically unfit who had to be turned back at the camp. A former roommate of mine who had incipient tuberculosis immediately broke down and had to spend months in government hospitals.

Believing they should support the government in every

way not prohibited by the principles of Christ, teachers and
students of the college at Cordell bought Liberty Bonds and
War Savings Stamps, helped in Red Cross work, followed
the food administration's request in using only corn bread,
but no wheat bread except on Sundays so that the cooks
could attend church, and went out to farms to help in
agricultural work. Students under Mrs. Armstrong's direction
presented a play which raised more than a hundred thirty
dollars for the Red Cross. Thirty-eight students and teachers
entered the armed services before July, 1918. Eighteen of
these had volunteered, including J. D. Armstrong, the
nephew whom the Armstrongs were rearing as their son.
These did faithfully every duty required of them, ran every
danger. When the flu was raging and men were dying like
flies, young Armstrong for a time was the only man at his
post able to sound taps or reveille.

Although this was a record perhaps not surpassed by any
school of its size, it was not sufficient to satisfy the local
defense council. Several of the students were conscientious
about taking human life but had gladly accepted service in
the medical corps, which became one of the most dangerous
positions because the Germans held that shooting one member of the medical corps would eliminate a hundred regular
soldiers. To protect the medics the army finally removed the
Red Cross arm bands which had identified them too clearly
for German sharpshooters. Unfortunately, however, Ben
Randolph, my former roommate felt that he could accept no
type of service. Armstrong and I had both tried to convince
him that obedience to the government in accepting non-
combatant service would not violate the teachings of Christ,
but he was unable to see it.

The consciences of these young men aroused the anger of
the local defense council. Certain members of the church who
had been involved in the fight against Armstrong ten years
before also helped to agitate the opposition. On July 24, the
defense council issued a formal order to the board of trustees
that the "institution be so reorganized as will unreservedly
conform to all military policies and requirements of the
government in order to successfully carry on the war and
that no half-way compliance will be tolerated." To this end

they demanded that President Armstrong, and all teachers and all members of the board who shared his views regarding a Christian's participation in war, be immediately removed and others be appointed that could support the war effort unreservedly. Since all teachers and all but one member of the board shared Armstrong's views, this meant a complete change in the nature of the institution. No charge of disloyalty, however, was placed against any member of the board or faculty.

W. D. Hockaday, president of the board, and D. R. Dial, secretary, asked for an informal meeting with the defense council but gained no concessions. They then asked the State Council of Defense for investigation and protection against the local council. Hockaday had already encountered the same violent prejudice at Granite. His nephew, who was never a student at Cordell, had felt that he could not accept noncombatant service. Though Hockaday was one of the most highly respected citizens in Granite, one morning he found his store windows had been painted yellow during the night.

When Supreme Court Judge Thomas J. Owens came over to investigate, Armstrong furnished witnesses who testified that no one at the college had done anything seditious and that no one was pro-German. He insisted that those opposing the school bring witnesses, but they brought none. Judge Owens exonerated the college fully. He announced publicly that, while the position of the faculty and board was unfortunate for them in time of war, many good people in the state held the same position and that they were free to proceed with their work if they wished. But Armstrong and the board agreed with Judge Owens that it would be difficult and unwise under the circumstances to continue, and Armstrong handed his resignation to the board. The board at once closed the school.

During these troubled days when emotions ran wild, Hockaday was a tower of strength. Years later Armstrong wrote:

"I looked to Hockaday as to no one else for moral support and backing. He always wanted a 'Christian' College, not just a college. If this made a large attendance he was happy, but if the attendance was small, he was happy because the school was Christian. His conception of a Christian school was a hundred percent correct. Through his administration as president of the board we had the best and most spiritual student body I have ever presided over, though I have been president of four Christian colleges."

The closing of the school left Armstrong with a debt of $1,500, including summer advertising and the catalog, which was never mailed out. This deficit he was able to pay by selling his home, and the college was left free of all indebtedness.

Fortunately all teachers immediately found positions elsewhere, Rhodes and I in Harper College at Harper, Kansas, and the following year Armstrong was asked to become president of that institution. When it became clear that the Cordell board did not intend to reopen the college, Armstrong requested that they donate the equipment to Harper College. It was a similar school, several Cordell teachers were now at Harper, and a number of families had moved there. At Cordell nearly all the moveable equipment had been furnished by Armstrong and the teachers, not by the board nor by outside assistance. The board readily approved the request and all college equipment was moved to Harper.

"This college did not die," Armstrong declared. "Rather it was a martyr for the convictions of the faculty and of its board." But these were convictions which President Wilson respected and for which he had tried to make adequate provision. Ironically, it was only a small group that caused the furor and deprived the city of a growing institution. Armstrong writes that the college to the end held the sympathy and good will of "every businessman in town except one," but people in time of war fear to speak out. Armstrong himself was invited back for a meeting with the college congregation the following year.

Ben Randolph from the college and Hockaday's nephew from Granite were sent to Leavenworth Penitentiary, along with others of like conviction. Armstrong visited them there and gave them what encouragement he could. But their sincerity was severely tested. A special representative, they understood from Washington, pleaded with them, and tears ran down his cheeks as he told them they would be shot at daybreak unless they accepted some kind of service. But all replied that they could accept none. Next morning they faced a firing squad, blindfolded. They heard the commands, "Present arms, aim!" But the word "fire" was never given. They were taken back to their ward and were used on the penitentiary farms with almost complete freedom to come and go. Only one other unpleasant incident occurred. A young officer ordered them out one Sunday morning.

"But this is Sunday," one of the young men said. "Let us first have our worship, and then we will go." But the young officer would not wait. When they reached the farm, the men refused to work. The officer ordered his assistant to tie them by the thumbs to the limbs of a tree with only their tiptoes touching the ground. About that time a superior officer came out, saw the situation, and released the men at once. From that time there was no trouble. Randolph was given work in the penitentiary library. After the war they were all released and paid full salaries for the time of imprisonment. But the experience had not been easy. Randolph died a year or two later, a very young man, and I preached his funeral. Another died a few years later in New York, and another suffered a nervous breakdown.

Shortly after the closing of Cordell Christian College, Armstrong, J. W. Shepherd, and Dr. J. R. Ward were sent as a delegation representing the churches of Christ to call on General Crowder, head of the Selective Service at Washington. The Selective Service Act had specified that members of religious organizations then existing whose "creed or principles forbid its members to participate in war" might be given non-combatant service. The Quakers, long recognized as opposed to war, were automatically assigned to non-combatant service. But the churches of Christ had no written creed except the Bible itself, and each member is allowed to interpret its meaning in the light of his own intelligence. Accordingly many members of the church understood Christ to condemn taking human life even in war or as an agent of the government; others disagreed with this position.

General Crowder received the committee with great courtesy. He had grown up from childhood among members of the church of Christ and understood their acceptance of the Bible as their creed and the freedom each member had in studying the scriptures and arriving at his own convictions rather than submitting to ecclesiastical decrees. He promised that members of the churches of Christ whose faith in the Bible would not permit them to kill would be treated in the same manner as members of other churches opposed to war.

To some of us the sudden closing of Cordell Christian College seemed like the end of the world. It was only the end of an era and the beginning of even more fruitful periods, for out of the school flowed an influence that continues to this hour. Hundreds of students like S. T. Tipton, Webb Freeman, the Hockadays, Terrys, Utleys, Hudsons, Lawyers, Merritts, Symcoxes, Blansetts, Carpenters, Tomlinsons, Cooks, Sasseens, O'Neals, and a host of others became preachers, missionaries, teachers, bankers, lawyers, businessmen, and leaders in the church in many capacities, and their children and grandchildren are now carrying on the influence of the institution that suffered martyrdom rather than violate its faith.

MR. AND MRS. ARMSTRONG AT
POTTER BIBLE COLLEGE, BOWLING GREEN, KENTUCKY

JAMES A. HARDING AND PATTIE HATHAWAY ARMSTRONG
AT CORDELL, OKLAHOMA

WESTERN BIBLE
AND LITERARY
COLLEGE AND
DORMITORY,
ODESSA, MISSOURI

CORDELL
CHRISTIAN COLLEGE
AND DORMITORY,
CORDELL,
OKLAHOMA

PRESIDENT
ARMSTRONG AND
MRS. ARMSTRONG AT
CORDELL, OKLAHOMA

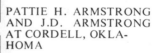

PATTIE H. ARMSTRONG
AND J.D. ARMSTRONG
AT CORDELL, OKLA-
HOMA

ADMINISTRATION BUILDING, MORRILTON

GIRL'S DORMITORY, SEARCY

GIRL'S DORMITORY, MORRILTON

MEN'S DORMITORY AT SEARCY

SCIENCE BUILDING AT SEARCY

MUSIC BUILDING AT SEARCY

DR. JOHN NELSON ARMSTRONG ABOUT 1936

Chapter 11

EDITOR AND WRITER

NO ONE BELIEVED more intensely than J. N. Armstrong in the importance of the message God had given to the world. Had he been prevented from proclaiming it, like Jermiah he would have felt a consuming fire within. Daily in classes and in chapel he could teach it in the most effective way, by personal word and example. But he longed for a wider audience.

Hence in October, 1912, with a group of dedicated friends he began publication of the *Gospel Herald,* a weekly religious journal. When the college at Cordell closed the *Herald* was moved to Harper, Kansas, and in 1923 as a result of its taking over the *Kentucky Evangelist* of Horse Cave, Kentucky, and the *Harvest Work* of St. Louis, Missouri, its name was changed to the *Living Message,* and C. C. Merrit became the office manager and Tona Covey the business manager. But Armstrong remained editor-in-chief and publisher till its close in 1934—twenty-two years of editorial service.

R. C. Ledbetter, when he heard Armstrong speak at Abilene, was so deeply impressed that he wrote, "I always look for his articles first." Many others were like him, for Armstrong's articles in a remarkable way reflected his personality, his deep convictions, strong faith, breadth of vision, tolerance, and love of humanity. The range of his interests was wide and he touched each issue with force, but with wisdom and fairness as well. The purpose of the *Herald* he explained was "to serve as Jesus came to serve."

"When this ceases to be the propelling power," he wrote, "may it have a decent burial, and may no tomb be built to its memory save a tomb warning against its failure . . . Every Christian, like Paul, owes a debt to the world. With a hope of stirring thousands to a realization of this debt and the only method of repaying it, the *Herald* enters the field of journalism."

The only consideration that could inspire caution, he said, was support, but that "never was entertained as a matter of fear by New Testament Christians."

"The very idea of support becoming a factor in making my decision to become a laborer in his vineyard is preposterously absurd in face of the emptied life of the blessed Lord. Hundreds of Christians are today abiding 'alone' and their lives are as worthless to the world as the life of the grain of wheat carefully placed in my desk drawer. The wheat must 'fall into the earth and die' to pay its debt to the world. So must every Christian die, give up life, sacrifice himself, to pay the debt he owes."

Journals naturally reflect the personalities and convictions of their editors and may therefore be limited in the truth they give to their readers. He hoped, however, to make the content of truth as broad and complete as the message God had given to men.

"This paper," he wrote, "contends for a full and free, and even-handed discussion of every subject in which truth is found. It is a firm conviction of ours that there is no other method by which to find truth as effective as by fair and Christian discussion. Just as black is never quite so black as when contrasted with perfect whiteness, so error is never quite so easily seen as when contrasted with truth."

Unlike many religious journals, the *Herald* would not

avoid, but rather welcome, constructive discussion and allow differences of view to be freely expressed.

"This does not mean," he explained, "that all the views expressed are approved by the editors." Many assuredly would not be, and if likely to prove harmful, would be answered, but always with courtesy and with respect for a different point of view, even if it were erroneous.

It would be the policy of the paper also, Armstrong stated, that no editor or writer would receive any pay for his work:

"Personally the managing editor believes most firmly that the paper can always yield a far better influence, can impart a spirit truer to our Master, altogether can accomplish a vast deal more good by being able to say that every cent paid by its readers goes into printer's ink, that nobody gets one cent of profit from the paper save that profit that comes through real sacrifice for the truth of God, the richest profit in the world. This makes it a service wholly sanctified to God."

Yet the writing and editing of a religious journal was a large responsibility.

"It takes two days of hard work on my part to do the writing for the *Herald* each week," Armstrong once said. "It is as hard as any work I do and I am as tired at the close of the articles as the farmer is at the close of the day."

The success of the paper from the beginning was extremely encouraging. It was a common thing to hear readers say, "The *Gospel Herald* is the best paper I have ever read."

"It is no little thing," he wrote, "to teach the immortal lessons of the Christ to thousands of hearts every week. He that would give up such a position to become president of this nation would stoop."

By 1915 subscriptions had increased to four thousand, and a cylinder press was installed. In a few months this was paid out, a new paper cutter added, and paper purchased to last through the summer. In 1916, however, because of the war, the price of paper rose, and many of the largest journals cut off all free copies. Not only the editors but the workers in the office had to sacrifice keenly to see the

Herald through. One of the office workers dropped out and found other work to buy a suit of clothes for another office worker.

F. B. Srygley reprinted in the *Gospel Advocate* an article from the *Christian Standard* bemoaning the financial woes of the religious journals. He added that he had seen a "dozen or more eke out a miserable existence for a few years," and then stop.

"My advice," Srygley volunteered, "to any brethren who have an aspiration to be editors is to try to work this aspiration off by writing a few articles for the *Gospel Advocate* or some other good paper that has already been started, and not injure themselves and the papers we already have by starting another paper which must of necessity be a rival. . .

Armstrong recognized the good business sense of this advice, but he also realized that not all values can be measured in length of time or in dollars and cents.

"What makes a religious paper a success?" he asked. "Is it the length of days that she lives? Is it the money it makes? How long must a paper live to be a success? How much money must it make?"

He pointed out that not only papers but many of the great books have not met their costs:

"Blind Milton and his heirs received less than one hundred dollars for *Paradise Lost* . . . the one great epic of our literature . . . God forbid that we should ever grow so selfishly commercial that we can have only books, papers, journals that can be given to us on a paying basis. May the world never be deprived of those spirits that launch great enterprises in their unselfishness to serve though they not only can't see a profit in the undertaking, but know well it means financial loss."

One of the chief purposes of the *Herald* was to show that the Christian faith was not a mere form but a vital, transforming power which should shape every attitude and motivate every act.

"Christianity contains not only forms, ordinances, precepts, that must be carefully and faithfully observed," he wrote, "but a spirit also that must permeate and saturate the lives of those keeping the forms, lest the very keeping be an abomination in our Master's sight. Cold, lifeless formality is the pit into which God's people have never failed to fall. Let us not forget that there are small and large, lighter and weightier matters of the law. May we not be gnat strainers and camel-swallowers."

He often quoted the old man in Kentucky who said, "If I could live the Christian's rule for one day, I would become a Christian." When asked, "What is the Christian's rule?" he replied, "Do unto others as you would have others do unto you."

"Could any mortal tell the changes that would be wrought in the world if all professed Christians should follow the rule just for a day?" Armstrong asked. "Daughters would lift the burdens from their mothers that they never dream of touching. Sons would become conscious of the burdens and cares of fathers in providing for the family. Husbands and wives would not ignore each other but would express the love they really feel, and we would reach out with sympathy and help wherever help is needed."

He was constantly shocked at the unconcern of even good people in trying to understand and accept the will of God:

"How forcibly am I impressed in every meeting I hold with the sad and fatal fact that there are few among the teeming millions of earth that will to do his will. Otherwise good honest citizens and kind helpful neighbors, but actually unwilling to do his will. God has made them religious creatures; but strange to say where God's word contravenes their pleasure, where his word calls upon them to give up things they like, they can explain it entirely out of the way."

Much of this indifference he attributed to ignorance of God's will.

"The greatest mistake now being made by Christians is their failure to read and study the word of God. Three-fourths of all Christians never read anything worthwhile. Hundreds of good faithful wives go for days and weeks without reading a word of print. They cook, wash dishes, sweep, scrub floors, make beds, wash and iron day in and day out. They are the greatest servants in the world. Their fault, and almost their only fault, is that they are cumbered

about much serving." He insisted that every one set aside
at least an hour a day for self-improvement, and be sure
that a part of that time was in reading the Bible and a part
in reading other good books.

Repeatedly in writing and in preaching, as well as in his
personal life, he emphasized complete and humble submission
to the will of God as revealed in the Scriptures, not allowing
one's own judgment to question a divine command, or place
one's pragmatic reasoning above the wisdom of God.

"God's children are not to decide the right and wrong of
a question, any question, by 'results.' We are shortsighted
and sometimes mistake results. But God's word is infallible
in its guidance, and we can rely implicitly upon it; where
results seem to indicate another path we are to distrust our
vision and rely entirely upon his holy word."

Expressive of his spirit of reverence and submission was
the prayer with which he closed one of his articles:

Lord, whatever other faults I may have, whatever
other wickedness I may fall into, grant that I may always love every word of thine and may reverence it as
thy word always. Grant, Father, that whatever else may
prevent my perfect obedience to thy word, it may never
be the terrible sin of rebellion, but may my heart be
always perfect to keep all thy commandments and to
please thee at any cost.

A remarkable instance of his personal submission was his
change of attitude toward what was then called "special
providence." When James A. Harding was preaching and
living the faith that God takes care of his children, he unexpectedly aroused violent opposition. In places it became a
"fighting" issue, and many urged that discussion of it cease
because it was an "untaught question." The *Gospel Herald*
had received from its readers even extravagant praise, which
had greatly encouraged the management in carrying the heavy
burdens of publishing it. But it was also condemned because
it taught "that God is a great loving Father, and that as
other fathers care of their children and provide for them, our
Father so cares for his children, but on an infinitely greater
scale." In answering the opposition Armstrong wrote:

From a great deal of teaching done today, one could
conclude that God has retired to private life and turned

the world over to natural laws on the one hand and to
men on the other. Each man is left, it seems from this
teaching, to work out his own success. Natural law must
simply run its course and produce the same effect,
whether you believe in God or don't believe in him,
whether you pray or don't pray. God is no more than
a stone image. God, who made this wonderful world,
has so fixed himself that the very laws he has made
are more powerful than he.

This is not the God of the Bible. He claims to have
control of all law and force. He has never acknowledged, so far as I know, that any law or nation was not
under his control and that he could use them any moment to serve his purpose. Just because God works in
and through natural laws and there is no manifestation
of his power we are apt to conclude that everything
happens solely as the result of natural law. In supposing
that, we are making a great mistake, for God can cause
natural law to work out the very result he desires.

But he understood the opposition because he himself once
shared it. "In my own case I was driven to the position that
God provides for his faithful. I was slow to believe it. I
thought it foolish doctrine and did not want to accept it.
But like Thomas of old I was driven to it, not by my 'experiences' but by the infallible word of God. I had to accept
the doctrine or cancel many passages of Scripture that are as
plain as 'He that believeth and is baptized shall be saved.'"

His own skepticism made him patient with others, but it
was characteristic of him that even his doubts and prejudice
gave way before the plain statements of the Bible:

The weakness of the human family is to doubt God.
In fact it is no easy thing to believe in Jehovah. All
men are afraid of him. True they don't mean to doubt
his goodness, but his promises are so astoundingly great
they doubt the fulfillment. They are not quite willing to
say they don't believe he is able to do what he promises, but really this is the seat of their unbelief. They
think his promises obligate him to do things that he
can't do within the reign of natural law. They never
mean to say he lies, but—but—and they keep "butting"
until they but him out of the count. They often explain
the promises by saying they do not apply to us, or that
they do not mean quite what they say. But the teaching

of Jesus in the Sermon on the Mount that we are to seek first his kingdom and his righteousness and all necessities of life will be added to us, and that we need not be anxious for food and clothing, is very explicit and is made to every one.

Once this promise of God is accepted with simple faith, he felt, it solves multitudes of problems. It relieves one of worry, even over bad situations. It enables a man to choose without fear the work in which he believes he can do the greatest good:

"The world lives to make a living. This is their business. Never do they enter a service without first considering how much there is in it for them. But blessed is the man who finds the work in which he can best serve humanity, and who gives himself wholly to it, losing sight of his own remuneration in his intense love and service for others. Making a living least concerns him. It is actually so insignificant that he loses sight of it. Such servants are the world's greatest benefactors."

Such trust in the Lord, he believed, was especially important for preachers. One of the problems to which he gave considerable attention in the *Herald* was the relationship between the churches and the preachers. He was concerned about the tendency of preachers to require definite contracts from the churches:

"In fifty years at our present rate," he said, "the gospel will be dished out—so much preaching for so much money. From a simple understanding as to how much I am to receive, a thrifty plant is growing among us. 'Well,' says one, 'I have to live and it takes so much for me to live on.' How much does this lack of making support the pivot of decision? Every gospel preacher in the world has a contract with the Lord for his support, and all he has to do is see to it that he complies with the conditions of the contract. God is always faithful and just. It is contrary to the spirit and principles of Christ to bind brethren in human contracts to get them to be honest, just, fair, and unselfish. This is not God's way of doing it."

He emphasized, to be sure, the responsibility of churches

to give adequate support to those who preach, but setting a price on preaching was a different matter:

"Churches and brethren who fail to divide with the teacher their carnal things are not just in their treatment of him. But the preacher must not forget that Christianity makes greater demands of him than simple compliance with the bare principles of justice. To wait until I am justly treated, to make just treatment a condition of my service to humanity, is as foreign to Christianity as a course could well be. To refuse to serve a people until they promise to treat me right, until they promise to be just to me in return for my service, is to refuse to follow Christ. It is being moved by a principle that would as certainly drive Christianity out of the world as that Christ came into the world. Were every Christian to do only what justice demands of him, and to demand all that justice would give him, the death knell of Christianity would be sounded. What do you think of the preacher who refused to hold a meeting for a small, young church because they could pay only $100. Yet that is on record!"

As the concern of both preachers and churches grew over the problem of support, Armstrong saw with dismay a trend toward a short-cut, crash solution. Many meetings in those days lasted a month or six weeks, or as long as the interest justified. But many churches saved up a certain sum for a meeting, and preachers soon learned that they would receive the same amount whether the meeting closed in ten days or in four weeks. So ten-day meetings rapidly became the fashion; a preacher could increase his income three, or perhaps four times, by shorter meetings. The church also felt the strain of attending twice a day for four long weeks, and they were happy to reward the preacher who reduced the strain to ten days.

"For years I have been a strong believer in long meetings," Armstrong wrote. "So often have I seen meetings practically ruined by quitting at the end of ten days." After two such meetings at one church he refused to hold another unless they agreed to run the meeting longer.

But along with concern for more pay and shorter meetings the tendency of preachers to locate indefinitely with well-

established churches, where salaries were good, was developing rapidly, to the neglect of large areas with no churches.
And wealthy churches would have it so, for they monopo-
lized the ablest preachers!

"If there is one plain outstanding truth in New Testament
history," he pointed out, "it is that the preachers were not
tied down with local churches, but were pushing out into
new fields and building up new congregations. What other
way is there to establish new churches?"

He believed that most preachers even yet would willingly
sacrifice to preach in destitute places, but the churches lacked
interest. Some were even "antimissionary." One of the persistent efforts of the *Herald* was to make the churches conscious of their responsibility. Under Armstrong's influence
in the school and through the paper more young people
dedicated themselves to mission work than ever before. The
list is too long to give of those who went not only to
foreign countries like China, Japan, the Philippines, South
America, and India, but also to the mission fields in America, choosing the hard places instead of the soft.

"Selfishness has been, is, and will be the greatest hindrance
to the progress of Christianity," he wrote. "It is the one
enemy to be fought and the battle never ceases till we quit
the flesh."

He pointed out that even a human government takes care
of its soldiers in war and cares for the widows and children
of the dead, but the churches make no such provision.
William J. Bishop, who had spent years in Japan, had just
died.

"He laid down his life," Armstrong wrote, "as truly as
many American boys did in Flanders; he fought for the
greatest and best cause in all the world. He is our dead
soldier. But what of his dependents? What provision have
we made for them? When he was compelled to leave his
guns, his faithful wife, like Molly Pitcher, took up the
fight while he went away to die. When he died he left a
young wife and dependent children. What have we done for
them? Our treatment of our soldiers! Ah, brethren, let us
hide our faces in shame rather than boast of our loyalty!
Even governments of the world are truer to the principle

of justice in their treatment of their soldiers' dependent ones than we to the soldiers of the cross!"

Again, when J. M. McCaleb had to return from Japan for removal of cataracts, Armstrong urged churches to supply immediately the necessary funds.

"Once I visited a home and observed two mules running on a beautiful alfalfa pasture. They were sleek and fine, but I noticed they were seldom used or worked, and I asked the owner why."

"Sometimes we work them in a push," he replied, "but not often."

"Why don't you sell them?" I asked.

"Oh," he replied, almost with tears in his eyes. "We are afraid they might fall into bad hands and not be treated well. We are keeping them and giving the best care on the place for what they have done. They helped us pay for this farm; they are almost as dear to us as members of the family."

"'Keeping them for what they have done.' Isn't that fine? Many years ago Brother and Sister McCaleb went to Japan while they were yet all but children . . . He went depending on the promises of God. When the McCaleb children needed to come back to America for further education, Sister McCaleb and the children came back, while Brother McCaleb stood by the work alone and lonely. Who can measure the loneliness of those years separated from Sister McCaleb and the children? Like Job, there have been none like him.

"He has never been a beggar or complainer. We are all ready to serve him now 'for what he has done.' May God help us to do our duty—no, not our duty only, but to use the privilege of dealing righteously with this unusual veteran of the cross."

To provide for the missionaries and ministers in old age or disability required money, and money required giving, and most Christians he felt had never developed giving enough to become a "grace" in their lives.

"If I were to wait till my family and I were clothed and fed before contributing to the Lord's work, we would never have anything to give," Armstrong wrote. "Besides this, we would make God second, which would violate one of the first principles of the divine Book. I would rather give God his portion and live on the leavings. This would be the spirit of Christ." But he reminded Christians also of the joy that comes from giving.

"There is no sweetness quite so sweet as that which comes to hearts through real giving. Truly it is the pathway of happiness. How we ought to covet opportunities to give! How like the Lord it makes one!"

A major purpose of Armstrong in the *Gospel Herald* was to encourage a larger vision of Christian unity together with the freedom allowed in Christ, a vision of the love which, in spite of many differences, should bind all Christians into a single world-wide brotherhood. His first series of articles appeared under the title "Undenominational Christianity." In simple language he pictured the beginning of the church, as thousands of believers at Jerusalem and all over the Roman world, both Jews and Gentiles, worked together with one heart and one mind, in one body, one church, perfecting the beautiful unity of spirit which the Master desired that "the world might know that he had sent them." This was undenominational Christianity as Jesus directed it. Following the same instruction and example would bring the same unity of faith to the world today. The articles were immediately published as a small book and a thousand copies sold the first year.

He was concerned also about the extent to which denominational thinking influenced even those who were trying to keep the undenominational attitudes of the early Christians. His next series of articles dealt with the church, in an effort to help people understand just what the church is which Jesus established and of which every obedient believer is a member. Under the many terms used in the Scriptures he illustrated with vividness and force the relations the Christian has to the Christ:

"We are so full of the sectarian idea of "church" that the simplicity of Christ's arrangement staggers us . . . Hence Christians move into a community where there is no church and they sit down and die spiritually just because 'there is no where to worship . . .In the simplicity of Christ . . .

wherever there are hearts dedicated to God there is a temple of God . . . Clean up the temple, sweep out the spiritual house, and be a holy priesthood there to offer up spiritual sacrifices, acceptable to God through Jesus Christ our Lord.'"

Armstrong was alarmed at the trend among Christians to follow traditions and leaders and ill-founded prejudices and to be unconcerned about the authority of Christ.

"Every true child of God," he wrote, "is anxious to know, not a part of the truth, but all the truth in every subject that pertains to eternal life. Like Cornelius, he lives 'in the sight of God to hear all things which have been commanded of the Lord.'"

"The only thing that hinders him from thus devoting himself to truth is that terribly blighting, blinding god, prejudice, whom we all serve. Sometimes I hear brethren say they are not prejudiced, good brethren too. I know they do not mean to tell stories, but I never believe such statements. They are not so. *Facts* in every field of advancement are waging an eternal war against superstition, predisposition, bias, and error. So it is better, far better, to understand our enemy. Superstition, early training, self-interest, bias, and error must be battled down by stubborn facts if we would advance in any field of thought. He that is not waging a truceless battle against these enemies must go down in inglorious defeat."

It was this constant fight for truth against prejudice, for unity against forces that threatened to tear the church into fragments, for the simple undenominational faith of the early Christians against a retreat into denominational creedism, for the freedom to teach all truth against a new bondage that would limit such freedom, that through the next thirty years, was to make Armstrong the foremost champion of Christian liberty.

When the Galatian Christians nineteen centuries before, under the fire of persecution, were returning to the traditions which Peter said were a yoke "which neither we nor our fathers were able to bear," and which had built a wall of hatred between them and the Gentile world, Paul had pleaded with them, "For freedom did Christ set us free: stand fast therefore, and be not entangled again in a yoke of bondage."

In the Reformation period courageous men had rebelled against the tyranny of the mediaeval church, which had controlled the minds of men and permitted no deviation from its central authority. These leaders, or their well-intentioned followers, however, had in turn formulated "creeds" defining what all their members must believe and teach and excluding all who differed from them. So the brave effort to restore the freedom of the New Testament church, where each member was responsible to God alone and to no human authority, had produced, instead of one, a multitude of "central authorities."

Against this "creedal" control John Milton, the English poet and independent thinker, pleaded for the right of every man to understand the Scriptures for himself and be free to express his views. Shortly after, John Locke, whose political and philosophical principles profoundly influenced our forefathers, urged Christians to accept the Scriptures alone as their authority and, with tolerance in minor matters, to unite in one universal body as the church of Christ. Rousseau, the brilliant but erratic philosopher of the Age of Reason, praised the simplicity and freedom of the New Testament church as the ideal form of the Christian faith, but he doubted if it could ever be restored.

About a hundred years after Rousseau, Thomas and Alexander Campbell, Barton W. Stone, Walter Scott, and a score of others, independently of each other, arrived at the conviction that the New Testament faith could be restored if men would lay aside all creeds and human authority and follow the Bible alone. In response to such conviction countless thousands, not only in America, but in many other countries, broke denominational enslavement to creeds to restore the unity and freedom of the early church. Even in our time thousands in Russia, India, Italy, Spain, Germany, and other countries have caught the same vision.

To the consternation of Armstrong and many others, however, signs were appearing that this new-found liberty was giving way before attacks of prejudice and intolerance, and Christians were in danger of going back to denominational bondage and division. In his youth, Armstrong heard many sermons on unity. They were beautiful lessons, attractive, clear, and ideal. But he had been rudely awakened:

"I had not observed how this ideal and perfectly scriptural lesson worked in churches composed of men, women, and children, of all stages and degrees of development."

To be sure, wide differences in the development of Christians have always existed. In the church at Jerusalem were Jews who had spent their lives under the shadow of the temple and who were steeped in Jewish traditions. There were also Grecian Jews who had grown up in a Gentile world. At Antioch and other places were Jews devoted to "the law" and Gentiles who had never heard of "the law." Yet so precious was the unity of all believers that the impassable chasm between Jew and Gentile, the difference in custom, tradition, and understanding of God was bridged by a love centered in Christ, which was greater than all differences.

"If Christians are allowed to keep their individualities," Armstrong wrote, "and are permitted to make individual progress in Christian growth, there will always be differences among growing, developing children of God." But in his youth Christians, like those at Jerusalem, had possessed a greatness of love that bridged all such differences, even serious ones.

When I entered the Nashville Bible School it was well understood that E. G. Sewell and Dr. Brents differed on the appointment of elders, on the millennium, and on other questions. So it was understood of Lipscomb and Harding, Taylor and Lipscomb, and others. Each freely discussed his side of the controversial point. That any one would consider another "unsound," "disloyal," or unworthy of the most hearty fellowship never entered one's mind. Such an idea would not have been tolerated for a second. The thing that is now causing trouble is this divisive spirit, this self-righteous, dogmatic, intolerant spirit, that has made a determined effort to divide an otherwise united brotherhood . . . As a result some have "lined up"; some "shut up"; and others suffered martyrdom for their convictions.

But what could be done about such a condition? Clearly it

was wrong to force men to "shut up." This would be bind-
ing on men a human creed, the views of certain cliques, the
very shackles the church had broken a hundred years before:

If there is one thing for which the church of the living
God has stood for through all its history, it is the freedom of conscience of all its members. No one has been
free to bind on another's conscience that which the other
man has not found to be the word of God. Every one
too, unto the humblest of these children, has been encouraged to teach what he feels to be his duty from his
own study of God's word, without intimidation. This
has been our heritage.

That heritage the church could never afford to surrender.
But next to freedom of conscience was the precious unity of
God's people.

"Except to surrender truth, principle, conscience," Armstrong wrote, "one can do nothing more heinous in God's
sight than to disturb the unity of the children of God.
Through my entire life as an active Christian I have stood
firm for shielding the conscience of every man. But we
should not make things a matter of conscience and a ground
of division till we are certain that division in all its hein-
ousness is justifiable."

But the freedom of men to teach, he believed, is always a
matter of conscience. If such teachings were erroneous, the
errors could be exposed by free discussion, and the unity of
the church preserved by patient toleration in the spirit of
Romans 14. The essential in the Christian life is not a
perfect understanding of God's will, but perfect loyalty and
faithfulness to him:

God is patient, longsuffering, and forgiving toward
the humble, docile, loyal, and meek heart. He abides
in watchful waiting as the weak, stumbling life reaches
for higher ground. He is "sound" with all his weaknesses, with all his ignorance. "Who art thou that
judgest the servant of another? To his own Lord he
standeth or falleth. Yea, he shall be made to stand;
for the Lord hath power to make him stand."

If the unity and freedom of Christ are to be preserved, he
held, the teacher must exercise patience with those who hear
but disagree:

"If one holds a particular doctrine that he regards important," he wrote, "let him hold it and teach it; but let him not stress it to the destruction of the peace of the brotherhood. Let him never forget that there are others just as loyal as he dare to be, that have just as much brain as he, just as much ability to understand the simple statements of the Holy Spirit as he was born with, that differ from him."

On the other hand, the hearer must also be patient with the teacher from whom he differs:

"Every Christian ought to rejoice at the preaching of any truth and all truth. He ought to be fair and just in his consideration. A Christian is not a partisan; he doesn't live north or south of the Mason and Dixon's line; he doesn't view matters as a Southerner or as a Northerner; but he is a Christ-man. He loves all truth and all men everywhere."

With a sufficient measure of God's patience and love every problem involving unity and freedom of conscience, he felt, could be resolved. "For freedom did Christ set men free," a freedom which all the world should share. Like Paul of old, Armstrong as editor pleaded with all those who had attained such freedom not, through blind prejudice and selfish contention, to go back to the bondage from which it had taken centuries to deliver them.

Chapter 12

A UNION OF COLLEGES

HARPER, KANSAS, had an unusual church. When Alexander Yohannan visited this country in the interest of Armenian missions and Armstrong urged the churches to receive him with kindness, the Harper church, it was reported, gave him over two thousand dollars. Such generosity in those days was unheard of even with large churches.

Armstrong's first acquaintance with this church was in 1913, five years before the college closed at Cordell.

"The brethren at Harper must be pretty good," he wrote, "or else they have a good way of hiding their meanness. Still I don't see how they could get on their Sunday clothes so quickly. For some of us slipped up on them. We came on a train that never ran before on Sunday. I don't know that it was special providence, but it was a special train. I do not remember ever going to a new place where I had never met anybody before but where I had such a delightful time."

At the time of this unexpected visit Armstrong never dreamed that his future would be so intimately and pleasantly intertwined with this church. Three years later, in

March, 1916, Dow Martin announced in the *Firm Foundation* that a new college had opened at Harper the previous September. The members of this remarkable church had in a few minutes raised an endowment of $55,000, which he believed would soon be increased to $75,000, and Professor N. L. Clark had agreed to become president the following year.

Armstrong was delighted at the beginning of a new Christian school, and particularly with the plan for an endowment. He believed it would be possible to raise endowments for all the colleges and ultimately make instruction free.

"I shall never be satisfied till this is done. We can make them free schools just as soon as we want to do it," he wrote.

The endowment plan at Harper called for each donor to make a ten-year pledge and pay five percent on the amount each year. The principal was never to be paid, but the annual income on $55,000 "living endowment" would be $2,750, which was no small sum in those days. Pledges would be renewed at their expiration and others obtained until the college enjoyed a perpetual, guaranteed income.

Dow Martin was president of the little college the first two years, but refused to use the title, preferring "Dean" instead. Clark was president in 1917-18, but Martin again the following year. Then in 1919 the board asked Armstrong to take the presidency. Up to this time the enrollment had been largely local, but when Cordell closed and Rhodes and I came to Harper, many families moved from Cordell to Harper and the enrollment increased. Armstrong stipulated that, if he accepted the presidency, the school must have a dormitory. Accordingly Z. C. Thompson, president of the board and one of the elders of the church, called a meeting to present the need.

A second factor made Armstrong hesitate also in accepting the presidency. The founding of the college had been inspired by Harper students who had attended Gunter College in Texas, an institution which opposed Sunday school classes, and the Harper church and college board shared this opposition. Armstrong wanted it clearly understood that he would not be limited in any way in teaching what he believed on this question as on all others. When the meeting convened he asked permission to make a statement. He explained that he approved Sunday school classes as they were conducted in the churches of Christ everywhere.

"If I come into this work, I would not press upon you or this church the class work. I would not disturb your good work here by agitating this issue, but I must be made free to teach on the subject when I believe I ought to. If you do not want me to be free at this point, now is the time for you to say so."

Through the winter Armstrong had lived in Harper when he was not in meetings, and the church had become well acquainted with him. When he sat down, Thompson took charge, and without reference to Armstrong's statement proceeded to raise the money for the dormitory. In a few minutes those attending the meeting agreed to assess all their property at market value and donate five percent of this total assessment to the new building. This meant $19,000 raised in a few moments of time, not from people of wealth but from farmers with moderate incomes.

Through the entire five years of Armstrong's presidency the church and the college worked in perfect harmony.

"No discrimination was ever made between preachers opposed to Sunday school classes and those that approved them. In our Thanksgiving programs men who believed and supported Sunday school work were our speakers, but there was perfect harmony between the church and the college although for several years every member of the board opposed Sunday classes." It was a beautiful example of Christian love and tolerance, the kind of unity with freedom to differ for which Armstrong so earnestly contended.

With Armstrong's presidency a new ten-acre campus was purchased south of town, and work began immediately on the new dormitory, a three-story brick veneer, which was divided into two sections—one for boys and one for girls with classrooms on the first floor to be converted later into student rooms.

Armstrong's connection with the Nashville Bible School

and Potter Bible College, his presidency of Western Bible and Literary College and Cordell Christian College, and his reputation across the nation as an educator, evangelist, and writer brought such a flood of applications that the building could not accommodate the enrollment. Z. C. Thompson immediately placed a mortgage of twenty thousand dollars on his farm and began the construction of a two-story frame dormitory for men. A contract was also let for a one-story science building with full basement, containing laboratories for physics, chemistry, biology, and home economics, class-rooms, and an auditorium that would seat two hundred.

On August 4, 1921, the college was formally accredited by the State Department as a junior college, and later became a member of the American Association of Junior Colleges. Enrollment had increased to 323 and enthusiasm over the growth and future of the school was high. The grounds were being landscaped, trees and shrubbery planted, the aquarium and lily pool had been finished, and the leaves of the water lilies were covering the water.

At Cordell Armstrong had carried all the financial burden. At Harper the board managed the finances, even to setting and collecting charges for entertainments. He helped the board increase the endowment, however, and at the Thanks-giving meeting in 1919 his stirring speech brought the endowment up from $55,000 to $130,000; by 1924 it had grown to approximately $300,000. The board advised with him, and he presented to them his recommendations for faculty and financial needs, but the board shouldered all responsibilities. It was a most pleasant relief.

It even gave Armstrong a little leisure time, and I was able to persuade him one Christmas to go rabbit hunting with me. It was a unique experience for him. He may have tracked rabbits in the snow as a boy, but had probably never hunted with a gun. Along a creek we found a corn field alive with rabbits, and in a few minutes we had seven, one of which to his surprise and delight he had bagged.

Though he was free from financial worries, increased enrollments require larger faculties, and by 1923 the faculty numbered seventeen. The preceding year Rhodes had left to teach at Abilene, but after one year of absence he returned. R. C. Bell also rejoined Armstrong from Abilene, and the faculty was the strongest it had ever been. But larger faculties bring heavier expense, and at times the board had difficulty meeting salaries. One month when the treasury was too low to cover all salaries, the president of the board was greatly distressed.

"Don't worry," Armstrong smiled, "these teachers will all be in their places Monday morning, check or no check." This was a tribute to the loyalty of the teachers, but a tribute also to Armstrong, who could inspire such loyalty. But salaries were seldom unduly delayed.

The greatest financial need, however, was a classroom and administration building. The enrollment had simply outgrown the facilities, and growth had to stop or more buildings be provided. In 1922 James A. Harding died. Thirty years before, Harding had started the stream of Christian schools in which every student, along with his other studies, carried a regular Bible class, and he had also served as president of the first two such colleges. He had been keenly interested in the success of all the schools, had spent one year on the campus at Cordell, and had spoken frequently at others. Many of the Harper faculty had been his students, and Mrs. Armstrong was his daughter. She and Armstrong got in touch with other students of Harding, and all agreed that some fitting memorial should be erected to honor the man who had given a greater impetus to this stream of Christian education than any other man of his generation. All agreed too that an administration and classroom building at Harper College would be a fitting memorial because it would carry on for generations the service to which he had dedicated his life. Consequently John E. Dunn, who had graduated with Armstrong at the Nashville Bible School, agreed in 1923 to head a campaign to raise $150,000 for such a building.

Almost immediately, however, the announcement met opposition. Armstrong had years earlier unintentionally offended two men of wide influence. In 1918, after the break between R. H. Boll and M. C. Kurfees, Armstrong was invited to hold a meeting for the Highland church in Louisville. Kurfees had earlier taken a fatherly interest in Boll, and the two had been warm friends. They were among the most gifted writers of the *Gospel Advocate,* Boll finally being given the prominent first-page space. Then a difficulty arose at Highlands, tensions grew, involving both men and the *Advocate,* earnest attempts failed to settle the trouble, and Boll was finally dropped from the editorial staff.

Armstrong was deeply grieved over the break between two men of such great ability and hoped the difficulty could in some way be resolved. Years before he had studied Hebrew under Kurfees and had always loved and honored him. Boll had been a student at Nashville and Armstrong loved him. Since the influenza epidemic of 1918 suddenly closed his meeting at the Highlands, friends suggested that Armstrong try to effect a reconciliation between the two old friends. He found Boll eager to cooperate, but Kurfees was so highly wrought that Armstrong despaired of any reconciliation. It was a sickening experience. He loved both men, and it was heartbreaking to feel that the chasm could never be bridged. His attempt at reconciliation, however, was to have unfortunate repercussions.

During World War I feelings had run high, and many who were conscientious about fighting had suffered reproach, condemnation, and imprisonment. J. C. McQuiddy, managing editor of the *Advocate*, had a particularly hard place to fill, for Lipscomb, the editor-in-chief, held that Christians should not engage in war. Many leaders in the church criticized McQuiddy because he did not stand more firmly for the conscientious objector in the columns of the *Advocate*. After the war closed, the whole matter might soon have been forgotten, but McQuiddy, apparently still stinging from the criticism, two years after the war gave Lipscomb some of his earlier articles and asked him to collate from them a statement about the Christian's relation to war. This collated article under the pseudonym "Daniel Quilp" he sent to Armstrong and to E. A. Elam to be published in the *Herald* and the *Advocate* if they thought it worthy. Both published it without comment. McQuiddy then revealed that he was the author, and that the attitude toward war expressed in the article showed that he had been unjustly criticized. During the war he felt it was not the time for strong condemnation, and his critics, he claimed, had finally followed the same course he had pursued.

"Although they were loud in their indiscriminate and unwise antiwar talk at the beginning," McQuiddy charged, "still, as soon as the government put into operation its military machinery to curb unnecessary, unguarded, and hurtful talk with yawning prisons . . . they suddenly hushed up with their antiwar talk and were in meek and instant subjection to the 'powers that be.' My course differed from those of my critics in that I not only adopted with them the same sensible negative line of procedure . . . but I did all on the positive side that I could conscientiously do to stand by the government and help its soldiers in all legitimate ways."

This very natural desire of McQuiddy to free himself from criticism Armstrong could easily have ignored and have let the matter rest. But he had seen his college at Cordell closed because of the frenzied war spirit. He had seen conscientious Christians held up to ridicule by other Christians, and when they were imprisoned their own brethren refused to help and were ashamed of them. He felt he must speak out.

He reminded McQuiddy that his sarcasm against those who hushed their antiwar talk when faced with "yawning prisons" was unfair, for McQuiddy's own attitude had suddenly changed after Mr. Douglas, the attorney general, had called him in.

"From that time on," Mr. Douglas had said, "Brother McQuiddy was satisfactory to the federal authority."

Whether the attorney general's warning had caused McQuiddy's sudden change or not, Armstrong reminded him that he had refused to publish a statement signed by E. G. Sewell, F. B. Srygley, F. W. Smith, A. B. Lipscomb, H. Leo Boles, W. L. Karnes, and E. A. Elam as to what brethren had taught on the subject of war, and had also refused to publish an article from Elam that contained nothing but excerpts from the Scriptures. Instead he had printed a strong article from the *Literary Digest* in favor of war and a weak one from a Quaker magazine, saying that each was as strong as could be presented from each point of view.

Armstrong also pointed out that the McQuiddy article from which Lipscomb had drawn twenty-five lines for the "Daniel Quilp" statement had actually closed with quotations from other papers that held the conscientious objector up to contemptuous gaze.

"Brother McQuiddy prepared an article and published it to many thousands of readers that could only increase the already inflamed passions of bitterness against the man who dared to say he had a religious conviction against going to war," Armstrong charged.

But Armstrong was also sympathetic, for McQuiddy, he said, had been in a hard place.

"I believe he, in his own convictions, has never accepted the antiwar position for Christians, but he knew that the *Advocate* had so led the readers to believe—many of them. So he tried to keep in line with the lifelong policy of the paper, while all the time his convictions were contrary."

It is dangerous, of course, to guess at another's convictions; yet Armstrong's explanation of McQuiddy's course during the war seemed the kindest defense he could suggest. But almost nineteen years later, as sentiment was growing in this country for entering the second World War, McQuiddy declined to print Armstrong's article "Lest We Forget." The article emphasized the separateness of the Christian's calling from the world with its passions and hates, cautioned Christians against being caught up again in the frenzy of war, and reminded them of the noble aims that prompted our entry into World War I twenty years before, only to produce a Hitler instead of a Kaiser. The article was accepted by the *Firm Foundation*.

Though years had passed, it was apparently hard for McQuiddy to forget the criticisms. The immediate consequence in 1922, however, was a denunciation of the campaign to raise funds from former students of James A. Harding for a building in his honor. To a question from A. A. Bunner whether it was right to "honor a man," McQuiddy wrote: "I am sure that James A. Harding would not approve of building a memorial to his name . . . I do not believe it right to build a memorial building to the name of any man and of capitalizing it in order to get money. It is selling the name . . . Only from a sense of duty have I written this."

Kurfees immediately agreed with McQuiddy. "No man ever lived," he wrote, "who would have been more outspoken and vigorous in his opposition to such a project than the beloved Brother Harding himself. All of us who knew him are ready to say, God bless his memory, and God be praised for the magnificent work done by the consecrated and godly James A. Harding . . . and if we wish to see a memorial to his name, behold the record of his life . . . 'Harding Memorial Building' indeed! If he were here and should speak out with the fire and force that characterized his opposition to such things while he lived, he would most likely speak of it as a desecration to his memory."

It is easy for people to imagine what the dead would do or say, for the dead cannot speak. Certainly when Harding was alive he never asked a penny for himself from any man. But he pleaded with people to give to many good works, including new buildings for the Nashville Bible School, though few responded to his pleading. It is strange that Kurfees and McQuiddy both forgot that when the Potters wanted to build and name, not merely one building, but a whole college, as a memorial to a son, Harding heartily approved such honoring of a man's memory! It is ironic also that Kurfees felt he understood what Harding would say better than Harding's own daughter, his son-in-law, and the others who, as his students and fellow teachers, had been far more closely associated with him than Kurfees had ever been. It is ironic too that when, after Lipscomb's death, the name of the Nashville Bible School was changed to David Lipscomb College to honor Lipscomb, there was never a protest from either McQuiddy or Kurfees, though the reverence thousands had for the Lipscomb name would be worth millions to the institution!

It is easy for the slightest pretext to discourage people from giving, but it is doubtful if the protests of McQuiddy and Kurfees had any great effect. Warm approval of the memorial building came in from many of Harding's former students and friends, and in a few months Dunn had raised in pledges and cash $25,000.

The opening of the school year 1923-24 seemed auspicious. The faculty was the strongest the school ever had, and the spirit of cooperation between teachers and students was perfect. When Brother Sheriff, a missionary from Africa, visited the school in the spring, the students voted unanimously to leave off fruits from their tables for a week in order to send canned fruits to the Shorts, former students who were being supported by the Harper church as missionaries in the Rhodesias. There were no disciplinary problems the whole year. Instead of buying class rings, the graduates of 1922-23 contributed $600 to the building fund, and the graduates of 1924 made an equally valuable contribution to the library.

As Armstrong looked back over the year he was constrained to say with Joshua, "We know that not one thing has failed of all the good things which Jehovah our God spake concerning us." God had wonderfully blessed the school and the new campaign, and the future looked bright. His prayer for 1924 was: "Father, we pray for wisdom for the year 1924. We do pray that if it be thy will, we may live it through and that we may by thy help make it the best year we have ever lived." And he closed with the beautiful request of Jabez: "O that thou wouldst bless us indeed, and enlarge our borders, and that thy hand might be with us and that thou wouldst keep us from evil that it be not to our sorrow."

This prayer was to be unexpectedly answered and in a way he had never dreamed. In spite of the enthusiasm of students, faculty, and board, all began to realize that Harper was too small a town for an institution growing as rapidly as the college was. Many families wanted to move to the school for the sake of their children, but Harper offered no opportunities for work or for new businesses. It became a grave question as to whether the college could afford to locate a new and expensive building on a campus whose "borders" could not easily be enlarged.

After much study the board, in the fall of 1923, sent a committee to confer with the churches in Wichita about moving the college there. The interest in Wichita was immediate, but moving a college is not a simple undertaking. At Harper the school had four buildings which it had already outgrown. To purchase a campus at Wichita and build larger facilities would require time and money. Yet the board was at the point of taking an option on a tract of land near the city limits, a part of which could be reserved for campus and the rest divided into lots and sold.

Before the option was taken, however, President A. S. Croom of Arkansas Christian College in Morrilton, and Z. D. Barber, treasurer of the board, appeared unexpectedly on the campus. A few years earlier Croom had taught at Harper and knew Armstrong well. He had dropped out to finish his Master's degree at Harvard and had then headed the effort in Arkansas, his home state, to establish a college there. Hearing that Harper College was considering a move, he and Barber came to propose a merger of Harper College and Arkansas Christian College at Morrilton.

Harper, they pointed out, needed an administration building and a location with larger opportunities; Morrilton already had, they felt, the finest administration building among the Christian schools, and the location in the heart of the churches of Christ would assure support in both students and money. In fact, money did not seem to be a problem at Morrilton. But the Arkansas school needed Armstrong and his faculty. "We have the building," Barber said, "but you have the college." Harper was accredited as a standard junior college, and Arkansas Christian, not yet accredited, was offering two years of college work. By combining all their resources the new institution could open as a first-class senior college.

These arguments were appealing, but there were two serious obstacles. Harper had already raised $25,000 for a Harding Memorial Building, and this money would have to be returned to the donors unless a satisfactory arrangement could be made with them. Croom then suggested that the new school be called Harding College, and all felt that the donors would be even more highly pleased at this recognition than merely naming a building for the founder of the Christian schools.

But a second obstacle was a debt of about $25,000 resting on the Harper institution and secured by a mortgage on Z. C. Thompson's farm. Thompson through the years had been a most liberal donor, and he expected no return from his gifts except the good the school was doing. But the mortgage on his farm was not a gift but a loan. Armstrong insisted that it must be paid.

"I stood firm for this money to be returned to Brother Thompson," he said, "and the mortgage to be cleared. I told the committee I would not consider consolidation until this was done." Croom and Barber agreed to try to raise the money in Morrilton to liquidate this debt. Upon this promise the Harper board agreed to the consolidation, and on May 1, 1924, Morrilton sent a check for $25,000—$22,000 as gifts from the citizens of Morrilton and $3,000 borrowed by the board from the bank.

A further difficulty, however, arose with the Morrilton board regarding the new name. Two board members objected strenuously to change. One elderly member of the board is reported to have protested vehemently, his voice thick with emotion.

"If we change the name of Arkanshaw Christshan College, we'll be shinnin' againsht God, we'll be shinnin' againsht the church, and we'll be shinnin' againsht the shtate of Arkanshaw," he cried. And Croom suggested that he was perhaps unconsciously arranging the "shins" in the order of their enormity. But the board agreed to the new name, and the two members who objected resigned.

At the time Morrilton had only one still unfinished administration-classroom building, but no dormitories. And dormitories would be absolutely necessary. John T. Hinds, head of the Bible department at Morrilton, had the year before published in Armstrong's paper a plea for help to build dormitories at Morrilton, a plea which Armstrong warmly endorsed.

Harper had a two-story brick and stone building with half basement, an excellent girls' dormitory, better than Morrilton was ever to have, a two-story frame dormitory for boys, and the one-story science building with basement. It had furnishings for two dormitories, and far more library, laboratory, and classroom equipment than Morrilton had. It also had $25,000 in pledges which it had raised for a new building, all of which it would turn to the new college. In addition it had the "living endowment" pledges of approximately $300,000, which were bringing in five percent interest annually to the school. Since these had been made to Harper College, it was understood that most of the donors might automatically stop paying, but Armstrong and the *Harper Board* urged all who would to continue paying their pledges to the new institution since it was in effect a continuation of Harper College on a new campus and under a new name, doing the same work on an even higher level. From these pledges Mr. Thompson selected a sufficient number, approximately $140,000, for their payments to liquidate the amount still due him and relieve the new institution of this burden.

In effecting a merger of the two institutions equipment, notes, and pledges could easily be transferred, but not the Harper buildings. Consequently the Harper board gave the Morrilton board a deed to the campus and buildings at Harper so that they could immediately trade them at a value of $55,000 for a hospital near the Morrilton campus which had cost $70,000. This became the first dormitory of the new college.

At the time the merger was proposed the Harper plant had a mortgage of $25,000 and uncovered obligations to Thompson of $7,000. The Morrilton plant, unknown to us, had an indebtedness of "some $45,000." Croom declared thirty years later that, had he known of "this cumbersome indebtedness ($32,000) against Harper College, it is doubtful whether he would ever have approached the Harper school with an offer. It may be equally true that had Armstrong and the teachers from Harper known the indebtedness at Morrilton and the financial strains they were later to suffer, far greater than they had ever endured at Harper, it is doubtful if they would have considered a merger. Croom at least did know the indebtedness at Harper before he proposed the merger to his board, and he could easily have withdrawn his offer. But Armstrong and his teachers learned only gradually and through painful experience the financial situation at Morrilton.

No one can know how each school would have developed had they not united, but looking back from the present, we may consider it a blessing that God so hides the future that we have to walk by faith. Armstrong, not knowing the struggles which lay ahead, wrote, "Faithful believers in God would be constrained to say, 'This thing proceedeth from the Lord.'" Even after the long struggle at Morrilton no doubt he would still have thought so.

"The new college was in every sense a consolidation," Armstrong said in the September bulletin of 1928, "not a 'swallowing up' of one school by the other. For every teacher in both schools who cared to remain and who could be fitted into the new organization was retained. Every member of both boards who would serve was placed upon the new board."

Two members of the Morrilton board refused to serve and resigned, and perhaps because of the distance C. Ray Thompson was the only member of the Harper board at first to serve. B. F. Lowery was added later.

But the great need at Morrilton had been for Armstrong and his faculty. Unknown to Armstrong at the time, unfortunate difficulties had arisen between President Croom and his students and some of his faculty that apparently made him feel he should turn the presidency to someone else, and made him even doubt the wisdom of remaining with the school in any capacity.

So, with the action of the two boards a new, formerly undreamed of institution began to take shape. Arkansas Christian College had been running for two years and Harper for seven. Harding College, however, was not even a dream until the spring of 1924, when a merger was proposed. Not until April 15, 1924, when the "Articles of Incorporation of Harding College" were signed by the new board, did it become a legal entity, and not until the two junior colleges closed their last sessions in June, 1924, did Harding College begin to function.

In the catalog statement that "Harding College was established in 1924," no disrespect was intended toward the fine work Croom, Barber, and their supporters had done the past three years at Morrilton, or to Dow Martin, the Thompsons, Armstrong and others for the equally fine service they had given through seven years and more at Harper. It was a mere statement of fact that Harding College did not legally start till 1924. Arkansas Christian College, Harper College, Cordell, and Western Bible and Literary College were all worthy predecessors, preparing the way, but were not Harding itself.

After the decision of the two boards to consolidate, a number of important decisions had to be made. Armstrong insisted that Croom remain with the school. In a letter of January 15, 1924, Croom said: "If I should stay I should want to be Vice-President of the College, with a division of the work that would release me from direct work with the students, where I am a failure, and give me work to keep the machinery of the thing moving properly, if possible. I should have to be content with the mechanical phase of the work and let you give it the soul."

And in a letter of January 24, he became more specific: "The matter I thought I should be best adapted to is the matter of organization of support for the school, development of outside interest, that is, interest among parents and brethren. I do not consider that I can succeed well in direct control of students. This you can do to perfection."

Croom's suggestion that he assume the financial responsibilities met with Armstrong's hearty approval. Armstrong had felt keenly the strain of financing the college at Cordell, and for five years at Harper had enjoyed complete freedom from financial worries. He was glad for Croom and the board to relieve him of this burden. But when he reached Morrilton he met an unexpected obstacle. Dr. Matthews, the president of the board, objected to Croom's having anything to do with collecting student fees because, he said (and Croom's letters seem so to indicate), Croom antagonized

the students. This objection Armstrong never mentioned to
Croom, for he did not want to hurt him, but he told Matthews that Croom was expecting to handle the finances and
that it would be unfair to change the arrangement. Dr.
Matthews then withdrew his objection, and Croom took
charge of current collections and disbursements.

Another matter to be arranged was the salary schedule.
Since the new institution had to complete the administration
building and construct a second dormitory—an expense which
would double its present indebtedness, Armstrong felt that
the salary schedule Croom suggested was unrealistic. Although he had no responsibility for the finances, he was sure
the college could not meet such a schedule. With reluctance
Croom insisted that the very lowest salary teachers with
Master's degrees could live on would be $1,800 a year.
The financial rating of the board, he pointed out, was
$350,000, and they were actually worth more. "Hence the
Board is amply able to share the financial sacrifice," he
added. "If they are willing, and, if they are not willing, I
see no use to start another school. The outcome is inevitable when the teachers alone undertake to bear the
whole burden. For a family to live and dress comfortably
nowadays, it requires such a salary."

But he said that he would be absolutely unwilling to receive a higher salary than the rest. "I won't even consider
it." He doubted, however, if John T. Hinds, head of the
Bible Department, or Z. D. Barber would be willing to
reduce their salaries to the proposed level, but since Barber
was not a teacher the board could pay him whatever they
wished.

The salary schedule was finally agreed on and approved
by the board, but Armstrong's judgment was unfortunately
right. The board had to borrow money the very first year
to meet the salaries, a loan which Armstrong himself had to
settle many years later.

A third matter was the teachers who would be retained
from each institution. Croom did not want to keep the head
of the business department at Morrilton because he lacked
the spirit of cooperation and ran up bills against the school
without authorization. He did not want to retain the dean

also and his wife or John T. Hinds because they had not stood with him in student discipline and had criticized him to others.

Time unfortunately is a traitor to memory, and thirty years later Croom blamed Armstrong for getting rid of Hinds:

"It was a great misfortune," he wrote, "for this godly man (Hinds) to be left out of the faculty after the changes made in 1924. Armstrong expressed a conviction that one could not be scripturally employed to teach only Bible in the school."

Croom's statement is incomprehensible. Armstrong clearly had no such "conviction." David Lipscomb had taught only Bible all the years at Nashville. James A. Harding had taught only Bible the last two years at Nashville and nearly always at Bowling Green, and in his last years Armstrong himself taught only Bible. He did believe that a Bible department under a faculty separate from the rest of the departments was not a wise and good arrangement. He felt that capable men like Rhodes, the Bells, himself, and others, would be better teachers of history, English, science, and Greek if they were also teaching a Bible class. In that way the influence of the Bible would be an integral part of every department, not just of one. In blaming Armstrong for eliminating Hinds, Croom had forgotten his own opposition. In a letter of January, 1924, (See Appendix A) Croom wrote:

The Board is standing behind me here in the fight I am having to make against teachers who have broken confidence and are indirectly doing their best to oust me by catering to all the whims and complaints the students have or can make against me. In other words, they are doing all they can, it seems, to nourish a student grudge against me for enforcing regulations in the fall. Perhaps I have made mistakes, but for a teacher to sit in a faculty meeting, help make regulations, and pretend his hearty cooperation and support of the same, to turn and knife you from the back by working among the students, is an inexcusable outrage in a school that calls itself Christian. Now if at any time the Board should fail me in what I consider being true to Christian principle, you might easily understand why I should dislike to be bound to you by my word that I would stay. Whether I stay or not, the field is open to you, and I am more than glad for you and your co-workers to enter. The teachers above referred to are Hinds, Sullivan, and Sullivan's wife. Strange enough Sullivans never showed any disposition but to love me and co-operate heartily with me until Brother Hinds went there to room this year. And Bro. Hinds did not until I tried to *choke him off his high salary*. He gained his point in regard to salary by secretly working on some members of the board . . . To be plain here is another point I should be unyielding on, and that is that *I will not teach another year in a school with a man of that principle posing as a Bible teacher, if I know it beforehand as in this case.* [Italics mine, L.C.S.]

With such emphatic opposition, had Armstrong wanted to retain Hinds, it would have been impossible. But if the Bible courses were distributed among various teachers as at Harper as Armstrong preferred, there would be no point in keeping a full-time man for it, and in a later letter Croom said, "If they (the board) then want to maintain Hinds at dead expense, it would be only for a year, because he would soon have no students as their Bible teacher, if we make it optional with the students as to their Bible teacher. Brother Hinds is a fine teacher of his type, however." But he had already declared he would not remain in the faculty with "a man of that principle posing as a Bible teacher."

Armstrong talked with the teachers at Harper about who would be needed in the new school and who would have to be left out because there would be no place. He left to Croom the responsibility of eliminating those at Morrilton whom he could not or did not want to keep. But no one was left out at Morrilton that Croom wanted to keep.

It is easy to understand Croom's feeling toward Hinds in 1924 and the change thirty years later. Time and distance often erase unpleasant memories, and attitudes become kinder, but it is strange that his attitude toward Armstrong seems to have changed to a strong dislike. Of this change Armstrong was unaware even to the day of his death. To be sure he and Croom were the antithesis of each other in many respects, but Armstrong considered such personality differences insignificant and loved Croom in spite of them. He regretted deeply that Croom remained with the new school only one year and always held the way open for his return at any time he might desire.

In the Harding Bulletin of September, 1928, Armstrong said: "Few Christians in the state know of the unselfish service rendered by A. S. Croom, the first president of the school (Arkansas Christian College), John T. Hinds, and the men and women who taught with them through the rain and slush that entered every crack and crevice of the un-finished roof of the administration building during the first winter. It was an unusually rainy season, and in the absence of walks even women teachers wore rubber boots to school."

In another account Armstrong says, "As the walls rose on the college grounds the classes move in. But there was no roof, and as the rains poured through the concrete upper floors or blew in at the paneless window openings the students sat with umbrellas over them and instructors lectured in rain coats."

Armstrong genuinely appreciated the unselfishness of teachers who had endured such conditions, but in the college catalog eulogies were out of place, and only a factual statement was made about the consolidation. The catalog contained a list of the graduates of Harper College, but if there had been graduates of Arkansas Christian College during its two years, no list was ever furnished Armstrong or me for inclusion in the catalog.

Croom's resignation at the close of 1924-25, he said thirty years later, was because Armstrong encroached upon the domain of finance, which had been assigned to him. Croom was to handle current expenses, but the board with Barber, its treasurer, was responsible for all finances, including liquidating the indebtedness and purchasing permanent equipment. When Armstrong learned that the indebtedness was far greater than he had been led to believe, he was concerned. He had the highest regard for Barber's ability to raise money, but he doubted if one man could do the job.

Thirty years later Croom blamed Armstrong for not talking to him before recommending to the board that Barber be given some assistants.

Whether he talked with Croom or not, Armstrong is not alive to testify, but for the president of a college to make recommendations to the board which is responsible for the institution is no encroachment on anyone's domain. It is a president's duty, and to the day of his death Armstrong did not dream of Croom's objection or his bitterness toward him. He considered Croom, though extreme in many ways, a man of honor and integrity. But even good men can be biased and can unfortunately misunderstand others.

During the tragic days of 1931, for instance, when Harding College was struggling almost with its last breath to stay alive, Armstrong made a speech about the difficulty of keeping a college going. He referred to a report he had just received that the board of one Christian school had been asked to guarantee the salaries of teachers for the following year or the school would not open. Armstrong prophesied that the board would not do so and that the college would have to close. Croom felt that the speech was a reflection on him, since he was at that time president of the revived college at Cordell, Oklahoma, and had apparently made some such demand of the board.

"In thinking this speech over," Armstrong replied to Croom, "I thought that, perhaps, I had unduly reflected on that board . . . I certainly was far from wanting, or meaning, to reflect on any one of the small groups in our school plants that are bearing the brunt of things. I honor every one of them. Nor would I even think of criticizing a teacher in these groups who should become tired of the burdens and should decide to walk out unless others equally bound would divide the burden with him. More than once I have said to our teachers who are the hub of our faculty that I did not want them to remain under the burdens one hour longer than they were willing to do. I should deeply regret to see them retire, but they would be entirely within the bounds of justice in doing so. But to remain is more noble and makes them akin to martyrs."

Financing a college has always been a problem. In the

Depression years it was especially difficult, and often impossible, for many colleges closed. Croom condemned Armstrong because, he asserted, "he was never willing to solicit funds from persons and firms individually and therein lay a major weakness. Schools successfully financed have always had to rely mainly on the President's success in raising money."

Armstrong, to be sure, never claimed to be a financier, but at Cordell from 1907 to 1918 and later at Morrilton his success was greater than Croom knew. In 1930-31 Croom was president of the revived Cordell College as Armstrong was of Harding. Both faced the same financial crisis. To meet it successfully, Croom asserted, each institution had "to rely mainly on the President's success in raising money." Croom had all Oklahoma and the Southwest from which to solicit support for Cordell, a much more lucrative field than impoverished Arkansas. But when he failed to get the support needed, he apparently, from his letter, asked the board to guarantee the salaries, and the school closed never to open again. Armstrong never condemned either Croom or the board. They did what seemed best at the time. But Armstrong's nature compelled him to a different course. Faced with the same problem at Morrilton, he and the teachers, at unbelievable sacrifice, carried the college through the black years to become the present Harding College.

In spite of Croom's tendency to interpret everything in a way prejudicial to Armstrong, in a private letter he showed a surprisingly admirable sense of justice. Ted McElroy, in an article in the *Bible Banner* in 1942, reported that L. R. Wilson had said Croom resigned from the college at Morrilton because Armstrong was a premillennialist. In a letter to Wilson, a copy of which he sent to Armstrong, Croom says:

> I left Harding College mainly on things Bro. Armstrong was doing, but the premillennial question was in no way related, nor had any bearing whatsoever on my leaving . . . For your further information, I can state that Bro. Armstrong insisted on my staying, and, sincerely, I am sure; then in 1930 he wrote me a long

letter requesting that I return to the school. (I have the letter just in case) [Parenthesis is A. S. Croom's] . . . No, in view of the above statements, it seems to me that you and McElroy through the influence of the Bible have a job to do. I have a bird dog (not much account), but if I did him as much injury as this article was calculated to do, I'd do something about my treatment of "Rusty"—the dog. What do you say? If I were you, Brother Wilson, I'd do a lot of thinking about this and especially when singing "Face to Face with My Redeemer" next time, and also would do something about it—not because of me, but because of a published false statement attributed to you.

The summer of 1924, preceding the opening of the new college, Armstrong spent in meetings in California—at Graton, Santa Rosa, and Berkley. It was a joy to meet many former students and old friends, and he thoroughly enjoyed his visits with Halliday Price, and the L. R., Luther, and James Sewells, and the trips with Felix Owen to places of interest in and around San Francisco. But he was concerned about the churches in the West and made an urgent appeal to those in the East to send evangelists for a ten-year period to build up the church on the coast.

Returning shortly before the opening of the first session of Harding College in September, 1924, Armstrong was pleased with the enrollment, which was about the same as that at Harper. It was pathetic, however, that, despite the important work Croom had done in starting Arkansas Christian College, in carrying it through the two years of its operation, and in suggesting its consolidation with Harper College, he may have been right in feeling that certain teachers at Morrilton had been working against him and that he was a "failure" in "direct work with students," for only two boarding girls from the preceding year at Morrilton returned. From Harper approximately as many boarding students came to Morrilton as could have been expected to re-enroll at Harper. But with students from twelve states the union of the two schools with their combined resources indicated bright prospects for the future.

Chapter 13

TAKING ARMS AGAINST A SEA OF TROUBLES, 1924-34

WITH GREAT ENTHUSIASM Harding College opened its first session, combining the faculty and resources of Harper College, accumulated through nine years, and the resources of Arkansas Christian College, accumulated through its two years of operation and two years of preparation.

The first dream of Arkansas Christian College had come from Mrs. Jennie Hill, whose husband, Wilmer Augustus Hill, was a student at the Nashville Bible School under James A. Harding. Hill became the first president of the Arkansas board and was soon joined by seventeen other members, including J. A. Mode, whose daughters had been students of Armstrong at Western Bible and Literary College.

Since a recession in 1920 slowed payments on pledges, the board of Arkansas Christian College had to borrow $25,000 to begin construction of the administration building. When the two colleges united, only the front section of the building had been completed, and the board of Harding College then borrowed an additional $50,000 to finish the rear section containing the gymnasium and auditorium and to construct a dormitory for girls. In the meantime the campus and buildings at Harper had been traded for a hospital building, a few blocks from the Morrilton campus, which furnished a dormitory for sixty students. The first year this was filled with girls, and the boys were placed in private homes.

In the spring of the first year the students, under the leadership of C. Ray Thompson, a member of the new board who had formerly been secretary-treasurer of the Harper board, in order not to add to the college debt purchased lots across the street from the campus and built a brick-veneer dining hall with seating capacity for two hundred fifty and with kitchen and storage facilities. This construction was financed entirely by the students and teachers who ate at the club without obligating the college board in any way. R. C. Bell, who had taught at five Christian schools and had been president of Thorp Springs, was deeply impressed.

"I have been intimately acquainted with most of our Bible schools for the past twenty-five years," he wrote, "and not one of them has made the rapid growth that Harding has. Never has one of our schools been so well supported financially by its board and home town. The school has not been without its detractors, to be sure, but apparently opposition has only increased the number and enthusiasm of its friends."

J. G. Allen, in "A Trip through Arkansas," reported enthusiasm all over the state. "All churches in the state are in harmony with it and have full confidence in its management. Armstrong is held in high esteem by all."

By the spring of 1925 families began moving to Morrilton for the school. "Last week," Armstrong wrote, "ten new dwellings were going up within five or six blocks of the Harding campus. Since the college came, there has hardly been a day that one could get a carpenter for a small job. All are tied up on new jobs."

The glowing prospects for the new school, however, were rudely shaken by three unpleasant developments which no one could foresee.

First was the unexpected difficulty in obtaining accreditation as a senior college. In the spring of 1924 I visited the University of Arkansas and conferred with Dean Jordan, Examiner for the University. He looked over the faculty for the new institution, the courses of study, and requirements for graduation, and promised to visit the college in the fall. He also introduced me to the heads of the science departments for suggestions regarding equipment. Our library of 3,000 volumes we knew fell below the standard, but after the conference at the university we ordered equipment in science sufficient we hoped to counterbalance this weakness.

After a careful inspection in the fall Dr. Jordan gave the college the same recognition the University gave the other four-year institutions. Since many students came from Texas, we wrote immediately to the Texas State Board of Education and also to the New York State Board and were placed on their accredited list also as a four-year college.

But accreditation, we found, was not as easy as we expected. The State Department of Education apparently had the feeling that Arkansas already had too many colleges— five state and nine private institutions besides the University. Accordingly, without previous notice, in December of 1924 they sent Dr. Elliff from the University of Missouri to inspect the school. The new laboratory equipment had not all arrived, and without understanding the purpose of Dr. Elliff's visit, our reception may have been less cordial than it could have been. Consequently his report was unfavorable, and we asked for a second examination. Dr. Elliff returned in the fall of 1925. This time the laboratories were fully equipped, and the library had been enlarged. Dr. Elliff recommended only deletions of certain courses and a new form for the academic records.

These recommendations were immediately met. Because Dr. Elliff could not return at once, the new academic records were carefully packed and carried to St. Louis for his inspection, and after a second visit in April, 1926, he recommended that Harding be granted the same recognition as other four-year colleges.

The State Board did not meet, however, till June 4, and our commencement program was set for June 3. The previous spring the college had six graduates, but since the

State Department had held up accreditation, and we could only tell seniors we "hoped for their approval," most seniors transferred to other colleges. Miss Ruby Lowery was the only one with courage to remain. When Armstrong announced that the State Board was not meeting till June 4, the students voted enthusiastically to stay over an extra day and see Ruby graduate. On June 4, only minutes before the program was to start, when everybody waited with increasing tension, the telegram came from Superintendent Ross granting approval "for one year." As Miss Lowery marched forward to receive her degree and the diploma, the audience rose in spontaneous applause.

The one-year limit made necessary another inspection in 1927. Dr. Elliff again recommended approval, but again two or three members of the State Board haggled and thought another one-year limitation ought to be imposed. Consequently in 1928, the State Board asked Superintendent C. E. Pickens of Batesville to examine the college, and upon his recommendation it was placed on the accredited list indefinitely. A reinspection was supposed to be carried out each two years, but this was never done. In a public statement Mr. Pickens said he considered "Harding College, because of the vast territory from which she can draw students and the great numbers of Christians in Arkansas, to have the brightest prospects for the future of any college in the state."

Because of the long struggle for recognition, Harding College had gradually strengthened its library, laboratories, and faculty until at the time it practically met the standards of the North Central Association, with the exception of endowment and salaries.

The second, and more serious difficulty for the new school, strange to say, grew out of the conflict between M. C. Kurfees and R. H. Boll of Louisville, Kentucky, the old friends whom Armstrong had tried unsuccessfully to reconcile in 1918. It may seem unbelievable to many that friendships could break up over what Jesus intends to do when he returns to earth, especially since human opinions will probably in no way alter his plans. But Boll's view, that Jesus on his return would rule over the earth for a thousand years (the millennium) before the final destruction of the forces of evil, was anathema to many. In the heat of emotion some forgot all Christian love and forbearance. When Armstrong moved his *Living Message* from Harper to Morrilton, it seemed to invade the domain of a journal published by E. M. Borden of Little Rock. Borden immediately printed an article by a Brother Hines charging Armstrong and the office manager of his paper with accepting the views of R. H. Boll about a millennium. Nineteen years later, about a year before Armstrong's death, Hines wrote an apology:

> Brother Armstrong, as I get older, I can see my weaknesses and I wish to express to you that I have through my zeal done and said things I wish were undone. I thought I was doing right, and maybe I was, but had poor judgment in the matter. If you hold any of these things against me, won't you forgive me! I must not leave this world without asking you this.

Armstrong had never held anything against Hines. In response to Borden's attacks, however, Armstrong defended himself in "An Open Letter" for Borden's publication. He pointed out that Abilene Christian College had used a professor three years who accepted Boll's views, that David Lipscomb College had Boll himself speak recently to their students, and that G. H. P. Showalter, editor of the *Firm Foundation,* two years before had preached in "Boll's pulpit" and also in Jorgenson's; yet Borden had never criticized any of them.

"We are certain that your deep concern," Armstrong wrote, "was not aroused by any questionable teaching done at Harding College or in the *Living Message.* I doubt if there has ever been a lesson taught by pen or word of mouth by any member of the faculty of Harding College on the kingdom question that you would seriously criticize, or that differs materially from your position . . . Nor has there ever been an article in the *Living Message* from its birth until this hour that is out of harmony with your position . . . Whence then came this interest and this suspicion? Why has our paper and Harding College been the scapegoat?"

Borden printed only excerpts from the "Open Letter" and

followed each with comments of his own. This was the kind of editorial treatment Daniel Sommer once gave to an article by David Lipscomb, which led Lipscomb to forbid Sommer's name ever to appear in the *Advocate* again.

Shortly afterward Borden appeared on the campus and asked to meet with the men of the faculty. Armstrong obligingly called the meeting but protested warmly against Borden's authority to hold an "inquisition" into the beliefs of men who had never spoken or written on the issues in question and had probably never studied them carefully. Borden said, however, that he only wanted to learn what the faculty believed on two questions: (1) whether the Jews would return to Palestine and Christ rule over them after his second coming, and (2) whether Christ would reign on earth a thousand years after his second coming.

Only one member of the faculty gave an affirmative answer: Professor Earl Smith said he was doubtful about the first question, but he believed in the thousand-year reign.

Uneasy about what Borden might publish, Armstrong suggested that Smith write what he believed and give it to him that he might know what he had to defend. Instead of giving the statement to Armstrong, however, Smith published it in the *Living Message* under the title, "A Thousand Years of Glory for the Earth." Armstrong was shocked. He loved Earl, and he loved his father, who had been for many years on his editorial staff. Earl was an excellent teacher, and Armstrong valued the great service he could give to Christian education. But on the appearance of the article, and in view of Borden's attacks, he greatly feared that the board would not renew Earl's contract for the following year. Rather than have this happen it seemed to him wiser for Earl to resign. He talked with Rhodes, R. C. Bell, and me about it. I have never known anything to grieve him more deeply, and he asked the three of us to accompany him when he explained the situation to Earl. The meeting was brief, for no one felt like talking. We were more nearly on the verge of tears. But in view of the board's probable reaction Earl too felt it best to resign.

"Nothing ever disturbed my high regard for Brother Armstrong," Earl wrote forty-two years later. "He was a good soldier. I have never felt any assurance that he made a wrong decision in what he did then. I thought his articles in the *Living Message* at that time were not explicit about what he believed about the second coming of Christ and the millennium. And it seemed to me he was putting us all, as it were, under a cover."

Armstrong did not dismiss Earl. In a letter to President Benson in 1943 he says: "I want to correct the impression you have about Earl Smith. He was never dismissed. I thought the board might ask me to let him out, and to shield Earl I went over it with him and advised him to resign. He followed my advice. Neither he nor I knew what the board would do, for he had some mighty strong friends on the board."

Borden claimed eleven years later that he was only trying to help the school, and that he had encouraged students to attend it. He said also of those who accepted Boll's views, "Yes, they are our brethren, and they can do a great deal of good in the world if they will preach that which they know is right and leave off so much speculation." Borden's comments on the millennium were not out of harmony with Armstrong's views.

But Earl apparently thought Armstrong had much more definite ideas about a millennium than he actually had. From the obscure reference to a millennium in Revelation, however, Armstrong felt that people could not afford to be dogmatic, and in another letter he said the continual emphasis upon it by some "has a tendency to disgust me, as if it were vital to the salvation of every soul in the world." Dr. T. W. Brents used to preach on the millennium, and his sermons are still printed and advertised by the *Gospel Advocate*. Armstrong always said his idea of the millennium was more nearly like that of T. W. Brents than of any one else, but that he did not accept all of Brents' views. Boll said in a letter to S. H. Hall, an editor of the *Advocate*. "If I felt about any subject as Brents is said to have felt about his sermon on the millennium, I wouldn't waste the time preaching it." Brents considered his views only "opinions." Unlike both Boll and Brents, Armstrong's "opinions" about the millennium were so tenuous that he could not bring himself ever to preach or write on it.

Advising Earl's resignation was not inconsistent with Armstrong's long fight for freedom of teaching. He regretted deeply losing Earl to the Christian school work over a "matter that is not even vital to the salvation of a soul," when a little patience and tolerance might have avoided it. To be sure, Armstrong could have gone to bat for him. He could have fought the board to retain him. But the board had ultimate authority over the school, and some members would have undoubtedly felt that the retention of a teacher could hardly justify the injury to the school that would result from a long and bitter fight within the board and administration and through the press. When an issue is so vital that men should carry the fight even to division and destruction of fellowship is a very grave question, one on which the judgment of good men may differ. Considering the consequences both to the school and to Earl himself, painful as it was Armstrong felt the resignation was the only sensible course. With this decision Rhodes, Bell, and I, and Earl himself agreed.

The incident did not affect Armsgrong's love for Earl nor the long friendship with his father. On hearing of Armstrong's illness in 1943, his father wrote: "We are praying for the Lord to intervene in your illness. There is a strong tie of love and friendship in my heart toward you that needs an outlet occasionally. I wish I were close enough to have a closer touch at this time when friends can give some encouragement. You and I are going on borrowed time and the time of our going home is not far distant. But if the Lord can use us to bless others a few more days we will praise him for it."

And in a letter in November he said: "I would be glad if we could have a heart to heart talk. There are few men in my life that I have felt as free to pour out my heart to as I have with you. The friendship is sacred to me." Smith was seventy-four at the time and Armstrong seventy-three.

Armstrong used to wonder why so much is said in the Bible about being longsuffering and forbearing. Later, he

said, he learned with astonishment that good and true men
differed from one another, and that such a condition will
always be so long as men are free to study the Bible for
themselves:

> To have a group of men tell us what the Bible means
> in every instance and what all must teach and believe,
> would be placing a human yoke upon the necks of us
> all. It would be signing away our very birthright. So
> long as men are made free to study God's book in-
> dependently, unfettered by ecclesiasticisms, priests, popes,
> and preachers, there will be honest mistakes in interpre-
> tations of the devout, the consecrated, and the most
> godly of God's children. It has always been so. And no
> church of our Lord has a right to pass upon the scrup-
> les of the most humble and untrained in God's house.
> "One man esteemeth one day above another: another
> esteemeth every day alike. Let each man be fully assured
> in his own mind . . . Who art thou that judgest the
> servant of another? To his own Lord he standeth or
> falleth.

Armstrong stood, like Paul, for the freedom of men's
consciences, not merely his own or those who believed with
him, and such an attitude is always misunderstood by those
with less spiritual maturity. Even opposition he took with
forbearance, recognizing that it is inevitable:

> A firm steadfast life against the world's evils, though
> it be lived with the gentleness and compassionateness
> of Christ himself, will arouse antagonism, bitter opposi-
> tion, and hatred . . . It is altogether an error for us to
> conclude that one can preach and live the truth in a
> wicked world like ours and not be hated and despised as
> was our Lord; yet there is a strong feeling among us—
> many are afflicted with it, I fear—that if one be wise,
> prudent, and kind, one can avoid such antagonism and
> keep the friendship of all. If it be so, it would be a
> reflection on our Lord's wisdom. For think not, my
> friends, that the life of the world has changed. It may
> have donned a new dress, but is still "enmity against
> God." So strong is the conviction in many that, if a
> man be prudent, wise, and kind, he can avoid antago-
> nism and keep the friendship of all, that when a man
> does find himself opposed, antagonized, and in trouble,

he is at once declared radical, extreme, or imprudent, when in reality these things come upon him through his unfailing faithfulness to the Word of God. His only way to have been "wise and kind" would have been to wink at evil and compromise with gross wrongs.

Partly to reassure friends of the college, Armstrong invited E. A. Elam, an editor of the *Gospel Advocate* and President of David Lipscomb College, to give a series of lectures on the Kingdom and the millennium during the Thanksgiving program of 1924. After a week on the campus Elam reported: "I am pleased to say all I preached on the establishment of Christ's kingdom, on Christ's second coming, and against speculation of any kind was most heartily received and endorsed by the faculty and the church."

But a third and far more serious difficulty arose almost from the beginning of the new college. When the consolidation was proposed, we at Harper understood that the indebtedness on the Morrilton plant was only $25,000, the same as that on the Harper property. Croom, however, stated thirty years later that the indebtedness at Morrilton "amounted to some forty-five thousand dollars." Croom, Barber, Billingsley and others had done a masterful job in collecting pledges. Mr. J. J. Scroggin of Morrilton had been extremely liberal and could also move the city to give. But in the spring of 1924 Mr. Scroggin died, and the college lost its most liberal donor. When construction started in 1921 many could not meet their pledges. Mr. Hill, president of the board, had pledged $10,000, and had paid only $1,000 when he lost nearly all his property in the recession of 1920. He later sent several loads of coal from a small mine, but the pledge was cancelled.

With the inability of friends to meet their pledges, by the time of the consolidation the indebtedness, according to Croom, had risen to $45,000. To complete the administration building and construct a girls' dormitory the new board borrowed $50,000 more, which raised the indebtedness to $95,000. This, however, is a very low estimate. Judge Strait, who from its beginning served without charge as attorney for the college, more than once told Armstrong that no one really knew how much the college owed when, in 1926, the board signed a chattel mortgage to "grant, bargain, and sell to the Peoples Bank and Trust Company of Morrilton" all real estate and other property of the college to cover a debt of $5,426.80 due them. This was a second mortgage, for the large first mortgage was held by the Home Life Insurance Company. Judge Strait believed that the full indebtedness could not have been less than $175,000 to $200,000.

To give the reader an understanding of the weight of this indebtedness in 1926, one must consider the value of the dollar, the per capita income in Arkansas and in the nation, the sources of aid, and the size of the college now in comparison with these factors in 1926. Considering all the data one computer figured the indebtedness the equivalent of a debt of $20,000,000 to $30,000,000 on the college today.

To Armstrong the revelation of the financial condition was staggering. Yet he blamed nobody. The board had borrowed heavily but believed it held reliable pledges and could obtain sufficient additional gifts to meet the obligations.

"The secretary-treasurer (Z. D. Barber) was one of the best men to solicit and secure funds I have ever known," Armstrong said. "So the board with all confidence and sincerity shouldered the necessary obligations to give Arkansas and many other neighboring states a Christian college. No men I think ever undertook to do a great work with more honest purpose. They believed the obligations would be met, and were determined to see that they were."

Croom placed the blame for the financial conditions at Morrilton chiefly upon President Armstrong, but not until the Depression struck in 1929 and the board gave up in despair did Armstrong have anything to do with the finances. The accumulation of debt came under the management of the board before the merger of Harper and Arkansas Christian and in completing the buildings and supplying the capital equipment needed for accreditation, but the board felt fully able to meet its obligations.

In 1925 the bank which the college owed, apparently fearing that other creditors might be paid first, took over the finances, and Mr. Moose of the bank became the paymaster.

As Professor Kieffer relates, a teacher had to give Mr. Moose a detailed account of his needs, and might then get a check for twenty-five dollars. It was a humiliating situation, but forced upon the board by the bank, and the teachers with sympathetic understanding made no protest.

Soon after this the board under the leadership of its treasurer, Z. D. Barber, accepted a plan by a Mr. M. G. Caldwell to lend the college immediately enough money to pay off all indebtedness and construct a new boys' dormitory, then repay the loan and create an endowment of three and a half million dollars through life insurance policies. Armstrong and I were both doubtful of the scheme, and I urged the board to investigate thoroughly before I left in the spring for the University of Chicago, where I was taking graduate work. Although Croom had left the school in 1925, he also wrote the board warning them against Caldwell. In spite of the warnings the board agreed to Caldwell's plan, and Barber and his assistants visited the churches to persuade each member to pledge one dollar a year for a ten-year period to apply on the insurance endowment.

Caldwell may have advanced the $19,608.75, which was applied on the Home Life mortgage in March, 1926. But if so, that was about all he ever did. Under his promise the foundation was laid for the new dormitory, but when he failed to arrange his promised loan, the work stopped. It is difficult to see how the board could have been so deceived by a promoter. Barber, however, was the one chiefly responsible for finances. Money raising was not an easy task, the debts were pressing, and Caldwell's glowing promise to pay off the debts and create an endowment was alluring. The board too readily followed Barber's recommendation and agreed to the plan.

In two years the project had failed. Barber soon after resigned from the board and left the state. Whether the plan actually injured the college and caused people to lose confidence in its financial stability, as Croom felt, is not at all certain. Members in the churches Barber visited were receptive, and many signed up to give a dollar a year. Some paid out their pledges in full, but many failed because other factors entered in. It is doubtful if Caldwell profited by the venture. Whether Barber and his associates could have raised more money by gifts to pay off the debt than by gifts to create an endowment is also a question. Anyway it was the judgment of Barber and the board; they were doing the best they knew, and Armstrong was in no way responsible.

In the spring of 1927 came the worst flood in Arkansas since Noah. The river valleys were under water until April or later, and farmers could not plant. Hundreds fled from the valleys and were fed by the Red Cross and housed in emergency quarters in Morrilton and other cities. In the college dining hall a great pile of cotton almost to the ceiling and rolls of ticking were hurriedly converted into pillows by students and teachers and given to the refugees.

With the loss of crops no one could have raised money. To relieve increasing pressures the board, in addition to the mortgage of 1926, gave the Peoples Bank and Trust Company in November, 1927, a Deed of Trust to all the college property and any future buildings and equipment to cover the present indebtedness to the bank and also $125,000 which was to be issued in first mortgage bonds bearing four percent interest. Few bonds were ever sold.

In 1928 Wood Rainwater, one of the bankers, undertook to raise $2,500 to help clear the mortgage at the bank. Apparently little was raised, and in 1929 the stock market broke and the Great Depression began, the worst financial calamity Arkansas and the world ever faced. Nearly every bank in the state closed, businesses and large industries went bankrupt, and millionaires became beggars over night. Hundreds of people in New York and other cities, some of them financiers like Fred Bell of San Francisco, lined up daily for thin soup and coffee, and their box of apples to sell on street corners. By apple selling a man could make a profit of ninety-five cents in a twelve-hour day and return to the "Municipal Lodging House" to shiver around a fire through the night.

Under pressure of local creditors the college had been paying from current funds some of the unsecured debts. To prevent this and to protect their own mortgage on the property, the Home Life Insurance Company of Little Rock in June, 1927, had obtained a judgment against the board with authority to sell the entire college plant. Action, however, was not taken till 1929, when the Home Life took over the property. Armstrong immediately asked Judge Strait to confer with the company, and at their invitation Armstrong and I met with the directors of the Home Life. The company agreed to permit the college to operate, but only under a new organization. Twelve members of the old board resigned and a new board of thirteen members took over. This action of the Home Life legally eliminated all other creditors, and all claims against the institution including salaries owed to teachers. This was not an action of the college or its board; it was an action of the Home Life Insurance Company. The college never repudiated a single obligation, but it was now impossible legally to satisfy any creditor until the mortgage to the Home Life had been paid off.

The reader must bear in mind that the heavy burden of debt had been accumulated by the board under the financial leadership of its treasurer, most of it while Croom was still with the school, but the debts were made in good faith and with full expectation of repayment. Armstrong was never consulted, never asked to help with the finances, and, though he advised that Barber be given assistance, he did not learn the amount of indebtedness until the board gave the bank the mortgage in 1926. But as members of the board became aware of the financial strain, and were required to sign notes personally for the school, even as great and devoted men as Joe Blue resigned rather than endanger their own property. Men with money declined membership, and the board came to the end of its resources.

When the Home Life foreclosed and demanded the reorganization, the board gave up and turned the financial responsibility to Armstrong. Had he refused to accept it, the college would have closed in 1929. The situation seemed hopeless. Even Mrs. Armstrong urged him repeatedly to resign. When all her pleading did not prevail, she wrote her mother, Mrs. James A. Harding: "I have pleaded with Jack to give up the school, but he won't listen. The board had made so many debts before we came to Morrilton and in finishing the administration building and the girls' dormitory that they have not been able to pay the teachers' salaries. Now the Home Life Insurance Company has foreclosed their mortgage. With the floods and the depression and people out of work it is impossible to raise money. The board is helpless and they want Jack to take all the financial responsibility. I don't see how the school can go on."

Sister Harding had faced years at the Nashville Bible School and at Bowling Green when it seemed that those colleges "could not go on," and only the faith of James A. Harding had kept them going. Her reply gave her daughter little consolation: "Your husband is a very wise man, my dear."

So in desperation, to keep the school from closing Armstrong bowed his shoulders under the financial burden that everybody considered impossible.

The college carried small deposits in two banks in Morrilton. Though we had equal confidence in both, we had transferred all funds to one bank, perhaps because the deposits were small. Then both banks closed along with more than a hundred others in Arkansas, but the bank that held the college funds was able to reopen so that the deposits were safe. Armstrong remarked, "It was just another blessing of the Lord in disguise. We are grateful."

Shortly after foreclosing the mortgage, the Home Life also went bankrupt and was taken over by the Central States Life of St. Louis, who, because there was no market for a college campus, permitted the school to continue its operation.

Critical as the financial conditions were, no one visiting the college would have known it. Activities went on with enthusiasm. Students and teachers working together beautified the campus by planting trees and shrubbery and by building a lovely lily pool, rock garden, and an ornamental rock wall. To lessen expense of utilities a driller was brought to locate a well, but his "witching" stick resulted only in a trickle too feeble to supply the campus. Attendance at Thanksgiving lectures from many states was large, and the dinners on the lawn were delicious and bountiful. Armstrong's spirit never failed, and students gladly accepted his leadership. Annually when lost and unclaimed articles from books to coats and umbrellas accumulated, he auctioned them off at a special chapel, sometimes "modeling" a hat as he called for bids. Students cutting across campus on the grass went back with a smile to the sidewalk at his gentle reminder. And when at chapel he asked the boy (or girl) who had broken such and such a window to please stand so the college would know whom to charge for the expense, the student unfailingly stood. His appeal once caught one of his grandsons who had accidentally driven a tennis ball through a window.

But nobody seemed to feel any financial strain, and everybody was happy. Only when at my insistence Armstrong played an occasional game of tennis with me, sometimes at the height of the game some problem of the school would suddenly occur to him and he would stand absorbed in thought while the ball flew past him. But he was never so absorbed that a student could not get his full attention and sympathy with any problem he had.

In 1930 the Depression was growing constantly more severe, but the suffering was increased by the worst drouth the country had ever experienced. All states except Maine, California, Oregon, and Washington were affected, but the worst suffering was in Arkansas and the central states from which the college drew its students and support. The *Arkansas Gazette* reported that in Conway county, of which Morrilton was the county seat, a thousand families were practically without food and many without water. There had been four years of failure in cotton crops; now there was no fruit, hay, grain, or gardens. Thousands of cattle were reported slowly starving to death in the sunbaked pastures. Wayne Largent, preaching at Smackover, wrote that people would gladly work for fifty cents a day but could find no jobs. Some lived on parched acorns to keep from being classed as "bums." With banks and businesses closing everywhere collections for the college were impossible, as Armstrong reported:

Always before we have been able to collect considerable on pledges and student notes, but this source of
income is nearly wholly cut off this year. Collections
are all but impossible. Every year before, we have had
our field men gathering up gifts, donations, and pledges
from the field. This year this is all cut off. So desperate
is the condition in our immediate territory that field
men asking for a college would have the dogs sicked on
them. You could ask bread for the children, or clothes
to keep them warm; but for a college an appeal would
not be countenanced. If Harding College had the money
that brethren lost in Arkansas by the closing of the
banks, it would be independent. Yet two days before
these banks closed, these brethren could not have given
a dollar—just didn't have it. Had these brethren given
these thousands of dollars they would now be as well
off financially, and far happier. We had hoped that
friends would understand the need and respond. A friend
in New Mexico did send a check for twenty-five dollars
for a Christmas present. Another good friend in Oklahoma sent a check for twenty-five dollars. He thought
about it. Then some friends in Arkansas got together
and sent twenty-five dollars. Thoughtful? I should say
so!

Armstrong says of the loyalty and courage of the faculty,
"Had it not been for a few brave souls and indomitable
spirits that kept on hoping against hope, there would be no
Harding College today." The *Morrilton Democrat* in an
editorial, April 25, 1930, commented on the loyalty of students, teachers, and friends: "The history of Harding College of this city is a story of pluck, heroic struggle, and
unbelievable sacrifice . . . The growth of the college has
been possible only through the loyalty of its students and
teachers, and the support of the people of Morrilton. Business men and friends of the school in town have given it
their unqualified support. The heaviest individual sacrifice,
however, has been made by the faculty, who in addition to
contributing indirectly about $10,000 each year by teaching
for lower salaries than they could easily secure elsewhere,

have put into the school directly out of their salaries approximately $40,000 in the past five years. Such loyalty can hardly be duplicated."

Looking back many years later, the teachers who came through those dark years could scarcely believe it possible, and Armstrong often spoke of it as a miracle. But it was his courage and faith above everything else that kept the faculty together and the college going. I had spent 1927-28 as a part-time instructor in the University of Chicago doing graduate work, and was invited to stay on. Even after returning to the college they asked if I would take a position in one of the large Northern Universities. I was tempted, but when I thought of leaving Armstrong under the load at Harding, I could not go. Other teachers must have felt the same way. With strong faith we had joined in building a great institution, and when the crash came we were ashamed for that faith to fail. As Armstrong said, "Surely when we are being tried we will not fail our Lord!"

Under the added burden of financial management which the board had turned to him, Armstrong wondered, in fairness to the teachers, if he should give a younger man a chance to carry the college on. We invited A. R. Holton, who had shown exceptional ability in connection with Thorp Springs Christian College, to visit Harding and take the presidency. Armstrong and I were both willing to step out that he might have complete freedom to direct the school. We went over with him the financial condition and suggested that he confer with members of the board, with the bank, and with others. As Holton left, Armstrong remarked, "He will never take it; only a fool would take it!" And Holton declined.

"What can we do now?" I asked.

"We'll carry the school on," Armstrong replied. "It simply cannot stop."

When the board turned the financial responsibility to Armstrong in 1929, at his request they appointed as a Finance Committee Professor G. W. Kieffer, Professor I. C. Forbes, and me to assist Armstrong in making collections and disbursements, raising funds, and purchasing. From that time forward no new debts, except to teachers, were ever made. Armstrong called the faculty together and explained the financial crisis, and the decision of the board to turn the responsibility over to him and the faculty. He said he would regret to lose a single teacher, but he wanted them all to feel free to leave at any time they wished. No one would blame them. He stated that he was renouncing his own salary entirely, and would divide the part that he should receive among the others. He promised that the finance committee would press for collections and funds and after paying necessary operating expenses would divide the balance equitably among the teachers on the basis of the salary schedule. Though the board had been able to pay only a fraction of the salaries since 1925, this new arrangement would keep the faculty informed about the income and assure them an equitable distribution.

It is astonishing, in view of the pitiful salaries, that so few teachers dropped out during the years that followed and that everybody seemed happy and optimistic. Writing to Professor Houston T. Karnes, Armstrong asked: "Would you be willing to head the department of Mathematics next year at Harding College? After paying all current expenses—light, water, fuel, etc.—ten of us teachers divide what is left from tuition and fees, and rents, and donations, as our salaries. This year a share varied from $25 to $75 a month. This has been humiliatingly small, but we have had to take more notes from students this year or force them out of school, and this has occasioned the small shares. We would not ask you to share entirely with us this extreme sacrifice if you come. But we would furnish you room and board and guarantee you $50 a month, and should the share be more than this, of course, you would get more." Professor Karnes, whose father had borne similar sacrifices at Potter Bible College when he taught with Harding and Armstrong, felt the challenge and came.

James C. Andrews, who dropped out to become head of the department of economics at Southwestern University, and later Dean of Men at Woodbury College, Los Angeles, wrote back after he left:

"With another Thanksgiving I think of you and Brother Sears and Harding College . . . Somehow I am now confident that my year with you will forever stand out as the most satisfactory and happy period of my life. Several times recently I've been almost at the point of foregoing salary consideration in favor of the real joy and satisfaction that comes with living in an atmosphere as wholesome as at Harding."

Professor Schoggins also wrote back, "I have not forgotten —nor shall I ever forget—the two years I spent as a member of your faculty—two years that meant more to me than I can find words to express. I can say, however, that I have never been associated with people I loved more, and I have never worked under a college president I loved so much as you."

Those who have accused Armstrong of poor financial management should remember that all the large debts were made before 1926 and for buildings and equipment. After 1926 few debts were made except unpaid salaries to teachers, and after Armstrong accepted the financial responsibility no new debts were made except for salaries.

But Harding College was not the only sufferer during those years. The state itself with its power to tax could not meet the salaries of teachers and other public officials and had to issue warrants which could not be cashed for months even at a fifty percent discount. I drove one student to a neighboring town to find a bank willing to cash his warrant at half price. The strain on private colleges was worse. Commenting on this in the 1930s Armstrong said: "One college in Arkansas closed last year with a deficit of about $30,000. This same college in previous years had a yearly deficit of about $19,000. Another college in our state through the past three years has run a yearly deficit of $17,000. Compared with these colleges Harding has through the five years of its existence run a rather small yearly deficit— between $6,000 and $8,000. Do you ask how this has been cared for? The faculty of Harding College has borne the burden."

In June, 1930, Armstrong was granted the honorary LL.D. degree from Central Indiana University, and in 1931 he was

invited to give an address at the dedication of two new
dormitories at David Lipscomb College. He spoke on "What
Do the Churches of Nashville and of All Tennessee Owe to
David Lipscomb College?" He had read with distress of the
burning of the old dormitories, but was delighted that within
less than a year they had been replaced with buildings better,
larger, and more thoroughly equipped:

> I doubt if we mortals could justly estimate the debt
> of love and service we all owe to this humble school,
> for only eternity can tell the story of the service it has
> rendered . . . Nashville—Davidson County—Tennessee!
> Who can measure the debt they owe? . . . For forty
> years, the lifetime of this humble school, there has been
> no city in all the world like Nashville for simple Chris-
> tianity . . . More than this, the ideals, the inspiration,
> and the uplifting vision coming from this school have
> caused to spring up other Christian institutions in var-
> ious parts of the country . . . Ninety percent of the
> teachers of these other colleges have been secured from
> the students and grand-students of this first school . . .
> Had it not been for the spirit and life of David Lips-
> comb and James A. Harding that filled the students and
> teachers of this first school, hampered as we have been
> financially, we could never have furnished our other
> schools with teachers.

In view of the debt Nashville itself owed to the school,
he pleaded for them to take one step more and make Lipscomb the first fully endowed college:

> Think of it! One hundred dollars from each one of
> these Christians would mean not less than a million
> dollars! This would enable David Lipscomb College to
> become a standard four-year college, giving her the
> highest rating bestowed upon colleges of this country
> . . . Why not do a thing that the disciples in no other
> state and city have yet done—endow your college so that
> it may enter the Southern Association of Colleges and
> Universities as a senior college with the same rating
> and recognition as Vanderbilt and Peabody? The million
> dollars of which I have spoken would make this pos-
> sible, but even then David Lipscomb College would be
> poor compared to its neighbor colleges. Tennessee Breth-
> ren, it is your opportunity. Will you embrace it?

It was a delight to meet scores of old friends, and he had high praise for A. M. Burton and Mrs. Johnson for their liberal gifts to Lipscomb. Of Burton he said, "He is a man of great vision. Added to this he is a money maker, but unlike most money makers he realizes that Christians should use the money that God entrusts to them for his glory, that they should give liberally and be 'rich in good works, ready to distribute.' I venture the statement that he had never given another fifty thousand dollars that will do such far-reaching service." If others could have the same vision, he declared, all our Christian schools could be endowed and made permanent.

He spoke also at the Central Church, which he commended for its benevolent work, furnishing a home for working girls and a lodging for strangers who had no money but who needed a room for the night. "Once they are persuaded that a step is scriptural," he said, "though no other faithful church has ever taken the step they are not afraid to take it." He had only one warning: "It would be an indescribable calamity were the church to forsake its work to become only a benevolent society. He who swells the ranks of Christians on the earth supplies bread to the hungry and raiment for the naked in the most effectual and permanent way. In other words, they who convert people to Christ, put his spirit into men, increase the great army of men and women who are here to minister and not to be ministered unto. Feed that hungry family today and it must be done again tomorrow; but put Christ into it, and tomorrow that family is seeking to feed the hungry at its own door. Therefore the greatest givers of all the world are those simple teachers of the word of God who are going into all the world to preach the gospel."

In 1931 the boiler in the college heating plant at Harding burst, leaving the girls' dormitory and the students freezing. Armstrong announced the disaster to the shivering assembly and asked students and teachers to pray that God would stir the hearts of friends to give the money for a new boiler. He and the students wrote friends, and the money came in immediately.

In the spring he called upon farmers to plant one or two acres for the college in the crop best suited to their land, or to devote a cow, pig, or other livestock to it, and urged salaried people to devote one month's salary to the school. There was a generous response to the appeal, and he was able to make the only payment on the mortgage which had been made since Barber and Baldwell's payment of $19,000 in 1926.

"Three weeks ago," he announced, "we wiped off the slate the ten-thousand-dollar mortgage. We were able to do this by a heavy discount from the bank holding the mortgage. The obligation has been removed and we are happy. This leaves but one other shadow on the property, and this can be cleared for $17,000."

The Central States Life, which had taken over the assets of the Home Life, evidently at a fraction of their worth, had reduced the original mortgage to this figure. Armstrong's statement applied to the mortgage on the buildings and grounds. There was a small second mortgage to the bank on the college equipment which later caused some concern.

In response to this reduction the students immediately started a drive with donations of more than $600 and a goal of $750 to pay the Central States mortgage. Students and teachers of Abilene Christian College and of Freed Hardeman College also sent gifts, "Just to say we are for you." The teachers again expressed their generosity by selling scholarships totaling $6,075 to be applied on the debt, money which should rightly have gone to their own salaries. So the goal of freeing Harding College from its original mortgage was now in sight.

Strange as it may seem, through the dark years from 1927 to 1934, when prophets of doom everywhere declared each year the college would never open again in the fall, students and teachers never lost faith. Somehow they knew it could not close. The enrollment continued to grow even during the depression and drouth. In 1929-30 the girls' dormitory was so crowded the college had to put three girls in a room and use the hospital rooms for students. In 1930-31, when the depression and drouth struck with greatest intensity, enrollments in nearly all colleges dropped, but the Harding enrollment increased 44.5 percent over the previous year, with students from twenty-one states and Canada. Dr. Charles Brough, former governor, gave the commencement address to the second largest graduating class and to more visitors than had ever attended a commencement. This was the hardest year financially, when the college had to accept school warrants and notes, and when there were grave fears in Morrilton that the city schools would all have to close.

From 1924 when the school had only seventy-five college students the enrollment had increased till in 1935 it had 328, and boarding students numbered 307 from eighteen states and Canada. Though this enrollment seems small it was larger than that of older colleges in Arkansas. A part of the increase may have been due to persistent efforts to keep expenses low. Board was given at actual cost of the food and service, and students voted whether they would increase costs by more food or reduce them. They could also suggest the quality and kinds of food they wanted, as when one student voted "No more peas of the English descent." With such an arrangement there were few, if any, complaints.

But the increase in enrollment and the happy spirit of the students came far more from the quality of leadership Armstrong was giving. He took a personal interest in every student. A mother wrote him about her son, away from home for the first time: "Try to be a bit patient with his clumsiness until he learns to manage (if he ever does) his clothing and such. I've had to work for years, and his training along some lines has not been the best or else boys just don't like being neat." Armstrong answered her letter, and was "patient."

In classes and at chapel he was an inspiration. He often told the students that the men and women who move the world upward are those who dream dreams and drive with energy toward them. "The world's average are "C" graders. But are you content to be average? Anybody can pick cotton or build a barn. But you have priceless qualities that you cannot afford to waste. In a class at Bowling Green sat two boys, one no more gifted than the other. But today Charles Paine is a doctor giving a great service to the world and to the church. The other boy is driving a wagon selling patent medicines. The difference was vision and drive."

He was always happy in facing a full chapel at the beginning of a new year.

"This is a great morning," he often said. "It is great just to live. But this morning is especially great because you are beginning a preparation that will fit you for great service to the world. We are happy that you are here, that we have the opportunity to operate on you, to cut off a few knots and shape you up, make you more symmetrical, more beautiful. And you need it; some of you look as if you had lost your last friend, or your best girl had forsaken you. But while we are operating on you, you will be working on us as well. One of the great blessings of my life is my privilege of working with young people; they have taught me much. They are the nearest thing to the fountain of youth we can find on earth."

He often reminded students of the sacrifices their parents were making for them. "I heard one mother say she would rather starve than do what she was doing if it were not for her boys, but she had to keep them in school. You ought to be grateful to your parents and not waste your time, but use every moment of it well, that you may justify the faith your parents have in you. Were you to see a boy standing on the bank thumping nickels into the stream, you would think him crazy. But he would not be half as foolish as one who wasted his time and opportunity."

To the graduating class he once said, "Pilate once wrote, 'What I have written, I have written,' and he refused to change a word of it. As you young people have finished your work, I might also say, what you have written, you have written; what you have done, you have done. But how much is that? You have learned some facts of history, some principles of English and science. But what have you become yourselves? Are you kinder now, more considerate of others, more understanding? Do you feel responsibilities more keenly, or have you learned to shirk them? Do you have a deeper reverence for God and the great principles he has given to us? The greatest gift of a college education should not be knowledge and facts, but enriched character and higher ideals."

No happier group of students could have been found on any campus. The activities were varied and stimulating. Armstrong had never had football at Odessa, Cordell, or Harper, but when he came to Morrilton he "inherited intercollegiate athletics," as he put it, including football. The first year, because of the death of the coach, only four games were played. The next year the college lost most of its games, and the town was unhappy. Dr. E. L. Matthews talked with us and promised that the town would support the athletic program financially if we would get a good coach, and that they would help obtain some good players. Without experience in such arrangements, and with much misgiving, we accepted this aid. A competent coach was employed and a number of good players were obtained. Two men alone almost constituted the team. One could throw a pass nearly the length of the field, and the other always made the catch and the touchdown. They defeated one college after another, including the second-line team of the University. The Athletic Association wrote Armstrong demanding to know how he obtained such players. With complete honesty he wrote back, "Like all the other colleges; the town is paying them to come." Harding was unceremoniously ejected from the Association, the football season was over, and our headaches were gone, for these superb players were rowdies on the campus, creating a lawless spirit that the school had never known before. With an adjusted program the college continued to lose games two years longer, then discontinued football completely.

Although Armstrong recognized the need of sensible athletics and always encouraged it, football seemed to put a different spirit into the school from that of other sports.

"We were never able to gain spiritually with the students till the season was over," he said. "Every week in which there was a game it was all but impossible to build interest for anything else. Everything had to be side-tracked for the game, else you were not 'supporting the team.'" Some players were always hospitalized after a game until nearly time for the next, when they were miraculously healed and able to play again.

Many were afraid that discontinuing football would injure the enrollment. Because of academic as well as financial problems a number of colleges like the University of Chicago, Dubuque, the University of Atlanta, and Reed had already dropped intercollegiate football, but none reported an injury to enrollment. Neither was the enrollment at Harding affected, but the spirit of the school was greatly improved through the fall term.

Though intercollegiate basketball and baseball continued and interest was high in intramural sports, Harding students took even greater interest in debating, dramatics, and music. Debating teams won the Mid-South tournament in 1929, the Championship Tournament, including the champion teams of the South, and the State Tournaments in junior and senior debate eleven times between 1929 and 1942. In dramatics the Campus Players gave five major productions each year. They won first honors in the state festivals of 1929, 1936, 1937, and in the Mississippi Valley Festival in 1929. The College Bison won highest honors in the state for the best feature articles, and by 1934 Harding graduates were holding important positions in education and business, and places of great service in the church around the world.

This success, when many predicted each year that the college could never reopen in the fall, Armstrong attributed to the unquestioning loyalty of students and teachers. The churches in general had never really supported the Christian schools in spite of the great service they were giving. They were supported by the teachers.

"I know of no other teachers of the word of God that have done teaching at a keener sacrifice and whose families have gone without the necessities of life so often and so continually as the teachers in our Christian schools," Armstrong testified. "Not even our faithful missionaries, I think, at home or abroad, have made such extreme sacrifices. The sacrifices those teachers have made and are still making are unbelievable. I would not dare to tell the story lest my veracity be questioned. It is the only secret Harding has ever kept. Suffice it to say, the faculty has 'stood by the ship' even when good business men have said it must sink."

To the students in 1930 he said:

> To you and the students of former years Harding College owes more for its unparalleled success than to any group of helpers in all the world. In every emergency, after making known our need to God, we have gone to you, and we have never been turned away. Our gratitude is without measure. Financially Harding College has always been on the rocks, never able at the beginning of any year to see its way to the end; but its management has trusted in God, and each time the victory has been all but startling. Through these six years our country has been going through what might be called a money panic. However, Harding College is closing her sixth year (1929-30) with the highest rating it has ever enjoyed. Yes, I know it is "luck" to those who look on, but to us who know and believe in Jehovah the explanation is simple. The faith that "climbed the Alps beyond which lay Italy" has had its seat in our faculty. Do you remember Robert E. Lee and his starving army that lived for months on parched corn, or General Marion, who invited the English general to dine and had nothing to serve him but a potato on a piece of bark? For a greater cause than either Lee's or Marion's your faculty has lived on a crust that Harding College might live and attain its high rating. They have indeed been "fools for Christ's sake."

He reminded them of how the students and faculty had raised the money to replace the furnace, how the students had built the dining hall and had furnished beds and mattresses for the dormitories, how the dramatic club had furnished the stage curtains and reroofed the college buildings—all without cost to the board. He told of asking his grandson Kern if he was going to one of the basketball games, and Kern had replied, "No, I can't spare the money."

"But, son," he said, "what you pay for your ticket goes

to Harding College, and the college needs the money." "Then I'll go," the boy replied. But Armstrong did not tell the students that he supplied the money for his grandson to go.

Nor did Armstrong ever tell that, during the years when he had turned his own salary to the other teachers and was living from his preaching, he had personally purchased the *Encyclopedia Britannica* for the library and was paying for it in small monthly installments "because the library needed it." Nor did he mention that during this time he occasionally supplemented the salaries of other teachers with income from his meetings. Nor did he ever mention that, when Mrs. Armstrong in an automobile accident sustained a broken neck, punctures of both lungs, and internal hemorrhages, the doctors' charges were $1,300 besides the long hospital expense, but that without medical insurance or outside assistance, he and Mrs. Armstrong over a ten-year period managed to pay the entire cost. Nor did he ever mention that when other teachers had heavy medical expenses he almost without exception obtained assistance for them, and in at least one serious case assumed the entire cost. These are only a part of the "secret" he mentions and which he never told.

It was fortunate, of course, that he was continually in demand for Sunday appointments, and his summers were filled with meetings. In 1927, he held meetings in England, Waldo, and Camden, Arkansas, and at Thyatira, Mississippi, for a church where Alexander Campbell once preached, and where his old friend R. N. Gardner had a small Christian school. "It is one of the best schools in the county, and Brother Gardner is known to be the most wide-awake and energetic superintendent in the county." His final meeting was at Mount Vernon, Texas, from which he returned to give the dedicatory address for the new church at Heber Springs, Arkansas. The summer of 1930 he preached for the church at Cleburne, Texas, but held one meeting at Russellville, Alabama. Most summers were filled with meetings.

Under the heavy burdens and through the darkest years, Armstrong's faith never wavered, the joy in his work never failed, and he imparted this same confidence and joy to others. In 1932 John G. Reese, who had become a member of the board, wrote the *Gospel Advocate:* "The future of the school never looked so bright. She is more secure than ever before. J. N. Armstrong, the president, is a great leader and one of the most godly men I have ever met."

To this S. H. Hall added: "J. N. Armstrong, as president of this institution, has no superior, and I sometimes wonder if he has an equal. He loves God and his truth, and all young men and young women who fall under his influence are blessed. We wish for this splendid institution every needed thing to enable it to go forward and upward."

Summarizing the progress of the school up to 1934, Armstrong wrote:

We have had three objectives: first, the faculty has given primacy to the moral and spiritual development of the students; second, we have worked for efficiency and strength in our faculty, making it constantly stronger; and third, we have sought to maintain equipment in every department adequate for the courses offered. As a result, in the greatest Depression the world had ever felt, each student body has been larger than the preceding one, each year's faculty has been stronger in scholarship than the one it has followed, and our equipment—library and laboratories—has been commended by both the state university and the State Department of Education. True to our aim, for the year 1933-34 we have listed the strongest faculty in scholarship the institution has ever had. Last year in place of A.B.'s we put two M.A.'s; this year in place of three M.A.'s we are putting Ph.D's. Besides this we are adding a vigorous young man of scholarship and experience to our mathematics department—Professor Houston L. Karnes.

So with enrollments exceeding the capacity of its buildings, with the strongest faculty in its history, with the depression beginning to lift, and with a growing fund to pay off the mortgage, the future of the college finally seemed assured.

LIFTING THE LOADS

UNEXPECTEDLY 1934 was to force upon Armstrong two of the most far-reaching decisions he ever made in his college work. At keen personal sacrifice he had brought the school through the dark years of the Depression. Payment of the mortgage was now almost within reach. But as at Harper, enrollment had outgrown the college facilities, and more buildings were urgently needed. The boys' dormitory could accommodate only sixty students. A tile and stucco veneer, it had been more poorly constructed than its original cost would indicate, and ten years as a boys' dormitory had not improved it. After the Administration Building with its expensive limestone trim, the board suddenly decided to go "economical." The rear projection housing the auditorium and gymnasium, therefore, had been cheaply constructed, and the girls' dormitory, a brick veneer, was poorly built. It and the Administration Building had required reroofing once, and it was much too small to accommodate all who wanted to come.

Two years before, the Methodists closed two colleges, and the well equipped plant at Searcy, Arkansas, was offered for sale. Armstrong and I in December of 1933 drove over to see it. The high fences which had once made the Galloway campus a lovely park for fifteen deer were no longer there. But the two arched entrances with their stone pillars and massive chains, which may long ago have been locked across the drive, were still symbols of the security Galloway had once offered its young women. The campus was covered with immense oaks, some more than a hundred years old, and leaves lay deep over lawn and walkways, for the campus had been deserted for two years. To the right of the circular drive through the grounds were three cottages, the first, large, rambling, old, but attractive, with an outside door to every room; the second, a large compact bungalow of later construction; and the third, a tall, slender, two-story structure with high ceilings and floors that shook as we walked across them, but with needed repairs a livable place.

Beyond a brick music building with large studios furnished with grand pianos, was a beautiful girls' dormitory, finished only a few years before. Morrilton had nothing to compare with it. The broad porticos with their massive stone pillars across each end of the building and for all three floors gave it an impressive appearance. It was not a brick "veneer" but was solidly built to stand for centuries. The reception room with its grand piano was attractively furnished. Student rooms had large closets and connecting baths, some even private baths. The tile-floored dining hall would seat twice the number of students we could accommodate at Morrilton, and the dormitory would house more than twice as many girls. There was a well equipped kitchen, store rooms, and other facilities.

Adjacent to the girls' dormitory at the center of the drive was an immense three-story brick structure, perhaps two hundred fifty feet long with wings extending back at each end. It was the oldest of the buildings, but when erected in the late 1800s must have been one of the finest college buildings in the state. With its long porch on the front, arched windows, and gray slate roof with its towers, it was still interesting and usable. There was a large reception room, studios with pianos, classrooms and library on the ground floor, an auditorium on second floor, and enough rooms on second and third to house more than twice the number of boys we could take at Morrilton.

Around the circle on the east was a three-story brick administration building with twenty-seven classrooms and laboratories, recently finished and fully furnished and equipped. There was also a small brick gymnasium, a white-tiled, steam-heated swimming pool, a facility none of our Christian schools had ever dreamed possible to have. There was also a fully equipped steam laundry, a central heating plant, and a three-story frame building, "Gray Gables," with sound-proofes walls for piano practice rooms on first, an apartment on second, and student rooms on third. Pianos were everywhere—forty all told, from uprights, to studio and concert grands. In addition there were garages and a large brick workshop. Altogether there were eight buildings for college use, three cottages, the laundry, and two service buildings—fourteen in all. The property was assessed by the Chauncery Court at $604,575.34.

The visit impressed us both, and we urged B. Frank Lowery to come from Davenport, Nebraska, to see it. Lowery had been a member of the Harper board, was a member of the first Harding College board, and for a year and a half during the depression he had left his newspaper in charge of his daughter Ruby while he headed the financial drives for the college at Morrilton. Lowery was also impressed. We learned that the entire plant with all its equipment could be obtained for $75,000. The down payment could be $7,000 and the balance paid $4,000 a year, including interest for eleven years and the rest the twelfth year. These terms seemed reasonable and possible to meet. The plant could accommodate two or three times the number of students we could take at Morrilton. By combining our equipment with that of the Searcy plant, Harding would be by far the best equipped college in the state outside the university.

At Morrilton also we were sandwiched between a state school at Russellville and one at Conway and two private colleges at Conway. Carloads of students commuted from Morrilton to Conway, and others boarded at Russellville to escape the tuition Harding must charge, low as it was. At Searcy there would be no senior college within commuting distance. With our need for additional space, if we applied all present funds on the mortgage, we would have no hope for years of constructing more buildings at Morrilton.

At the moment also our campaign had not yet obtained the amount needed to retire the debt. The Central States Life had finally reduced the settlement to $13,000. The college was raising $10,000 and had asked Morrilton to supply $3,000, which had not yet been raised, and the company was pressing. On November 18, 1933, they wrote, "Would your board be willing to deed over the property, possession to be given at the end of the present school term, if possession was desired by the company?" They wanted to avoid the costs of foreclosure, but the letter also meant their patience was running out.

Other members of the board visited Searcy, and on March 27, 1934, the board voted eight to three to purchase the Searcy plant and establish the college there, to draw up a Charter and appoint a new board, and to arrange a settlement with Central States Life. Since the company had already asked for a deed instead of payment, a satisfactory arrangement seemed possible. Armstrong immediately suggested to the orphans' home in Fort Smith that they take over the Morrilton property at the low figure of $13,000 finally made to us. They or others may have got in touch with the Central States Life, for on June 2, the company wrote Armstrong again, urging a deed to the property as soon as possible. "As you know, other parties are figuring with us, if we become owners of the property, and too much delay would defeat those matters."

The college had recently received $10,000 in cash and $3,000 in bonds from the Will of Mrs. C. A. Adkins of Hope, Arkansas. Croom in his "history" puts the legacy at $20,000 but this is incorrect, as John G. Reese testifies. Mrs. Adkins' total estate may have amounted to $20,000, but half went to the orphans' home at Fort Smith.

Croom complains that no one ever publicly recognized Brother Reese's unselfishness in turning this bequent to the college instead of permitting Mrs. Adkins to will it to him.

We understood that Reese had obtained the bequest for the college and we were deeply grateful to him, but he never mentioned to Armstrong or to me, to my knowledge that Mrs. Adkins had planned to include him in the will and that he had urged her instead to leave her estate to the college and the Orphans' Home. This was unselfish indeed, and the more unselfish in that he never mentioned it.

Reese's assistance was publicly acknowledged more than once and was permanently recorded in Armstrong's article, "The Moving of a College Not So Unusual," which appeared in nearly all the religious papers. Considering the warmth of Reese's statements about Armstrong after the bequest was made and used, and the enthusiasm with which he worked for the school, I doubt if he felt hurt by any lack of recognition. It is regrettable, of course, that much of the good which people do goes unknown and unrecognized, but it is a comfort to know that even a cup of water is recorded by One who has a better memory than we. I am glad that Croom has given the additional information that Mrs. Adkins had originally intended the legacy for Reese. We have always appreciated him, and now even more.

Fearing that someone at Morrilton might learn that college funds were on deposit in the Worthen Bank in Little Rock and might run an attachment on them, Armstrong asked his grandson Jack Wood Sears to drive him down that he might move the deposit to the Postal Savings in Searcy. Usually Armstrong cautioned his drivers to go slow, but this time, afraid the bank might close on Saturday at noon before they arrived, he kept asking, "Can't you make this thing go any faster?" "We're doing sixty now," Jack Wood finally replied. "That's the speed limit. How fast do you want to go?" So grudgingly, but conscientiously, he held his impatience within the law.

There was a possibility, however, that after the campus and buildings were deeded to the Central States Life, as they insisted, they might then seek a deficiency judgment and take the equipment also, which was under a second mortgage to the bank at Morrilton. On the advice of the college attorney the board on March 16, 1934, unanimously assigned all equipment and part of the Adkins legacy to five of the teachers to whom the college owed most and in whom they had confidence. These were J. N. Armstrong, G. W. Kieffer, S. A. Bell, B. F. Rhodes, and L. C. Sears, to whom the college owed $11,481.91 in back salaries since the Home Life had foreclosed the mortgage in 1929. Croom called this assignment a "bogus" transfer, implied that these teachers and the board were defrauding other creditors of their rights, and indicated as a compliment that "not one of the original members of the board were involved" in this transfer.

True no members of the first board were involved because many of them had resigned, some because they did not want to become involved in what seemed a hopeless financial debacle and others for different reasons; the rest were excluded when the Home Life foreclosed in 1929 and demanded a reorganization under a new board. Croom however, insinuated unethical manipulation when he said, "Armstrong gained control of the board to the extent that he was able to carry through his desire to leave Morrilton and purchase the Searcy property." But of the men who composed this new board three were hard-headed bankers, one a newspaper man, one a planter, one a nurseryman, one a barber, two teachers, and a preacher. These men thought for themselves. Moreover, Armstrong was never a dictator, as those who taught with him can testify. If he swayed the board or the faculty toward any decision, it was always by presenting views that were so practical and sensible as to win support.

In the board's transfer to these teachers there was nothing bogus, fraudulent, or dishonest. It was clearly understood by all that if the college were permitted to move to Searcy, we would then reassign the equipment to the school; but if the Central States Life Insurance Company, after receiving a deed to the campus and buildings, compelled a sale of all equipment as well, the teachers who had borne the burdens for years had prior right to compensation.

To avoid undue complications not all teachers were included in the assignment, but it was also understood that if the equipment had to be sold, every teacher would receive his proportionate share. Neither would this action of the

board defraud any creditor, for since the Home Life's fore-
closure, it was impossible legally to pay creditors before
1929, including teachers, until all obligations to the mortga-
gors and to the teachers since 1929 had been paid. Satisfactory settlements were being negotiated with the two mort-
gagors, and the assignment protected the rights of the teachers.

Shortly afterward the mortgage held by the bank was
cleared. The Central States Life Insurance Company was
satisfied by a cash payment and a deed to the campus and
buildings at Morrilton, which they soon after sold to the
Southern Christian Home for an orphanage. Consequently
every cent Christians had put into Morrilton buildings and
grounds was preserved in an institution that would serve
thousands of children. At the same time the church had
preserved for it an educational institution which, in its more
favorable location, could give far greater service than ever
before. Without the move to Searcy both these advantages
would have been lost. Thus the church gained in two ways
by the move.

With the creditors satisfied and the college free for the
first time from debts contracted, not by Armstrong, but by
the board between 1921 and 1926, the way was open for
purchase of the Searcy property. Unexpectedly, however, a
new obstacle arose. Some members of the church at Morrilton obtained an injunction in an attempt to gain legal title
to all the Morrilton property—buildings, grounds, and equipment. This made necessary a hearing in Chancery Court, but
the hearing was brief. After a statement of the plaintiffs
and the defense, only Armstrong, Rhodes, and perhaps one
or two others were called as witnesses. Armstrong was asked
if he did not feel any concern for the loss Morrilton would
sustain by his moving the school.

"Yes," he said, "this is not the first time we have been
sorry for Morrilton. We were sorry when the banks closed
and people lost their money. We were sorry when Morrilton
lost the cotton mill and the $100,000 the citizens had invest-
ed in it. But this college would have closed six years ago
had not teachers working for $25 a month and sometimes

for nothing kept it running. During that time some here who are opposing its move did not even pay the tuition of their children."

Asked about "defrauding" the teachers of their salaries, Armstrong replied that all income was divided among the teachers according to a fixed salary scale and their need. "When they were pressed and had to have a dollar, they came to the office and if there was a dime in the fund, or we could get it, they got it. The president and dean have got less than others. But these teachers have stood by the school and would resent as an insult the implication that they have been defrauded."

He also stated that neither the town nor the church had any legal control or title, but that all college property was held by the board, and the board had voted for the move. When Rhodes was questioned as to how he felt about the salary he had never received, he replied, "I just kissed it goodbye!"

Judge Atkinson called the two attorneys into his office for a brief consultation and then gave the decision: neither Morrilton nor the church had any legal rights to the college property and that the board was free to move the school to Searcy if they wished. He expressed sympathy for Morrilton at its loss, but also for the college for its lack of support.

With regard to this court action Croom cites Paul's condemnation of Christians going to law with Christians, but he does not point out that these teachers and the board were not the ones who brought the court action. It was a small group in the church at Morrilton who brought suit against the board and the teachers. When charges were brought against Paul, he defended himself eloquently against his accusers and even appealed his case to the supreme court—Caesar. When charges were brought against the board and these teachers, they had no recourse but to defend themselves as Paul had done. It was a shame the court action was ever brought, and those involved in it must later have regretted it, especially since they had to pay all costs of the action.

"Not since the great World War," Armstrong said, "have

some of us carried on our hearts so great a care as the opposition to the acceptance of this gracious opportunity (the move to Searcy). Not that the opposition ever had the least chance . . . for the large majority in the board favoring the move from the start assured the removal."

Morrilton, however, not happy about the decision, took a minor punitive action. Since the equipment of the college had been assigned to the five teachers, and was therefore "privately owned," the city quickly assessed a tax of $500, which had to be paid before the equipment could be moved. After the move all equipment and the portion of the Atkins legacy were reassigned to the college and no teacher received a cent from the transaction.

The College Dining Hall and kitchen, owned by the "College Club," had never belonged to the board but was held in trust for the college by separate trustees. The mortgage on this property, held by Union Savings Building and Loan Association, was paid off, September 29, 1934, and after its sale the "College Club" at Searcy purchased a forty-acre farm east of the campus for a dairy. After Dr. Benson's accession to the presidency in 1936 the "College Club" was discontinued as an independent organization and the property was used for teachers' homes and a college park.

Actually Armstrong hated to leave Morrilton. As he said in the *Gazette,* "Harding College and her management have been in love with Morrilton; we are grateful to her for her unstinted moral support." But it was true that since the death of Mr. Scroggin the city of Morrilton had assisted the college very little financially even at the earnest solicitation of Wood Rainwater. During the ten years the college was at Morrilton it had brought into the city far more money than the city had ever contributed to it, so that financially the college had paid all costs of its residence and could leave in good conscience about being an expense to the city.

In explanation of the move Armstrong in "The Moving of a College Not So Unusual" pointed out that Peabody College had many years ago abandoned a beautiful campus with its magnificent buildings and moved miles across the city of Nashville against the wishes of people who had bought property around it; that Texas Christian University, once located at Thorp Springs, had become convinced that it could not grow there and had moved several hundred miles to Waco and later to Fort Worth, where its location contributed to its present development; and that even Abilene Christian College had moved to the other side of the city for a better location. On the other hand, Thorp Springs Christian College was convinced of its unfavorable location, and C. R. Nichol had tried hard to move it to Cleburne where it was offered a campus and a hundred thousand dollars, but some people who had moved to Thorp Springs for the school objected. The school was not moved, and it soon died.

"Our only reason for moving Harding College to Searcy," Armstrong said, "was and is the great advantage of obtaining a plant that the brotherhood of Arkansas could never build . . . That any Christian should have opposed our board in accepting this gracious offer is too bad and is enough to cause us great sorrow . . . At Morrilton we were crowded to every wall—dormitories and classrooms—even to the jeopardizing of our standing educationally."

Armstrong was hopeful that those who opposed the move would later see the wisdom of it, or at least become reconciled, and the hope apparently proved true. Mr. Tucker, the president of the board and his family remained friends, the secretary-treasurer, Walter McReynolds, received Armstrong with warmth on his trip to California. Mrs. Hill, whose dream was the origin of the college at Morrilton, invited him to dinner at Fresno.

"Sister Hill seemed as happy as I ever saw her," Armstrong wrote home. "Orpah her daughter is a beautiful girl. She married a grandson of T. B. Larimore. He seems to be a fine young man, gentle, refined, polite, thoughtful . . . 'I have heard many good things about you,' he said. So I suppose the Morrilton influence against the move did not affect them much."

Regrettably the minutes of all board meetings before 1934 have been lost. I was in the University of Chicago and could not have received them, and to my knowledge they were not given to Armstrong. Since Brother Tucker, president of the board, and Brother McReynolds, the secretary, were at the time so opposed to the move, and since the Harding College that moved to Searcy was being incorporated under a new charter, we presumed the president and secretary of the old board kept the former records.

All that is long ago. These were good men, but with opposing views. Time blessedly blots out memories and softens attitudes. Armstrong was happy at McReynolds' greeting in California, and some years ago I was called to preach D. A. Tucker's funeral. He was a man whose integrity I had always admired. So opposition in time gave way to the affection which had earlier bound us all together.

Jesse P. Sewell and Mrs. Sewell visited Searcy in the spring of 1934, and his praise of the new facilities is enthusiastic. "With the equipment of Harding added," he said, "more could not be desired."

G. H. P. Showalter, editor of the *Firm Foundation,* who attended the Thanksgiving lectures in 1934, wrote glowingly of his trip through the Ozarks with their "infinite variety of changing autumnal scenery of ineffable beauty and glory." He praised the college plant, "most of it new and strictly modern . . . No such property is held by any of our other schools." The judgment of able men gave unqualified approval to the wisdom of the move.

The reception of the college in Searcy was equally enthusiastic. Someone at Morrilton sent people in Searcy an annonymous pamphlet warning them against the college and charging "all sorts of dishonesty, mismanagement, and the like," but the Searcy *Citizen* pointed out that any man or set of men who are unwilling to sign their charges and assume full responsibility for them are unworthy of being believed. "It may be true that Harding College has had its financial troubles, same as other small colleges and universities," the *Citizen* said, "but we have not as yet heard any charges of dishonesty or mismanagement against those in charge of this institution, coming from responsible and dependable sources."

When the Armstrongs brought one hundred fifty students to visit the campus in the spring, Mayor M. P. Jones and members of the Kiwanis Club met them outside the city, and thirty car loads of people greeted them at the campus and drove them around town. Searcy lost its heart when it lost Galloway College, and it had not dreamed of being able to have another school. On June 27 the *Citizen* said, "The people of Searcy and all of this part of Arkansas feel that the coming of this institution into our midst is nothing short of a God-send."

Armstrong ran an advertisement in the Morrilton *Democrat* requesting notice of any unpaid account, and all current obligations were cleared up so that the college could move with honor. People in and around Searcy furnished trucks and moving vans, teachers and students at Morrilton helped load equipment and unload at Searcy. The campus was a hum of activity all summer long as buildings were cleaned after a two-year vacancy, furniture repaired, and rooms repainted.

At the opening in September the auditorium and stage were crowded not only with students, but with the most prominent people in Searcy. The enrollment instead of being 400, as the *Citizen* had suggested, was 461 in all departments. There were more boarding students than the college at Morrilton could have accommodated, and the following year twice as many as it ever had at Morrilton.

The friendship of the townspeople for the Armstrongs grew stronger with the years. The Wyatt Sanfords each year, until Mr. Sanford's death, sent them a generous Christmas gift. In a note of thanks to Mr. and Mrs. Sanford in 1939, Armstrong said, "This is just a note expressing our thanksgiving to you for the kindness that added to our joy this Christmas. I believe you have remembered us every Christmas since we have been in Searcy. We do not know why you should have been so considerate of us. We count it God's goodness to us through you and your company." But in addition to the Sanfords, no one could have been kinder and more helpful than the Deeners, Dr. and Mrs. Rodgers, Judges Brundage and Neeley, the Baughs, the Huddlestons, the Smiths, the Vaughans, the Joneses, the Cones, and a host of others, too many to name, who quickly won their love.

Happy as the new year opened, however, it was to have two rough spots. For the first time in the history of the school there was trouble in the faculty. A new teacher criticized some of the social regulations as being too severe, and students quickly joined the criticism. It was in the days before student rebellions and mass demonstrations, but emotions were aroused, and even a few young student preachers were involved. It reached a climax at chapel one morning when all the boys sat on one side of the auditorium and all the girls on the other. J. D. Bales, who was unaware of any trouble, came in late, but when urged to sit with the boys, refused and deliberately sat with the girls. Though the group was good natured, Armstrong felt that things had gone far enough, and he turned the chapel into a lecture on the purpose of the school.

"Young people, when Harding was started," he said, "we were not trying to be popular or shape the regulations to please all you students. We were trying to build a school that would satisfy our consciences and be pleasing to the Lord. We are trying to build the kind of men and women the world needs. If we can accomplish that, we will do our best to sell the idea to you. If you do not care for it, we are deeply sorry. When we require daily Bible study and daily chapel attendance and the observance of sensible social regulations, we do not force them on anybody. You are free not to attend Harding College if that should be your decision, but we cannot depart from the principles for which the school was founded. If you choose to leave, we should regret it deeply. We never see a student leave that our hearts do not grieve, for we realize how much he will be missing that he cannot see. But any one is free to go whenever he decides he cannot live up to the standards of the school."

This ended the "rebellion," and students wondered later why they had ever been drawn into it.

The second, and more unpleasant, occurrence was the defection of Professor Wright, which caused Armstrong weeks of anxiety. But details of this episode and of Wright's later murder of his mother are given in the appendix.

In the spring of 1934, Jesse P. Sewell spent a week on the

campus and was impressed with Armstrong's youthful vigor. "Few men, if any, have made larger or better contributions to the development of Christian education than J. N. Armstrong," he wrote. "Brother Armstrong is in good health and is full of energy and love for God and humanity. He is as radiant with enthusiasm, hope, and confidence as he considers the future of Harding College as any youngster could be. I see no reason why he should not give to this great service many years of constructive leadership. No man has perhaps had more loyal support in his work than Brother Armstrong has received from B. F. Rhodes, S. A. Bell, and others of his co-workers."

Sewell's reference to the loyalty of Rhodes, Bell, and others cannot be overemphasized. Repeatedly Armstrong had said that if three or four of these key men had left, he would not have known how to replace them, and the college would have closed. This was a dramatic expression of his deep gratitude, and might have been literally true if all had left at once; but in the years past, when Rhodes, R. C. Bell, and S. A. Bell had left for different periods of time, and when he felt he could not go on without them, somehow he had managed until they returned.

Armstrong's devotion to Rhodes, who had fought the battles with him against Daniel Sommer years before, and to both Rhodes and S. A. Bell for their enduring loyalty, could not be measured. If any teacher had to be paid slightly more, or rather was guaranteed a definite salary, as in the case of Professor Karnes, these men approved the arrangement. The Finance Committee always considered the size of families and their other income before making distribution of funds. To assist Rhodes with the family expense he was placed for a time in charge of the boys' dormitory in Morrilton, and Mrs. Armstrong and Mrs. Sears spent days personally scrubbing floors and repainting woodwork to make their apartment livable. When that arrangement was changed, Rhodes took a large house across the street from the dormitory and kept a number of boys, whose room rent supplemented his income. Mrs. Rhodes also bought any groceries and supplies she wished through the

College Club at the wholesale price at which the Club could obtain them, a policy which prevailed as long as Armstrong was president.

When the school moved to Searcy, Bell and Rhodes were given the two better cottages on the campus rent free, and I took the one with the shaky floors, which, however, was burned with nearly all our possessions. Brother Rhodes rightly felt that his house needed renovation, and Mrs. Armstrong offered to raise the money for that purpose, but Rhodes wrote her, "I most heartily appreciate your helpful spirit. I should be a very poor learner if these thirty years of experience did not prove the good qualities of your thoughtfulness." But he felt that to make an appeal to repair a house for him would be humiliating, and he would prefer to wait until the repairs could be made from regular college funds. Since Armstrong shortly after turned the presidency to Dr. Benson, it is presumed that the needed repairs were made later.

To help further with Rhodes' living expenses, his son Frank was employed as secretary in the dean's office, his daughter Juanita was manager of the College Book store until Armstrong's resignation, and his daughter Maurine was given a place in the faculty. Croom states that her salary was only $28 a month, but this is an indication of what the Finance Committee considered equitable on the basis of what other teachers were receiving. She was free, of course, not to accept the offer, but she shared the generous spirit of those who were trying to preserve the college till the dawn of a more prosperous day, and she did accept.

As a final mark of appreciation and love, on May 11, 1943, a year before his own death, Armstrong made an appeal to President Benson, his successor, of which Rhodes perhaps never knew: "For several years," Armstrong wrote, "I have thought of making the following suggestion: B. F. Rhodes has worked in this school work as a teacher since 1905—thirty-eight years with, perhaps, one or two years in this long period in which he was not actually teaching. He has done this at extreme sacrifice, a cost that many would never have paid. So he has made an unusual contribution to this exceptionally fine work." In view of this Armstrong recommended that the college confer on Rhodes the honorary LL. D. degree at the next commencement. He suggested that similar honors might also be conferred upon Mrs. Cathcart and Mrs. Armstrong for their long and distinguished service.

S. A. Bell had a little more income than Rhodes from meetings and monthly appointments, but to supplement this his daughter Catherine was employed as bookkeeper for the College Club, and the other children were given employment of different kinds. It was the policy of the college to employ students who wanted work, for this helped both the students and the college, and students were usually the most faithful workers we could find. The Bell children were especially efficient.

Truth is, the faculty had to live as best they could within the income of the college during these hard years, and Armstrong felt so keenly the sacrifice they were making that, as already said, he renounced his own share of the income and divided it among the rest, and at times even supplemented from his own preaching the amount going to the others.

Croom refers to Mrs. Armstrong's salary of $100 a month as manager of the College Club as being the best on the campus. Theoretically only. For Mrs. Armstrong had all the generosity of her father and her husband. But managing the dining hall and kitchen, buying and overseeing the workers was a seven-day-a-week job with long hours through the nine months. Through the summers there was no salary, but she spent an equal time without pay in upholstering and repairing furniture, cleaning, painting, and redecorating rooms, and overseeing workers at these tasks and on the campus. She bought most of the tools for campus work herself, and personally raised thousands of dollars for the auditorium chairs at Morrilton and furniture for the reception room in the girls' dormitory, and from her plays reroofed both the girls' dormitory and the Administration Building at Morrilton as well as those at Cordell. In one way or another most of her salary went back into the school.

Notwithstanding the youthful enthusiasm which impressed Sewell, Armstrong's burdens were beginning to tell more than

any of us realized. Only he could have brought the college
successfully through the depression, but it had been at a
cost of more sleepless nights than we knew. Outwardly he
never reflected the strain that would have broken a man of
less faith. The unexpected opposition to moving the school,
from friends with whom he had worked so closely, grieved
him. The Wright affair sickened him. He began to feel that
he should turn more of the responsibility to younger
shoulders.

The college was now in the best condition it had ever
known. The enrollment of 1936 was approximately five
hundred. More than fifty families had moved to Searcy for
the school, and new houses were going up. With the addition of Dr. Roy Coons in chemistry and Dr. Callie Mae
Coons in home economics, the faculty was stronger than ever
before. No university in the South had a professor of home
economics as well qualified as Mrs. Coons, who had turned
down a five-year contract at the University of Southern
California to return to Harding. Only sixteen women in the
world held Ph.D.s in her field, and her original methods in
research had attracted the attention of leaders over the
nation and brought a request that she conduct a special
session on research at the national meeting of the Home
Economics Association in Seattle. Her suggestions to Washington on the need of wider research in nutrition and child
development started large regional research projects in the
Northern states in which she had been asked to advise.

The inspectors who visited the college in the spring of
1936, Armstrong wrote, were "frank in saying that no other
college in the state included in its survey is more strongly
equipped. It admitted that in some respects we are better
equipped even than its own institution . . . The committee
was complimentary of the conditions found in our business
office (Bursar C. D. Brown headed the office) . . . It
pronounced our books in the best order it had found in its
visit among the colleges." Income from students had increased, and the college laundry was clearing $600 a month.

Though no one would have taken the presidency during
the depression, the college was now in condition, Armstrong

believed, for a younger man to carry it forward. He talked with me, and we both agreed that we needed a man who had the ability to raise money and would be willing to devote his time to financial promotion, a task for which I had no inclination. We consulted other teachers and members of the board.

At a special meeting on April 22, 1936, Armstrong told the board he believed the time had come for him to retire and to introduce the new president while he would still be able to help and advise. He recommended that the board elect Dr. George S. Benson to succeed him. The motion was then made and seconded that the board accept Armstrong's resignation on condition that he remain as President Emeritus and active Dean of the Bible. The motion was carried unanimously.

It was immediately moved by H. H. Dawson that the presidency of the school be offered to Dean Sears; but this offer I declined, because I believed I could give my best service to the school as dean. A motion was then made by Rhodes that Benson be elected president, and the motion was passed. A committee of the board then drew up the following Resolution which was also adopted unanimously:

Whereas, President J. N. Armstrong has asked to be relieved of the heavy responsibilities demanded of the college presidency to take a less heavy burden, but an equally useful service in the work of the college—We, the Board of Trustees, regretfully grant his request, on the understanding that he remain with the college as President Emeritus and as active Dean of Bible.

We appreciate as fully as we are able his long and honorable record in Christian education and his thirty-nine years of useful life which has been given to teaching in one or other of the colleges maintained by the Churches of Christ. For twenty-nine of these years he has served as both president and teacher—a double load.

His service has been outstanding . . . His heart has been open to the students entrusted to his care. Their burdens, their cares, and sorrows, their safety by day and by night have engaged his time.

In view of the service he had rendered, and in view

of the fact that today students who have been trained under his care are outstanding teachers in the schools in the homeland and in foreign fields and that others are successful business men and home makers, rendering useful service, in fact, in almost all honorable callings and professions of life; we do well to honor him to the fullest possible extent.

But we must not fail to add this final tribute to his outstanding worth. Young men who have been trained under his sympathetic care are now preaching the gospel of Christ in half the continents of the world. In China, Japan, South America, South Africa, the Philippines, by scores, and in the United States and Canada by hundreds—a glorious host of stars for his crowning reward.

The next morning in chapel the announcement of the change was made by John G. Reese, president of the board, who praised Armstrong for his long years of service and especially for his influence on students.

In an announcement in the *Gospel Advocate* and the *Firm Foundation,* Armstrong said:

For thirty-nine years I have taught in Christian college work. For twenty-nine I have served as president and Mrs. Armstrong as dean of women. Our home has been a girls' dormitory where we have been on duty day and night throughout these long years. As we look back, we wonder how we have borne the weight of the burdens—both mental and physical—that have often been placed upon our shoulders. But . . . there has never been a time when we were not glad to have the privilege of spending our lives in Bible school work. We are thankful to God for the great opportunity it has given us to help mold the lives of thousands of boys and girls . . .

With the rapid growth of Harding College, with its attendant increase in administrative work, we believe we need younger blood. Mrs. Armstrong is now fifty-seven and I am sixty-six. We believe, by ridding our shoulders of a part of the load, we shall be able to help guide the destiny of Harding College for years to come. For this we pray . . .

Dr. Sears, our son-in-law, who has taught with us for twenty-one years, serving as dean eighteen of these years, and who has borne so many of my burdens as well as his own; and Mrs. Sears, who has been her mother's chief helper from childhood, would of course have been our first choice as our successors, as well as the first choice of the Board and of the student body, had we not known for years that neither of them wanted our jobs . . .

Dr. Benson knows the work and the spirit of Harding College, for he is not only an alumnus, but he was a member of the faculty in 1925 when he resigned to take up his work in China . . .

In handing over my portfolio to Brother Benson I hand to him the best of all, this priceless loyalty (of former students)! For, while Mrs. Armstrong and I have had our part in building this devotion and while this loyalty has often been our only salaries through these years, I believe the loyalty is more deeply rooted than to a personality; I believe it is rooted in the cause we have all supported. So in this confidence I . . . believe that the great body of ex-students and alumni and that other great body of friends and supporters of the college, composed of our children's parents and other lovers of Christian education, will endorse the change being made and will receive the new president with open arms, pledging to him the same loyalty they have given me.

At the opening chapel in the fall he paid a warm tribute to Dr. and Mrs. Benson and urged wholehearted support for him in his new responsibilities: "Brother Benson, Mrs. Armstrong and I commit to you our child, whose steps we have guided from childhood to the strength of youth, with full confidence that you will fulfill the sacred trust of carrying on the ideals for which it is established, and we pledge you our unstinted loyalty and support."

Unexpectedly on November 24, 1936, the Board of Governors of the Eugene Field Society conferred on Armstrong Honorary Membership in the Eugene Field Society for "having by his writings made an outstanding contribution to contemporary literature." This was a recognition he never mentioned, which I discovered only among his long-forgotten papers.

Unexpectedly also Armstrong was able to assist Dr. Benson in a remarkable way in the new campaign to lift the mortgage from the college. In the spring of 1936, before Dr. Benson returned from China, Clinton Davidson of New York, riding the caboose of the little freight from Kensett to the front of the campus, knocked at my door in old "Gray Gables" and asked where he could find Armstrong and R. N. Gardner. Davidson had been a student at Potter Bible College under James A. Harding, Armstrong, and Gardner, and loved them all. During the intervening years he had become financial adviser to a group of men and women whose combined wealth at the time exceeded a billion dollars and grew to more than two billion as he continued to help the college. On moving to Searcy Armstrong had brought Gardner back into the faculty and asked him to edit a small journal, the *Truthseeker*. A copy Davidson received brought memories of the Bible school flooding back, and he resolved to do something for the college.

He had saved five thousand dollars, but he wanted Armstrong and Gardner to decide whether to use it immediately for salaries, or to promote a campaign for further funds. In characteristic fairness to the faculty Armstrong called a meeting and asked the teachers to make the decision. They voted for Davidson to use the gift to obtain larger funds from his friends. When Armstrong explained to Davidson that he was giving up the presidency, it was decided to wait till Dr. Benson arrived to start the campaign.

At the board meeting in November H. H. Rowland, president of the Elliot Paint Company of Chicago, also placed before the board suggestions for a campaign and promised personal help. Armstrong in his youth had idealized Mrs. Rowland's father, Jesse Phillips, and during the years when Mrs. Sears and I were in Chicago this friendship with the Rowlands was renewed and deepened.

Benson's first efforts to raise money among the churches were unexpectedly blocked by the opposition of B. G. Hope of Paragould and E. R. Harper of Little Rock. Davidson then offered to pay a finance company $10,000 to prepare a movie and direct a campaign among his millionaire friends. He also obtained some very favorable publicity in newspapers over the nation. But it was Armstrong who gave him his first lead when he visited the college.

"Clinton," Armstrong asked, "through your contacts could you get some very important men—presidents of large corporations—to come to Harding and make speeches?"

"Yes, I think I can," Davidson replied.

"If you can," Armstrong said, "we can get instructors and professors from colleges all over the state to come to our auditorium to hear them."

The first of his clients, whom Davidson approached about speaking turned him down, but later gave the college several hundred thousand dollars. But the idea soon caught on, and a number of prominent industrialists and educators became speakers, beginning with Sterling Morton, president of the Morton Salt Company, who later gave the college a farm along with other gifts.

In the summer of 1938, Armstrong held meetings in California, and at Los Angeles Mr. and Mrs. George Pepperdine had attended the meeting and invited him to dinner. Pepperdine was a native of Kansas and knew of Armstrong's work at Harper. He had also been impressed with the fact that at that time nearly all missionaries of the church had come from the colleges. Accordingly in 1937 he had established and endowed George Pepperdine College in Los Angeles, and Armstrong had written a warm commendation of his great gift. The Pepperdines, with their new college, were interested in Harding and in Armstrong's long experience in Christian education. When they were planning a trip to New York in 1939, Armstrong urged them to visit Harding on their return.

In New York Pepperdine spent an entire morning with Davidson, whose advice he was seeking on financial matters. In connection with his advice Davidson asked Pepperdine to give $25,000 to help clear the mortgage from Harding College, and Pepperdine left the impression that he would do so. At Searcy he and Mrs. Pepperdine seemed to enjoy their visit with students and with the Bensons and Armstrongs. Mrs. Pepperdine said they had heard of the Armstrongs forever and had enjoyed meeting Brother Armstrong in California, but so much wanted to know them both. Pepperdine did make the gift of $25,000, as Davidson understood he planned to do.

Previously Davidson had helped obtain $16,000 from one of his best friends, who later increased it to $25,000 or more. With a discount of $2,300 from the Booth family, who held the mortgage, with Pepperdine's gift and some others already obtained, the mortgage could now be paid and the college freed for the first time in its history.

On Thanksgiving day, 1939, President Benson announced that the mortgage was cleared. He expressed gratitude to Armstrong and the faculty who had preserved the school through the Depression, and in appreciation he presented the cancelled mortgage to Armstrong, who was given a standing ovation from the audience.

The meeting adjourned immediately to the campus, Benson lighted a bonfire, and Armstrong placed the mortgage on the flames as the spectators broke into the strains of the "Alma Mater."

The board at its meeting in December expressed appreciation to Davidson for his aid in removing the mortgage. With modesty Davidson pointed out those, he felt, who were really responsible: "Of course I appreciate this feeling on their part (the board), but as I see it my work was secondary. The primary work was done by two men who make one of the best teams in the country today, and may I say right here that I hope these two men will work together as a team in double harness until parted by death. I refer to J. N. Armstrong and George S. Benson."

"Brother Benson has real ability, in my opinion, for the work assigned to him in the raising of these funds. I was pleased in working with him, and I am not easy to please in this respect. I do not know where you could have found a better man for this work than Brother Benson. I do not forget, however, that Brother Armstrong is responsible for the record which was used to get men who live so far away from Arkansas to send money to Harding College. A college must have an unusual record if it is to get people who live a thousand miles away and who are interested in colleges and churches in their community to contribute to it.

"As I see it, Brother Armstrong's leadership plus the sacrifice of the rest of the faculty over quite a number of years made the record, and Brother Benson used this record in the most efficient manner possible."

Actually clearing the mortgage could hardly have been done by one man alone. Had Armstrong not preserved the school through the Depression and had he not seen the opportunity of gaining a physical plant worth more than $600,000 for only $75,000, there would have been no Harding College at all. Had his work not developed unselfish men like Davidson and appealed to others like Rowland and Pepperdine, there would have been no heritage worthy of assistance. Though Davidson felt that his contacts and aid were responsible for at least three-fourths of the amount raised, he could probably have done little without Benson and Armstrong. The ultimate success was really due not to any one man but to all of them.

Davidson's generous aid in later helping to start the college endowment and in raising funds for the building program belongs to a later period and can only be mentioned here, but with deep and lasting appreciation.

Now, at last, after twenty-five years of unbelievable sacrifice, the burdens were finally lifted, not only from his own shoulders, but from the college which he loved, and Armstrong could look forward to a period of rest and peace.

Chapter 15

THE WILL TO POWER

RELIEVED AT LAST of financial and administrative burdens Armstrong could now give himself to the work he had always loved best—his teaching, preaching, and writing. Though the *Living Message* had been discontinued when the college moved to Searcy and the *Truthseeker* ran only a short time, he wrote often for the *Gospel Advocate* and the *Firm Foundation*. About 1935 he also began a weekly radio broadcast which continued till his death.

In 1935 he spent a week with the Grove Avenue church in San Antonio, Texas, speaking twice a day. Jesse P. Sewell wrote:

It is the unanimous judgment of this congregation, as well as others who attended the services, that no stronger, more fundamental, heart-and-life searching series of pure gospel sermons has ever been preached in San Antonio . . . Personally I consider this the most complete and most perfectly balanced presentation of the entire content of Christianity I have ever heard in sixteen sermons.

James H. Childress, who had taught with Armstrong a year or two at Harper, came from Houston. "It is very difficult for me to refrain from being envious of Brother Armstrong's school work," he said, "because the churches all over the country need so much the type of preaching he does."

Armstrong was almost unequalled in giving to churches, not just the easy first principles of the Christian faith, but the broad and basic concepts which underlie and enrich the whole Christian life. He was recalled to San Antonio in the spring of 1938 for another meeting. In 1937 he held meetings in Kentucky and Michigan. At Flint it was said that "more outsiders were preached to in this meeting than in any other meeting ever held in Flint." People drove from Canada and from many places in Michigan to hear him.

The summer of 1938 he spent in California. At Sebastopol friends drove him out to "Cal Armstrong's Grove" with its natural "theater" seated with redwood logs, electrically lighted, and arranged for concerts and large audiences.

"The trees grow up to the sky," he wrote home. "You nearly have to stand on your head to see the tops."

He had just opened the meeting when a telephone call insisted that he come to Fresno to preach the funeral of a Brother Arteburn, whom he knew long ago at Bowling Green. He left by bus at 11:40 p.m., following the evening service, arrived the next morning at 6:30, had the funeral at 8:30, took the bus back to Berkeley, arriving just in time for the evening service—no sleep for thirty-six hours. He said after the evening service, "I was tired, but felt fine the next morning and am full of gratitude to God for my physical health and strength." But the strain was too much and he had two degrees of fever from the trip.

"Two nights past," he wrote, "my preaching was 'punk,' but I couldn't help it. I ought not to have preached either night. Night before last I didn't close my eyes one time all night. About 5:00 a.m. I dropped off for thirty minutes. I just wasn't sleepy, eyes wide open. I counted and tried to read, but nothing availed. Awake I was for the night. Last night I slept very well, but my voice sounds as if I were in a gourd."

The many old friends were a delight, but physically also a burden: "I closed at Berkeley Sunday night with the hardest day of the year;" he wrote home; "in fact I do not remember another day so hard. Three services, dinner on the ground, and fifty people pulling on me to ask, 'Do you know me? You don't remember me, do you? Don't you remember me? I met you at Possum Trot fifteen years ago,' and so forever. Well, it's simply terrible, and by night I am a frazzle, and especially when I am sick to begin with. The last days of a meeting are terrible!"

At Los Angeles the church arranged a room for him near a cafe where he could take whatever meals he wished. "I don't know whether I shall like the cafe or not, but to get away from folks, folks, a minute is a joy unspeakable. I can get up when I please and go to breakfast when I want to, and choose what I want to eat once anyway." But the morning meeting began at 10:00, and was followed by visiting till the evening service. "Almost every day people present themselves to know whether I remember them," he said. "Of course, I do and I don't. Last night five people came up in a bunch, old friends from Cordell. Last of all John O'Dowd, the fightingest of the Texas fighters, presented himself. I have in the past seen him a few times, but I was not looking for him and did not know him. That was too bad, wasn't it?"

He loved people and would have been deeply disappointed if old friends had not come to greet him, but he had never been physically strong, and the constant strain of speaking twice a day and visiting into the night was almost more than his strength could bear. He spoke to six hundred people at an orphans' home in Southern California, and was delighted that the contribution taken after the speech was the largest ever received.

In spite of his illness and the strenuous schedule, he enjoyed the summer greatly, and especially meeting the Pepperdines and visiting in their home. To one of the old students he wrote, "I enjoyed my summer out there more than I can tell you. I think it was one of the greatest summers of my life. Never was I quite so busy through eleven weeks as I was there. With the exception of one day when I was ill and one day on the bus I preached every day through those weeks, twice a day most of the time, and three times on Sundays."

The following year the alumni on the West Coast wanted him to attend an area-wide meeting in the interest of Harding College, but unable financially to make the trip, he sent a message instead.:

It moves me greatly that you alumni and friends of Harding College in the far West have planned this rally in the interest of your Alma Mater. You are the declared dividend of the investment we have been making through many years. The teachers at Harding have almost lived on a crust, but you men and women scattered around the world are our pay for the service we have rendered. We are proud of you.

Mrs. Armstrong and I will soon be out of the picture, but we are counting on you to carry on this unparalleled effort in Christian service. You will find many problems along the way, but your greatest difficulty will be keeping our schools and colleges Christian. This effort will be forever drawing on all your resources. Mrs. Armstrong and I will be praying here, and even in heaven, that your faith fail not and that your strength hold out.

Every great movement makes its checkered history. But this is not discouraging. On the other hand, it is a source of inspiration. In fact the period in every important movement in which its "checkered" history is made (its life-and-death struggle through failure to success) is one of the most interesting chapters in its history. It is in that period that true heroism is displayed; it is then that the impossible is done.

These busy, happy summers, however, were soon to be interrupted. Long before most of us were aware, Armstrong saw the second World War approaching. With agony he had seen his boys suffer on the battlefields and in prison during the war to "end all wars," to "make democracy safe to the world," but despite these noble ideals the twenty intervening years had given rise to the worst forms of absolute tyranny the world had ever known—Nazism under Hitler and Communism under Stalin.

In 1939 Hitler launched the campaign that he declared would "decide the future of Germany for a thousand years."

In 1940 Armstrong wrote Mrs. Coons, "All of us are troubled about the impending danger of our being involved in the European troubles. This distresses me more than I can say . . . Surely all of us are praying that our country may not become involved, and still it seems to me that it may be in less than six months." It was slightly more than a year.

Armstrong tried hard to warn Christians not to lose the Christian attitude in the fever of war. "To hate our enemies only hurts us," he said. "Remember, there are volumes of history behind this world crisis, and unless we think deeper than Hitler and the German people we can never find the cause of our trouble."

At the opening chapel in 1943 he said, "This is a sad-happy day. Sad because our boys are scattered over the world, not to preach peace but to kill men. How they could like to be here this morning! But they were forced into a job none of them wanted. These boys gave up goals they prized highly—some of them forever, for many will never return. And back home are aching hearts, dreading each telephone call, fearing to read the headlines of the paper. Yes, the world is full of heartaches and distress. Who can measure it?"

He was anxious for Chirstians to see clearly their relationship to war. Governments are God's instruments to execute his wrath, but Christians are urged not to give place to wrath, for vengeance belongs to God. The Christian is to return good for evil and "heap coals of fire on the head" of enemies. "We cannot join in the hating, the bitterness, but must keep the spirit of Christ, and try to heal the wounds of the world in the love of men." In a touching speech the following Tahnksgiving, in what he suggested should be an "International Prayer in Time of War," he said, "With shamed faces we would confess before Thee our nation's mutual share in the universal guilt that has issued in the current horror that engulfs the world . . . In this dread hour of the world's crucial agony and woe, we turn again to Thee, O God, for comfort, for strength, and for direction. O Thou Spirit of infinite wisdom and love and might, overrule for good, we pray Thee, all the hatreds and horrors, all the evil and selfish designs that flare and flame in war . . . Reveal to us our guilt and call us to repentance, forgiveness, and reconciliation. O God, with whom are the issues of every human conflict, hasten the triumph of the right. Set in motion those unseen forces which will fulfill Thy purposes of grace for the world."

In an article "Lest We Forget," which was published in the *Firm Foundation,* he tried earnestly to make clear again the Christian's attitude toward the war. He recalled the high hopes of men in the former "war to end war," with the result that in twenty years we were in another war to "save democracy" in Europe. "The problems of the world are not ours to solve," he wrote. "Whether our statesmen in putting the nation into war are wise or otherwise is not ours to decide; whether it is right for this nation to join England or whether it is wrong, is not our responsibility. We are sojourners and pilgrims, strangers on our way home . . . So we Christians are not in the war; it is not our war. We are not on either side, any more than we would be, if we were Citizens of Germany . . . In neither country is the Christian in the war. If faithful to his Lord, he cannot partake or share in the hating, the starving of men, women, and children, the bombing, the killing, the murdering, and all the other wicked works that are essential to war. But the distinct mission of the Christian is to be "the light of the world," and to love even "your enemies, bless them that curse you, do good to them that hate you, and pray for them that despitefully use you and persecute you; that ye may be sons of your Father who is in heaven."

A critic immediately denounced the article as condemning Christians' giving aid to the nation. Armstrong corrected the impression:

"I do not know a government that has gone so far to meet the requirements of the Christian conscience as our government has done. For this magnanimous treatment all Christians owe a debt of unstinted loyalty to the government which entails upon us obedience, limited only by our consciences."

"Now if my critic's conscience approves his giving an 'all-out effort' to aid the nation, my article in no way hinders him. Let my critic also quiet his nerves concerning the evil influence of conscientious objectors. For in the first world war there were only a few conscientious objectors compared to the present number, and among them were those who could not do even non-combatant service, and they were sent to prison. But today such objectors are treated royally by our government, and camps are created especially for them in which they are doing service of national importance. There are, I think, more than twenty such camps in this conscience-respecting nation, and in these camps there are more than five thousand objectors. So we see that these despised conscientious objectors of 1917-18, by their stand for their consciences, preached a great sermon, a sermon that has moved the whole world. If our next war is delayed twenty-five years and the sermon these present 'witnesses of the right' are preaching today is as effective as the former sermon, my critic may himself learn the truth by the next world war."

Armstrong was happy to see the growing numbers who were conscientious about war. As World War II drew near, "Practically all the free churches in England and Scotland," he said, "put themselves on record to endorse and back all the conscientious objectors in their memberships, when and if they seek exemption from military service." The Methodist Church drew up a resolution "that conscientious objectors to war . . . are a natural outgrowth of the principles of good will and the Christian desire for universal peace; and that such objectors should not be oppressed by compulsory military service anywhere or at any time . . . We ask and claim exemption from all forms of military preparation or service for all conscientious objectors who may be members of the Methodist Church."

"Finally," Armstrong said, "I want to repeat that we as Christians are staying out of carnal war; we are not taking sides. The world struggles to 'make democracy safe,' to 'end war,' or to overthrow Communism, Fascism, or Nazism, and to establish permanent peace in Europe. I crave all these results. But we are followers of the Prince of Peace, and we ourselves are peacemakers, and there can never come permanent peace in Europe or in the world, save through us, the followers of the Prince of Peace. We are the salt of the earth, the light of the world. Our Lord came to bring peace, and his followers are men and women of peace . . . But their program for bringing peace was made out in heaven for them, and through it alone peace may be established on the earth."

He was happy at the concerted effort of J. M. McCaleb, Wade Ruby, R. N. Squire, James Lovell, Boyd Field, and others to raise money to pay the expenses of Christian boys in the camps. The numbers had increased to a hundred and the historic Peace Churches—Friends, Menonites, and Brethren—had spent $11,500 helping the boys from the churches of Christ whose parents, friends, and home congregations were not helping them.

Though Armstrong respected the consciences of these young men who took the extreme position that they could do nothing whatever under military orders, his own position was different. "Personally," he said, "I have felt that it makes no difference who gives the orders, whether it is military or civil authority. I can obey as a Christian as long as the orders do not conflict with Christ. So I would register, were I a young man, as one able to do service in the non-combatant branches of service."

Armstrong's opposition was not to war itself. His opposition like that of Lipscomb, Harding, and others, was based entirely upon the Christian's obedience to the Lord. J. D. Bales remembers stating in a Monday night meeting once that from the standpoint of modern youth it seemed ridiculous that a young man should work hard to get an education only to be shot down in war. When Armstrong arose to close the meeting, with his characteristic gesture of chopping the palm of his left hand with the heel of the right, he said, "Young men, it is not a matter of how you feel about war, but of what God says about it." Bales reports that at the close of his rebuke, he felt so low he "could have put a ten-gallon hat on his head and walked out under the rug without touching it."

To Armstrong the Christian's position was perfectly simple.

He belonged wholly to the Christ, but loyalty to Christ obligated him to follow the Golden Rule in his relations to all men, and to obey every ordinance of man except those conflicting with the will of God. He recognized the difficulty of maintaining the Christian position. But if the Christian's position is difficult for him, it is equally difficult for the government under which he lives. Armstrong cited the cases of two distinguished Canadians who had applied for citizenship in the United States. Both were willing to swear allegiance and to support the Constitution, but Dr. MacIntosh, a Professor of Theology at Yale, who was beyond the age for military service, said he must refuse to bear arms unless he felt the war was just. Miss Bland said she would defend the Constitution "as far as her conscience as a Christian would allow." Both were denied citizenship by the Supreme Court.

"The United States thus is on record by its highest tribunal," Armstrong wrote, "to the effect that making God and his will first disqualifies for citizenship in what is perhaps the highest developed and most Christian nation in the world. By this decision this highest tribunal denies God the right to exercise supreme authority over its citizens, even over their consciences, and declares at the same time that the American citizens cannot become servants of the Most High, unless they do so with the understanding that their first duty is to the United States. This calls the very hand of the Almighty; it challenges God to contest. These facts establish that the United States is a rival of God as to who shall have first place in controlling the conduct of men under its authority."

This conflict of authority over the consciences of men Armstrong recognized as one which required great tolerance and understanding. The Philadelphia *Register* declared that "national allegiance with reservations" seemed a dangerous experiment, and the Boston *Transcript* said that, if citizens are to choose their own wars, "it is only a question of time before our unity as a nation ceases." Here was a direct conflict, "a contention for supremacy—allegiance to the one arrayed against allegiance to the other." But Armstrong rejoiced that reverence for God was so fundamental and so strong within this greatest of all nations, that, even if it would not grant citizenship to the foreign born, it could still respect the consciences of its own citizens without loss of its national power.

The Christian's complete obedience to his government as long as such obedience does not conflict with the will of Christ, Armstrong recognized, created problems which only the individual Christian could resolve. For instance, he felt he could not logically vote for presidents and congressmen without becoming responsible for their decisions, because they were politically his representatives, or agents, doing what he wanted done. Since congress declares war and he could not conscientiously bear arms, he must decline the right to elect congressmen. Others, however, just as conscientious, have interpreted their vote as merely a preference, a judgment as to the man best qualified for a position which some one will fill whether they vote or not. It does not mean endorsement of the decisions or the responsibilities of the official so elected.

In answering the question as to whether Christians could serve on juries, Armstrong's reply is as usual based on the authority of the Scriptures. "The only question a Christian can ask himself when an officer of the law asks of him service is, Does the doing of this service involve a conflict with his obedience to Christ? If it does not, he must do it or be disobedient to Jehovah."

To see exactly what is demanded of a juror he went to the courthouse, sat through a trial, heard the jury impaneled, the judge's charge, the evidence, and the jury's verdict:

"The duty of the jurors as set forth by the judge was to consider the evidence, weigh it, and reach a decision, 'guilty' or 'not guilty' of the charges made. Then it was the judge's duty to assess the penalty. Personally, I cannot see wherein it would conflict with any principle of God for a Christian to hear evidence and decide honestly about the guiltiness of a person charged. The court's business is to punish crime, and I think it's the duty of Christians everywhere to cooperate with and to assist the officers in every righteous way in their efforts to find the guilty party. For instance,

I could volunteer knowledge of a criminal; I could testify against a criminal . . . I should feel guilty with the criminal, should I refuse to do so. So I can be a witness, and could have sat on the jury I have described above. I know of no conflict with God's teaching. I could not have taken the oath. But usually, so far as I know, one may be excused from taking an oath."

In June, 1944, Berlin fell and the war in Europe ended. With thanksgiving Armstrong recounts the church bells at midnight waking the people of Philadelphia with the good news. One hundred eighty-nine churches in Seattle, ninety in Cincinnati, all the churches on Woodward Avenue in Chicago, and thousands more across the nation held day-long services, and the whole nation was on its knees in thanksgiving. It was the most remarkable day of religious devotion in the nation's history.

Unhappily Armstrong was not to see the surrender of Japan and the close of the great war. Nor did he live to see the horrors of Hiroshima and Nagasaka and the rise of the terrible atomic power that could conceivably bring an end, not merely to war, but to all human existence, and leave earth spinning aimlessly for eons through infinite space, unless God chose to use it for Peter's "new earth wherein dwelleth righteousness."

Chapter 16

THE FIGHT FOR FREEDOM

JESUS WAS NOT a "rebel," as he is sometimes pictured. He created no riots, started no insurrections. Instead he lived and taught the eternal principles of honesty, integrity, human kindness, mercy, justice, and love—even to "love your enemies": "As you would that men should do unto you . . . " But since these principles often antagonize the world, as they did when Jesus lived them Christians were to understand that they were the "Lord's freemen," free to follow their Lord's way of life no matter what pressures might be brought against them.

Unfortunately, however, instead of opposing tyrannical power religious leaders too often have sought to exercise it. Christ himself was crucified by men with closed minds who loved traditions more than the great principles which could open the eyes of the blind and set free the human spirit. So strong are the shackles that bind men that even those who were liberated by the truth which Jesus brought had to be begged to keep that freedom: "For freedom did Christ set us free; stand fast therefore, and be not entangled again in a yoke of bondage."

Of this freedom Armstrong said: "There is great need to stress the importance of maintaining freedom of speech in the kingdom of God. Intolerance is dangerous to the future growth of the church. Most of us have an aversion to anything except what we ourselves believe and teach, and as a consequence, we are intolerant of the teaching of anything that antagonizes our doctrine. All progress of truth—scientific truth, political truth, or religious truth—all truth—has always depended on free speech and progressive teachers who were not afraid to teach their honest convictions, even though it cost life . . . It takes no courage to teach the things one's audience already believes . . .

"I am well aware of the fact that free speech has its dangers and that progressive and fearless teachers have given the world untold trouble. But are we ready to surrender free speech and to deny ourselves teachers who are not afraid? Even our deliverance from such a possibility must come through free speech and courageous teachers. If our great-great-grandchildren enjoy the truth we hold dear, it will be due to free speech and courageous teachers."

Armstrong's concepts of Christian freedom went back, not only to the free discussions of James A. Harding and David Lipscomb and to the great principles of the Campbells and others who led the Restoration Movement, but to the Scriptures themselves. In the *Living Message* of October 23, 1924, he had stated this freedom as the policy of the paper: "The columns of the *Living Message* are open to any faithful and sincere student of the Word, who in a kind and respectful manner presents his honest convictions on any Bible subject. Even though he may differ from the editors and managers of the paper, it has been our policy to make him free to set forth his position. It is our firm conviction that the humblest and most unlearned child of God should never be intimidated from teaching any lesson that he believes the Word of the Lord teaches. This freedom of speech is a blood-bought liberty."

With reference to a specific issue Armstrong wrote: "Some have criticized us for this freedom extended to other writers. A notable case is our attitude toward Brother R. H. Boll and others who are supposed to agree with him in some interpretations peculiar to him . . . Brother Boll knows that I do not agree with him in his peculiar positions . . . I have not only not agreed with the positions occupied by him and his associates, but I believe the positions needed to be criticized, but in a brotherly manner. I have never believed that Boll needed to be ruthlessly handled and then crucified as I consider has been done . . . "

The fight started by E. M. Borden in 1924 against Armstrong and Harding College over the teaching of Boll gradually subsided, but was renewed eleven years later when Earnest Wright sent his letter to Showalter (see appendix). From that time until his death in 1944 Armstrong was in continuous battle to maintain the unity of the great brotherhood which he devotedly loved and yet preserve the freedom of teaching for which others had so valiantly fought. Again and again he stated the real issue: "It is right for each of us to present his honest convictions concerning any difference of teaching he may hold. Having done this, let us leave it with that, and not try to force our teaching upon each other. An effort to force always produces opposition, strife, bitterness, and finally division. What we need is to love one another and magnify our agreements."

Armstrong recognized the right of every man to decide in his own mind the things that he considered important to teach and the things he did not care to teach.

"The way to unity and good fellowship," he declared, is not in deciding what is 'essential' and what is 'non-essential.' This line cannot be fixed except by a dictator or a pope. God has not fixed it. To submit to a line here would be nothing less than submitting to human wisdom and . . . it would be deadly, as I see it, in its reflection on the wisdom of God."

From his youth, Armstrong had considered the single reference to a "millennium" so obscure that he actually knew nothing to say about it beyond repeating the words of the biblical text. The Lord had not seen fit to give details, and whatever was to take place was the Lord's responsibility.

Though Armstrong wished fervently that Boll and others

did not feel that their theories about the millennium were so important and would cease voluntarily to teach them, he was strongly opposed to forcing them to desist. S. H. Hall, an editor of the *Gospel Advocate,* wrote Boll in 1939: "It seems unthinkable to me that we should ask a man to stop writing and talking about anything the Bible talks about. But if your views on Revelation 20 are such that you believe I can be saved without knowing and receiving them . . . for you just to retire from writing or talking about these two subjects unless asked to do so. I could do this if I were in your stead. If you feel in the least disposed to do this, I will be glad to get together men, *just* men, and help you formulate a statement that would be *just* to you as well as the great cause we both love."

But Boll had replied: "Would it not be adopting a bad principle which might lead to, no one knows what extremes of official censorship and creed-making in the church, if a man in Christ had to keep silent on some parts of Scripture in order to preserve fellowship? And who could say just where the line would run, and what should not be mentioned? But as I have often stated, as a free man under Christ, I would be glad to use wisdom and consideration, and in all my teaching to confine myself faithfully to the declarations found in God's word. Consider these things and may the Lord direct our hearts."

Since Hall, like Armstrong, could not conscientiously compel a man to cease teaching on any biblical subject, but must leave the matter to the man's own judgment, no further developments came from the correspondence.

In 1939 G. C. Brewer also published an appeal to the whole church to cease for a period all teaching on the millennium. He suggested calling a "conference" of representative leaders of the church to settle the "Boll problem" if the Boll group would "agree before the conference meets that they will cease the objectionable teaching."

Armstrong wrote Brewer that he read everything he wrote and agreed with about all of it, but he asserted that neither Boll nor any other man could conscientiously agree to cease teaching what he believes the Lord wants him to teach.

"I care nothing for the doctrine involved," Armstrong wrote, "and I wish these brethren would agree with me about this. But I do care about the principle that would allow *men* to say what I shall teach, and I will fight this effort to the last ditch. If men can do this one time, they can do it another time, and the fearless aggressive teacher of the word would never be left safe . . . "

To Armstrong's letter Brewer replied: "I agree absolutely with what you say. I know that we can set up no human authority to limit any man in his study and teaching of the Word of God . . . But I have come to the conclusion, Brother Armstrong, that the best way to defeat this radical element that wants to set up a sect governed by human authority, is to bury the issue. I believe if the brethren would agree to cease teaching anything about the thousand years and conditions that will prevail during that period, we would disarm these men and defeat them, and then later on, men would once again be free to teach what they believe they find in the Word of God."

Brewer was right in believing that men would soon forget the issue if no one continued to write or speak about it. But the impossibility was in getting such an agreement. The only sensible course left, therefore, as Armstrong pointed out, was the course recommended by Paul to the Romans. In the church at Rome were both Jews and Gentiles with widely different customs and convictions, Armstrong explained:

The matter of observing days as a religious service was not really an indifferent matter. Truth and error were involved. Those who regarded "every day alike" held the truth, and the others were in error. Their error was vital enough to divide the practice of the church, and they were setting brethren at naught in their effort to force their position upon others. This teaching needed to be corrected. But that was not the *primary* need at the moment. Their attitudes toward one another were unchristian, their feelings were running high, and it was no time to correct doctrine. So not one word of condemnation for either group as to their positions or differences of doctrine was given at that time. Each group is left to abide in its own doctrine. The Holy Spirit did not approve the one that regarded every day alike, nor did he condemn those that regarded one day above another. But he emphatically told all of them to leave each other free to decide the matter for himself, being fully assured each in his own mind.

It would surely be unfair to the apostle to assume that those brethren in error were never to be taught correctly on the matter. But the Lord showed them first how they could be brethren and preserve the unity of the Spirit as they learned the truth more perfectly. Their outstanding sin was their way of dealing with their misunderstanding and their differences. Efforts to bind on others even the truth before those others have discovered it to be truth destroys the peace of the church and makes division. Failing to let each conscience be fully persuaded *within itself* breeds trouble, parties, faction, and divisions. No one has a right scripturally to *bind* his teaching, even his teaching of truth, on other consciences. He who does it imposes a human creed on all who submit.

Though Armstrong could not conscientiously force men to limit their teaching to doctrines prescribed by a group, even of good men, he nevertheless was grieved that Boll could not take some step that would help to alleviate the strife.

"The calamity of the age," he said in a letter to Don Carlos Janes in 1939, "is that Boll and company allowed this to be done. I cannot believe that Boll saw the result and what his enemies have finally done to him. I see a number of steps that could have been taken to have avoided what we've got and nobody's conscience been hurt . . . Even if everything Brother Boll and the rest of you teach on the matters involved were true, these things are not vital enough for the cost you pay. How much better are the best churches among you than the best churches out of your circle? You have paid too dear for your whistle . . . "

G. C. Brewer in the *Firm Foundation* in 1925 had urged a debate between Boll and some representative man like C. R. Nichol, R. L. Whiteside, or J. B. Nelson to see just what the issues were.

"Frankly," he said, "I do not believe the issues are worth discussing—don't think they are of any practical value—but they are being discussed; then why not treat them as we do other issues—fight them out with their strongest opponent."

This article Armstrong reprinted in the *Living Message,* and added: "I want to give this suggestion a hearty amen. For eight years I have wanted such a discussion. I have all these years too been asking 'Why deal with this issue differently from other issues?' I heartily agree with Brother Brewer in his conviction that the issues involved are not of any practicable value."

In 1927 all the issues were explored in a written discussion between Boll and H. Leo Boles, president of the Nashville Bible School and an editor of the *Gospel Advocate.* At the close of the discussion H. Leo Boles stated: "Brother Boll and I hold many things in common—enough to fellowship each other as brethren in the Lord . . . We differ as the reader knows; our differences and a discussion of them do not keep me from esteeming him very highly as a brother in Christ."

This conclusion was the judgment of many other leaders in the church. Earnest Beam wrote from California that a group there had studied the Boles-Boll debate and "notwithstanding the individual convictions represented in our group out here (and Brother Foy E. Wallace was one of the group) (Parenthesis is Beam's), there was unanimity of persuasion that we need not disfellowship over this matter."

In spite of the reasoned judgment of prominent leaders, a group of preachers were still determined to disfellowship, not merely Boll and all who believed with him, but even all who disagreed with Boll but who refused to disfellowship him. Pressure was brought against preachers, the religious journals, and the colleges to "line up." Two radical new papers sprang up to lead in the elimination of Boll and all who would not disfellowship him.

Because of Armstrong's outspoken defense of the Christian's freedom of conscience and freedom to teach, he became the constant target of this group. Following Wright's letter to Showalter (see appendix), Armstrong published a series of articles, including "For Good Understanding," "A College Professor Goes on Record Again," "The Undenominational Stand and Plea for Unity," and others. Warm approval came from leaders all over the country.

Though Jesse P. Sewell commended the articles highly, he also added:

"The religious politicians have been forming a block to get you and Harding College, and they feel they are just about to succeed . . . The facts are, a lot of these fellows, I am convinced, don't care what you believe and teach. You just don't "belong." You don't fit into their political schemes. You don't make any contribution to their leadership and party plans. Harding College has never fit in . . . But stay in there. For a while it will be hard. They have a strong political combination."

When it became known that Armstrong was turning the presidency of Harding College to Dr. Benson, the political group planned its first attack. E. R. Harper of Little Rock arranged an elaborate "preachers' meeting" at Fourth and State Street church, for December 4-8, 1936, apparently for the purpose of putting pressure on the colleges, and especially Harding College, to "line up" in disfellowshipping all "premillinnealists" and also those who refused to disfellowship them. E. H. Ijams, president of David Lipscomb College, James F. Cox, president of Abilene Christian College, N. B. Hardeman, president of Freed-Hardeman College, and George S. Benson were all on the program to speak on "Policies, Plans, and Attitude on the Kingdom Question."

S. H. Hall, a member of the board of David Lipscomb College and an editor of the *Advocate,* wrote Armstrong immediately:

"You brethren have stated your position time and again on these questions . . . I think it's time to ignore all such. They have tried hard to hurt you and Harding College. Have they done it? You know they have not. The harder they fight you, the more you grow. I think I know this brotherhood of ours—seventy-five percent of them are tired and disgusted with it (the fight against the colleges, etc.) I so much wish the heads of David Lipscomb College, Harding, and Abilene would ignore all such (meetings) and go on with your work." In a second letter the next day Hall wrote:

"As to going to Little Rock, you and Benson take it to the Lord in prayer and be governed by your own good judgment. Your situation is different from some of the others. But if you go, stay with that position you took in your early discussions of this question following your first statement. That position is invulnerable, and the brethren as a rule, can see it, will see it, and endorse it. But the best of all, God will."

We did attend the Little Rock meeting. At the noon luncheon a leader in the Fourth and State Street church said to me, "I'm sorry for Brother Armstrong."

"Why?" I asked.

"Because of what they are planning to do this afternoon," he replied.

This was my first alarm about a plot against him. He and I were both scheduled to speak in the afternoon on "Why We Need Our Colleges." Instead, the afternoon meeting opened with a direct attack on Armstrong. L. R. Wilson read a list of twelve charges against him, denouncing what he termed his erroneous teaching and demanding that he reply to the charges. All were the old complaints which he had answered in numerous articles in the *Gospel Advocate* and the *Firm Foundation*. To the repetition of such charges, like Jesus before the Sanhedrin, Armstrong felt it was useless to reply. Nothing he could say would satisfy his critics except a declaration that he would no longer fellowship Boll and his associates, and this he had repeatedly declared he could not conscientiously do.

When I saw he was making no answer, I could no longer remain silent. But as I arose, I saw him shake his head with a wry half-smile at the hopelessness of any reply. I pointed out, however, that all these charges had been answered again and again in various articles and publications, and that Armstrong had made clear that he did not agree with Boll in the ideas that were causing dissention.

Though Armstrong would not speak in his own defense, he did speak out in defense of another. Wilson read a statement from Dr. C. H. Roberson, head of the Bible department at Abilene, which seemed to indicate a belief in a future millennium, and turning to President Cox, he asked, "In the light of this statement, Brother Cox, do you plan to keep Brother Roberson in your faculty or will you dismiss him?"

"I will have to talk with Brother Roberson about it, to see what he meant," Cox replied.

"May I answer that question?" Armstrong interrupted, and Wilson nodded.

"Certainly, I would keep him if I were Brother Cox." Armstrong said. "And may I ask you in turn, who gave you and Brother Harper the authority to demand the dismissal of any teacher from Abilene Christian College? The faculty at Abilene are responsible to their board of trustees, not to any convention of preachers anywhere!"

That comment applied equally to the faculty at Harding College, and effectively ended Wilson's "inquisition." To change the temper of the meeting Rue Porter, a well-known minister from Missouri, arose and warmly praised the faithfulness and long service of Armstrong. Harper was visibly nettled and disappointed. He could not permit the meeting to close on such a note of harmony and good fellowship. So he arose and said, "These brethren have left the load all on me," then launched into another attack on Harding College with the old charges that had repeatedly been refuted.

Though the meeting did not accomplish its purpose, the pressure on all the preachers present was great. As John G. Reese, president of the board at Harding, finished his speech on "The Purpose of Christ's Second Coming," he publicly offered his resignation from the board of the college because he was being branded a "Boll sympathizer." He wanted to clear himself of all suspicion of being "lined up" with the Boll group. Harper immediately urged him to stay on the board and sent letters to influential men everywhere to write the board to retain Reese and give him their full support in lifting "the cloud of suspicion" and "in demanding the resignation of those hindering such a move and place in their stead men on whom rests no suspicion regarding the 'Boll Question,' either with the theory or with Boll, who is its chief apostle," and he urged that Boll be disfellowshipped.

To accomplish Harper's purpose the board would have had

to dismiss practically all the faculty as well as the board itself, for nobody could approve Harper's extreme position. Reese was in a hard situation, because what Sewell called the "religious politicians" could close many churches to him, but he had no wish to turn against Armstrong. A year later he wrote Armstrong a warm appreciation of his radio sermons: "We enjoy them so much. I think the type preaching you are doing will do much good."

During the Little Rock meeting C. R. Nichol had remarked to Armstrong, "The only trouble with you, brother, is that you are too friendly to R. H. Boll." But friendship was not the trouble. Armstrong loved M. C. Kurfees, Boll's bitter opponent, and others who were opposed to Boll, as much as he loved Boll. It was a matter, he felt, of treating men right.

Following the Little Rock meeting Armstrong wrote C. R. Nichol, "I wish I had an opportunity to talk over with you the Little Rock meeting and some developments since. I attended the first preachers' meeting in Oklahoma. Some thoughtful brethren then opposed such meetings as potential of the convention type. I have lived to see such meetings convene to 'put over' a move, something 'decided upon' by a group . . . "

Nichol replied, "As I now recall there was a council in the second century of the Christian era, and since then there have been many more. To attempt to recount the harm which has followed such meetings would require a tome of no small proportions. Some meetings have been called when the very purpose for which they were convened was wrong when proposed." This was clearly true of the Little Rock meeting.

In spite of his failure at Little Rock, Harper was not one to give up. Through Judson Woodbridge, minister of a church in Fort Smith, Arkansas, a meeting was arranged there on April 17, 1939. The attendants proved to be a picked group from over the state but included President Benson and me, Clem Z. Pool, then president of the college board, and T. H. Sherrill, an influential minister in Searcy and over the state. Armstrong was markedly left out with no invitation. Presuming the meeting was to build interest in the college in that area and unaware that Harper was back of it, we attended. Our eyes were quickly opened when Harper made a speech accusing Armstrong of premillennialism and urging his retirement on pension or with an arrangement to preach for some church. To our surprise Clem Z. Pool, the president of our board, whom Harper had evidently won over in advance, arose and agreed with the suggestion.

The charge of "premillennialism" was quickly refuted. Then Benson demanded bluntly: "Are you men ready to say, 'Armstrong, you have given your life to the school; you have carried it through the dark years when you had to go without salary to pay the other teachers; you have given it your life-blood; but now since it has become a great school, the enrollment increased, safety and permanence assured, and you can begin to enjoy the fruits of your long service, we intend to kick you out and take the school over ourselves. We didn't sacrifice to make it, but now since it is going well we want it.' Is this what you men mean?"

When faced with this picture of themselves Harper was silent, but after a moment he suggested keeping Armstrong but adding another man who would teach against premillennialism. He even offered to help raise his salary. The board at its next meeting voted unanimously on motion by H. H. Dawson that "under no conditions may any be added to the faculty of the college who is partly paid by any outside funds," and that Harper's suggestion in the Fort Smith meeting "be ignored."

It was surprising and regrettable that Brother Pool allowed himself for the moment to be so influenced. But in a letter of June 14, two months after the Fort Smith meeting, Pool made a formal statement:

To Whom It May Concern: I wish to state that as a special Bible student one year in Harding College, and since then for seven years as member and president of the board, I have been intimately associated with the school and with the Bible teaching. During all these years I have never known of any speculative teaching on unfulfilled prophecy in the school.

Every Bible teacher has expressed himself emphatically on the disputed premillennial theories and I have every reason to believe that their teaching on this question is perfectly safe. No group of teachers known to me have been more unselfishly devoted to the truth. Perhaps no man in the brotherhood has such fine influence on young men and women in molding their lives in harmony with Christian ideals as Brother J. N. Armstrong . . . It is because I know so well the men who handle the Bible, and have such close touch with their teaching, that I express my complete confidence in them and in the institution.

Armstrong was rightly indignant at the injustice of the Fort Smith meeting, and he wanted to believe that Woodbridge, a former student, was unaware of the plot, but he could not understand Woodbridge's insistence that it was all a "friendly act."

"Bring charges, try me, and exclude me without hearing me at all, and that too when my absence was planned! This surely was high-handed dealing. And you want me, Judson, to accept all this as a 'friendly act!' If you call this a 'friendly act,' fair dealing, Christian treatment, I leave it with you."

Willing to go the second mile, however, to pacify Harper, Armstrong suggested trying to get Dr. W. B. West from Pepperdine College, whom we had already discussed, as Professor of Ancient Languages and Associate Professor of Bible. When this suggestion was submitted to Harper he agreed to call off his fight against the college and so announced before audiences of more than five hundred at Little Rock and also in the college auditorium. As soon as his announcement was known, however, a storm of condemnation broke upon him from a handfull of his supporters in a preachers' meeting. The *Bible Banner* also declared it would never again turn its columns "over to someone who hits and runs," and accused him of "surrendering to save your scalp," and of "compromise and whitewash."

At this unexpected and withering condemnation by his former associates, Harper pleaded in an article in the *Firm*

Foundation, "Brethren, please don't crucify me!" In a second article he declared the agreement was not a compromise, not a whitewash. "It was but a 'shifting of battle grounds' to carry on the fight. We were hoping to get 'inside the camp' where the fighting could be at 'close range' and the 'bull's eye' more easily hit. It might have been a mistake, but it was an honest one, not a 'compromise nor whitewash.'"

Further down in the article he says he was hoping "we could work our way into the Bible department." From this confession Harper's agreement to end the fight was merely a ruse to place some one inside the faculty who would support him. He even suggested teaching some classes in the department himself and of being on the college board.

In response to our invitation, when Dr. West visited the college and also conferred with Harper in Little Rock, he declined to come. West had a secure position as head of the Bible department at Pepperdine, and with Harper's attitude no one could blame him for avoiding an unpleasant situation. The college had fulfilled its promise, however, in trying to get West, but in a further effort to conciliate Harper it did add Batsell Baxter to the Bible faculty, a man with wide experience as president of three different Christian colleges, whose "soundness" not even Harper could challenge.

But the addition of Baxter did not satisfy Harper, and misrepresentations continued to be created and circulated against Armstrong and against the college. It was reported that students who wanted to attend a debate on premillennialism at Fort Worth were threatened with expulsion. The fact was that, although the faculty felt missing all classes for a week was too high a price to hear a debate which they could later get in print, they not only permitted the boys to go, but excused all class absences. As Armstrong said, "We are not teaching a 'kid' school at Harding," and the decision to attend was left to the young men.

Armstrong's speeches over the radio and his letters answering questions were constantly misrepresented, so that he often hesitated to answer a letter. "Some things I have written in the last few years in letters and otherwise have been ruthlessly treated, and I have been made to say or mean what I did not say and never dreamed of saying, so that I am nearly afraid to put out anything lest I be abused."

Some one told Jesse P. Sewell that he had actually seen a statement signed by Armstrong that he believed Christ would return to earth, reign on a throne in Jerusalem, and direct a war with carnal weapons to conquer the world. In answer to Sewell's inquiry, Armstrong replied:

> Now, Brother Sewell, I am going to use some strong language. I do not know the man who made this statement or its equivalent, so what I am saying cannot be personal; but this man either is an outright liar, or he saw a forgery. He never saw a letter from me or a statement that had anything like this with my name to it unless he saw a letter written by some one else with my name forged. I never said or wrote this, or anything equivalent to it. I have never believed what this statement contains nor have I ever made or written anything like it. I have always said I was positively unable to agree with Brother Boll in his theory about "David's throne." I believe that Christ is now reigning on all the throne he will ever occupy on this earth. I do not believe he will use carnal weapons, nor have I ever uttered anything that could legitimately be construed to mean this; so that "good" brother either way, as I have said, a forged statement or he himself is guilty of a lie.

Friends all over the nation sympathized deeply with Armstrong in the relentless fight, but few felt they could speak out. In a letter, September 26, 1941, S. P. Pittman of David Lipscomb College said he did not want to become involved, but "I can't keep from feeling that some of us have been guilty in our silence, and that we should have boldly stated in the beginning of the heat and controversy that we will *not* stand for ostracizing and bitterness, that we will not make the question (premillennialism) a test of fellowship regardless of what the persecution may be. We've 'kinda' 'softsoaped' the thing, it seems."

And in a letter of January 7, 1957, Pittman wrote, "To me the persecution Armstrong received at the hands of far less worthy men caused him to shine more brightly."

G. C. Brewer stood courageously with Armstrong in the long struggle, but he also joked him about his lack of "self-advertising" at which so many of his antagonists were adept. In a letter of August 14, 1942, Brewer wrote, "I think you should contrive to get the news into the papers that *you baptized a Baptist preacher.* I did that two years ago, but I am rated as 'sound' on that point. I've debated with Bogard—that fixes it."

Armstrong had also debated with the Baptist "fire-eater" Nunnley many years ago, but caring nothing for "self-advertising" he did not proclaim it across the nation, and not even his family knew of the "Baptist preacher."

While the college was being so severely condemned Brewer humorously added in the same letter, "I feel like 'exposing' that college (Harding) for not 'norating' the fact that you gave G. H. P. Showalter (editor of the *Firm Foundation*) the LL. D. degree. Don't you know it was published just two years ago that *no true gospel preacher would accept* such an honor? And it was even said, 'Imagine G. H. P. Showalter or C. R. Nichol accepting such a degree!' Send a news item to the *Bible Banner* stating that G. H. P. Showalter did accept!"

The bitterness of the attacks against Armstrong and the gross misrepresentations irritated, but in no way embittered him. In the homiletics class a student asked him about the viciousness of some of the attacks, and after a moment's thought Armstrong said, "Whether it is in the pulpit, the press, or in private conversation, a preacher ought to be careful never to say anything that he will later regret as long as he lives."

He was thinking of some who had made statements about him that they later regretted, but his comments about others even in the height of controversy were usually generous and kind. When James M. Laird, who had once criticized him, was asked to hold a meeting in Searcy, he wrote Armstrong, afraid of how he would be received. Armstrong replied: "I want to say that in regard to any matter that ever came between you and me that it is all forgotten and the slate is clean. I have no attitude toward you but the very best, and we shall be glad to welcome you to Searcy . . . So forget all the past that was unpleasant and come along and you will be received with open arms."

Harper's fight, however, continued as long as Armstrong lived, and when W. W. Otey published a brief appreciation of him after his death, Harper wrote urging him to retract his commendation because he felt it reflected on him. He was unable personally to criticize the statement because Showalter, Otey wrote, would not allow Harper to attack Armstrong in the *Firm Foundation* while he was living and of course would not permit it after his death.

To Harper's remonstrance Otey replied:

> Dear Brother Harper: On first reflection I was inclined to write you at length in reply to your last letter. On more mature reflection I will write briefly . . . Our situation is this: I made a brief statement of my appreciation of Brother Armstrong which you asked me to state in the *Firm Foundation* is not true. I still believe my statement true. You have attacked him bitterly and persistently for years, and many who are not premillennialists have a suspicion that it was part of a concerted plan by a number, to force Armstrong out of the college and elevate one of their choice to that position. I say many have suspected this. Now since he is dead you still want to pursue him with bitter attacks even to the grave, and ask me to aid in the attack. Once and for all, I have never, and never shall, become a collaborationist in this sort of unholy work. I did not agree with him in everything, but his memory will still be held dear when some of his bitter enemies who attacked him unjustly will be forgotten.

Because of great differences in nature, background, and experience it is difficult for people to understand each other, and it is possible that Harper could never understand the magnanimous spirit of Armstrong, who could differ radically with others and still love them as brethren. These unhappy events have long passed, and no doubt feelings and attitudes have been tempered by time. But to understand Armstrong's long struggle for freedom, tolerance, and love the reader must know the things that once happened.

Although for years Armstrong bore the brunt of the extremists' attacks, hundreds of church leaders believed as he did. He did not agree with Boll, he was not interested in the millennium, but he was intensely concerned about the unity of the church and the liberty men should have in Christ.

In reviewing his article "Free Speech and Fearless Teachers," John T. Lewis had implied that Armstrong's ideas on the millennium were so vitiating and destructive that he was unworthy of fellowship, that the difference between Armstrong and Boll was merely the difference "between tweedledum and tweedledee."

In reply Armstrong reminded him that he had stated again and again that his position was about the same as that held by James A. Harding and Dr. T. W. Brents:

I conclude that you judge the difference between J. A. Harding's position and R. H. Boll's position on the millennium is the difference between "tweedledum and tweedledee." If so, this brings us face to face with this reality: If James A. Harding were living and were preaching on the millennium as he did in his day, you brethren would be in a determined fight to exclude him from the fellowship of the faithful . . . You know, and I know, that these two men (Harding and Brents) preached their sermons on the millennium when they got ready . . . and nobody said them "Nay." But now it turns out that the difference between their position on the millennium and R. H. Boll's is the difference between "tweedledum and tweedledee." . . . While I have believed about the same as Brents and Harding on the millennium, there is quite a difference . . . They persisted in teaching their convictions, and I have never felt that it was important enough to teach; hence, in my forty-five years of active preaching I have never spoken on the subject.

In a second letter to Lewis, Armstrong made clear again his only interest:

I hold that the unity of God's people is so important that it is sinful to break fellowship and make division in the body of Christ over differences that may arise among brethren who hold the common faith and who are faithful to the commandments of God and whose lives are worthy—differences that do not hinder obedience to Christ and that do not change in any way the work and worship of the church—differences in which nobody's conscience is bound by the other's teaching, but each one is left free to think, believe, and act as he sees God's word leads him.

Armstrong then reminded Lewis of H. Leo Boles' statement at the conclusion of his debate with Boll, that they held enough in common "to fellowship each other as brethren," and that their differences "do not keep me from esteeming him very highly as a brother in Christ Jesus."

The freedom in Christ emphasized by Paul to the Galatians, Corinthains and Romans, was the perfect answer to the prayer of Jesus for a unity that would prove to the world that God had sent him. It was a unity that would combine into a universal fellowship and brotherhood all of every nation and tongue who were obedient to the Will of God. This had been the achievement of the early Christians, no matter how great the differences in their backgrounds. It had been the plea of Thomas and Alexander Campbell, Barton W. Stone, and scores of others who had urged men everywhere to give up special names, doctrines, and traditions not clearly based upon the Scriptures—traditions which had caused and cemented enmity and division among believers in Christ. It was a plea to accept as the only authority in religion what Christ and his Apostles had taught, speaking only where the Bible spoke and being silent where the Bible was silent, and never imposing human opinion on others. It was this freedom and unity which were now threatened by men who had lost the world-wide vision of the Christ.

To maintain such freedom and unity, Armstrong insisted, would require a large measure of love and tolerance, not only of teaching, but of practices which do not affect any one's obedience to Christ. In an interesting correspondence with W. E. Brightwell, News Editor of the *Gospel Advocate,* Armstrong had asked him to define how much error Christians may have before he would reject them for fellowship. He reminded Brightwell that Paul knew that the law of

Moses requiring animal sacrifices and the observance of the Sabbath and other days had been done away and that Christians were no longer bound by such commandments; yet Paul did not condemn those at Rome who were still observing days, and at Jerusalem, at the urging of James, he himself offered animal sacrifices and paid for the sacrifices being offered by others—fifteen sacrifices in all. This was to prove to the Jews at Jerusalem that he also "walked orderly keeping the law."

He asked Brightwell if he would fellowship anybody today who taught that Christians should offer animal sacrifices or keep the Sabbath day.

> Both of us agree that the oneness of the church is of prime importance—second only to truth itself . . . So I am anxious for you to come to the problem: how shall we deal with these differences in a church not creed-bound; in a church in which every one must be left free to study God's word for himself; in a church into which is to be received even the weak, the ignorant, and the backward—"but not for decision of scruples."

Brightwell, in explaining the "observance of days," and Paul's offering sacrifices at Jerusalem said that "revelation came little by little," that the "understanding of people was always 'progressive' and that sometimes their understandings were 'a few steps behind revelation.'"

> "Just so," Armstrong replied, "and those 'few steps' make room for all the differences of which I am speaking. Paul's case is a most excellent example of delayed understanding."

But he reminded Brightwell that James's understanding was also a "few steps behind revelation," for he not only approved the offering of animal sacrifices, but effectively pressed this false teaching on Paul. But most important of all in this affair was the attitude of Jehovah:

> If no Christian in all the country understood that it was false teaching to urge the offering of animal sacrifices upon the church, Jehovah himself knew it. Yet He stood by and said nothing while his Apostle enforced, pressed, his false teaching on others.

> Now one of my questions to you was: "Did the Lord himself receive and acknowledge as his children these Christians . . . in spite of their errors and false teach-

ing?" In answer to this question you say: "The Lord was patient with them." Fine, if you mean by this that Jehovah accepted them into his communion and fellowship with all this bundle of errors in doctrine and practice, and waited for their understanding to catch up with revelation. But later you say: "I cannot endorse any man who teaches men to practice the sacrifices of the law;" yet, God did endorse these preachers; with his perfect understanding, he did accept his church . . .

Certainly it "was God's affair." But do you mean by this that God's patience here is no example to us and that, though God in his patience, with the full light of the gospel, fellowshipped and endorsed a people, we should not fellowship and endorse the same people? Had you been there with "the full light of the gospel," would you have refused to endorse God's action and have led a party to disfellowship and to reject James and Paul instead of waiting for their understanding to catch up with revelation, as God did?

As these thousands of Christians at Jerusalem came into a fuller knowledge of the truth, you will not contend that, in making those "few steps in which they were behind revelation," they all made them with the same speed; so, before this church was thoroughly delivered from its false teaching and practice it, no doubt, had the two groups—some that kept on offering animal sacrifices, and some who had learned better and had dropped the practice. Hence, only by being "patient" with one another, as God had earlier been with them all, could they have maintained the unity of the Spirit.

Verily, Brother Brightwell, this divine record of the Jerusalem church, of God's patience with it, is illuminating. It gives us an example of a church emerging from error, from early training and education, into the glorious light and liberty of the gospel. The members of every church today are emerging from ignorance, from early training, from the religion of their fathers—even from the false teaching of gospel preachers who, like James, were struggling for light while teaching the best they knew. The conditions call, not only for the patience of God; but also for the patience of those who have been more highly favored and in consequence have emerged the faster. Certainly Paul did not violate his conscience in being patient with Sabbath keepers; he was simply following God's example.

In contrast with the offering of animal sacrifices by Paul, James, and perhaps hundreds of others at Jerusalem, and in contrast with Christians at Rome and through Galatia who still insisted on keeping the Jewish Sabbath and other days according to the law, the errors of R. H. Boll about an obscure reference to a millennium in Revelation 20 seemed utterly insignificant. Yet a small group of determined extremists were urging Christians everywhere to disfellowship all who held such views or who refused to go to the same extreme in disfellowshipping them. It was this issue that Armstrong proposed discussing with Brightwell: "Resolved: That the teaching of R. H. Boll, stated and defined by himself, on the millennium, on David's throne, on the Kingdom of God, on the second coming of Christ, and on the return of the Jews is so dangerous that it hinders obedience to Christ and his gospel, and so changes and modifies the faith and practice of a congregation in which the teaching is done that it ceases to be a Church of Christ, worthy of the fellowship of the faithful."

This proposition Brightwell refused to discuss, saying, "I have not suggested the premillennialists be disfellowshipped, nor has anybody else, so far as I know."

To this denial of disfellowshipping, S. H. Hall wrote, "I was amazed when I read (that) . . . Brightwell undoubtedly knows too much to make a statement of this kind. The fact of the business is the whole trouble that now exists over these questions grows out of the fact that they want to make it a test of fellowship . . . If Brightwell will not affirm this proposition why does he not stop this forever trying to make it a test of fellowship and even making it such a test as to want to disfellowship all of us who will not make it a test of fellowship."

In a letter of February 5, 1937, however, Brightwell said, "I have already agreed to affirm that fellowship should be withheld from those who teach this doctrine." But the discussion apparently did not go beyond Armstrong's "Open Letters."

In all the long struggle beginning in 1924 and ending only with his death in 1944, Armstrong was not interested in a defense of Boll or of any millennial doctrine—pre-, post-, or non-. He was interested only in the unity of the church and the freedom in Christ to learn and to teach.

At the invitation of Mr. Murch and others of the Christian church a series of "Unity Meetings" was arranged in the late thirties to see if the Christian churches and the churches of Christ might resolve the differences which had divided them and might all again be united as a single body. When Armstrong and Benson agreed to speak on the program in May, 1938, G. C. Brewer wrote, "I told Brother Benson that he would make a mistake if he lined up with (Claude) Witty in these unity conferences. I have not changed my mind one particle and I think you and he had better stay out of these meetings." Brewer himself refused to speak on the program. Armstrong had little hope that any significant results would come, but he could not refuse an invitation to plead for the unity for which Christ prayed.

"How can we turn a deaf ear to men of brains, learning, and success," he asked, "who come to us and want to sit down and find a way to work and worship with us? The way in which the Witty-Murch undertaking is being treated by those who have stood for the unity of all believers is humiliating to me. The spirit—'you fellows went away and if you want to come back, get on the mourners' bench for a time and the door's open to you'—will never save sinners."

His appeal at the Detroit meeting for unity on the principle of speaking where the Bible speaks and remaining silent where the Bible is silent was well received. Daniel Sommer, sitting on a front seat, was the first to congratulate him warmly, all the old antagonism over the Christian college now long forgotten.

Though the "Unity Meetings" seemed to produce no immediate results, Armstrong had at least contributed his "mite."

It is difficult to evaluate with any accuracy the results of Armstrong's long fight for freedom of conscience, freedom to learn and to teach, and for Christian forbearance over differences of view. It was disheartening at times, for hundreds who believed as he and G. C. Brewer, S. H. Hall, and H. Leo Boles did were afraid to speak out. The unchristian attitudes were reflected chiefly in the religious journals, which in turn scared into submission local leaders and preachers. In a letter to Armstrong, February 3, 1937, S. H. Hall commented on the state of the religious journals:

> It seems that our papers have lost all sense of justice and fairness. I've tried and tried and tried till my soul is almost worn out to get Leon [McQuiddy, business manager of the *Gospel Advocate*] to take a firm hand and see that our paper here stays on a high plane. But in spite of all this he lets the old heads slash at this one and that one, and then they edit your replies and make you say what they want you to say in reply. Along with this there is an alliance between two of the writers and Jim Allen and his paper, and the things they cannot get said in the *Advocate* they get Jim to say.

Hall informed Armstrong that all needed funds had been offered to buy a controlling interest in one of the existing papers or to start a new one, and asked his judgment about what was best to do. "If a new paper is started or even one bought, we would want a hundred percent cooperation on the part of you and your associates."

Later Armstrong attended a meeting in Nashville with G. C. Brewer, S. H. Hall, E. H. Ijams, president of David Lipscomb College, Ben Harding, member of the Lipscomb board, E. W. McMillan, Clinton Davidson of New Jersey, Jesse P. Sewell, James F. Cox, president of Abilene Christian College, and perhaps others, to discuss plans for buying or starting a new paper which would be fair to the colleges and kind in the discussion of all religious issues. The decision of the group was to purchase the *Christian Leader* of Cincinnati, enlarge it to twenty-four pages, and attempt to make it a model of fair, Christian journalism.

"It is the purpose," Hall wrote, "to give a paper that you can hand to your neighbors and friends. There is to be no fighting or gouging of different writers. It is to teach firmly and steadfastly the truth. Issues are to be discussed, not men."

Clinton Davidson had agreed to furnish the money for the new enterprise. To continue the publication of the *Leader* from Cincinnati, where it had long been published seemed wise, but Armstrong was uneasy about obtaining subscriptions from the South. He pointed out that when *The Way* was combined with the *Leader,* Southern subscribers dropped off and it was difficult to obtain others south of the Mason and Dixon line.

With MacMillan as managing editor, A. B. Lipscomb, I. B. Bradley, and James L. Lovell contributing editors, and Jesse P. Sewell, editor of the Sunday School Literature, the *Leader* set a new high standard in religious journalism, but financial obligations compelled Davidson to relinquish his support.

The change in the *Leader,* however, was only one of the developments in the improvement of the religious papers. After the Wright affair (see appendix) there was a significant improvement in the *Firm Foundation,* and, as Brother Otey has said, Showalter apparently refused to accept personal attacks on good men. A change also came in the *Gospel Advocate* with the appointment of B. C. Goodpasture as editor. Armstrong was pleased with this appointment, but felt that Goodpasture would not have been made editor had it not been for the change in the *Christian Leader.*

With the passing of years the great guns that once thundered in the long and bitter war are now silent, and their echoes have grown fainter and far away. Many of the present generation are unaware that such a battle for unity and freedom was ever waged, and that the hearts of strong men bled with pity at what was happening to a people trying to reflect the love of Christ to a world filled with hate and fear. The wounds are not completely healed, but with time and patience we may hope the freedom and the unity for which Armstrong earnestly longed and for which Jesus prayed may yet be attained. As new issues arise to trouble the church, as they inevitably do and will, perhaps this glimpse at one of the bitterest of the long struggles for freedom in Christ will lead a few "hot heads and cold hearts" to see the wisdom of the healing patience of God.

Chapter 17

PEACE AT LAST

WITH THE PERSISTENT, often bitter attacks against him through his long fight for Christian liberty, it is amazing that Armstrong could always remain calm and sweet tempered. In a letter to John T. Lewis he said of the effort to oust him from the college, "It does not trouble me." He was never concerned for himself but for the church.

He repeatedly told students, "Happiness does not grow on trees, nor is it found on street corners, but must grow in the heart." Often in the morning he came by our house and greeted Gretchen Hill, who was preparing breakfast, with a teasing, "Are you up so early this morning, Gretchen?" Teachers who met him on the campus, in his immaculately white suit, remarked that his warm greeting always made the day brighter.

Naturally, after guiding the college successfully through years that saw the collapse of many institutions, he was concerned about its future. Since the board ultimately determines the spirit and character of an institution, he was uneasy about putting men of wealth on the board who had never attended a Christian school. For years some of the faculty had served on the board because they knew better than any one else what a Christian college should be. There had never been a distinct separation of faculty and administration; all had worked together as a unit. Now, new trends emphasized a separation of faculty and administration, with different measures of authority assigned to each. Because it seemed undesirable for members of the faculty to serve on the board, it was agreed that a certain percentage of the board should always be chosen from former graduates who knew the spirit and ideals of the school. Since Armstrong's death, however, this requirement has apparently been dropped. Writing to Everett Evans in 1940, Armstrong said: "Our work here is progressing nicely. It is hard to keep a work in harmony with the ideals of the old school. Sometimes I get discouraged at things that appear to mean we are slipping in holding up the standards we used to have, but we are working at it."

He was opposed to involving the college in political actions. He was willing for faculty members to follow any political course they chose, but he objected to aligning the college institutionally with political groups. In a letter of 1943 he said: "We should not do wrong to get money . . . Certainly we all approved of Clinton's (Davidson's) original plan to interest men in Harding College. But did this mean to turn the campaign into a defense of the U. S. Government, to regulate its tax system, even to support a political group? Who dreamed it would lead to this? . . . Money is not worth this much, as I see it . . . I repeat, Harding College was not established to save some form of government or to reform it."

He was discouraged about the decrease of enrollment in 1938 and the lack of advertising in 1941. "But why should I worry," he commented. "As Mr. Kraft (of Kraft cheese fame) said, 'I have shot my bolt.'" Nevertheless he did worry, for giving young people a Christian education depended on getting them to the school.

He was deeply disappointed that the college did not arrange financially for the children of Will and Delia Short, former students and for years missionaries in Africa. Mrs.

friend of missionaries, helping raise their support, and furnishing money for emergencies that the churches were not immediately prepared to meet. In a letter to Homer Rutherford, Armstrong lamented the "bitter and distressing attacks on Janes' Will, which had appeared in the religious journals,"

"Showalter has been nicer and kinder," he wrote. "I am sorry Janes thought the doctrine (premillennialism) was so important, but he did, and again it was his right."

Armstrong's weekly radio programs through these last years were heard by thousands from distances of more than seven hundred miles. John Maple wrote from Kansas, "I think they are too good not to have them in print, and if you will put them in pamphlet form I will help bear the expense. The world is starving for just such kind of food, and we ought to send it to them."

Armstrong's long struggle against bigotry and prejudice, his fight for freedom of conscience and for unity through love and tolerance rather than through coercion aroused bitter enmity, but also won the loyalty and devotion of good hearts everywhere. His personal qualities inspired confidence. He was frank and open and had an astonishing measure of good judgment and realistic foresight. These qualities, combined with a keen sense of right, helped him to make wise and good decisions often baffling to those who opposed him. A minor instance was his letter to a Luis Gomez. Armstrong had never heard of the "pigeon drop racket," a treasure to be divided with one who would furnish the money to obtain it, a swindle which the government later reported had victimized scores of people eager for a "fast buck." But he wrote Gomez: "I am ready at any time to help anybody out of trouble that ought to be helped out, but with no more information than you give me in your letter, I certainly would not want to be involved in an effort of this kind. If you are really honest and sincere and unjustly imprisoned, I should be delighted to aid you without compensation, but unless you are willing to give me more information about your trunk, where it is, why you are in bankruptcy with all that money stored away in your trunk deposited in the United States somewhere, I am forced to wonder. If you are justly imprisoned, then I have no desire to interfere with the lawful proceedings."

Needless to say, he never heard from Gomez again.

Armstrong's keen observation and wit were often a surprise and a delight. J. R. Waldrum tells that when Armstrong in a meeting at Tom Bean, Texas, was staying in the home of the local preacher Barrett Scott, he and his wife drove up in a car. Scott said, "There's a couple wanting to get married." But as Waldrum got out of the car and started toward the house, letting his wife get out as best she could and follow, Armstrong said, "That couple's been married a long time."

Though he was always kind, he could also be firm in discipline. Waldrum relates that "On one occasion I quit the college club. Others were thinking of quitting. My action was about to disrupt the working of the club plan (by which students obtained meals at cost). He did not hesitate to call me into his office and rebuke me severely. I accepted the rebuke and thanked him for the advice he gave me. He was slow to rebuke and exercise discipline, but when necessary he gave it in a way that corrected the error without incurring the wrath of the student."

Armstrong's natural inclination was to agree with people whenever possible, to be kind and unselfishly helpful. He shrank from disagreements, but when he considered issues of truth or right to be involved, he could also be a determined fighter. R. C. Bell once remarked, "I would hate to get involved in a fight with him." He had an uncanny way of remembering everything an opponent ever said, wrote, or did. When Virgil Bentley once was being severely criticized about an article he had written for the student paper, Armstrong called him in and said he knew nothing about the problem of which he had written nor of its merits, "But sometimes pressures can be built up that are hard to resist. I don't believe in causing trouble if you can help it, but if you really have convictions about the matter and feel that something should be done, then stick to your guns and don't be intimidated."

He encouraged students, instead of becoming discouraged and quitting, to turn defeat into victory, and told the story of John McDonough's falling in love with a beautiful girl in New Orleans who refused to marry him. "I'll be remembered when you are forgotten," McDonough declared. At his death he left his whole estate to the city, the interest from which had built thirty-four "John McDonough Schools" in New Orleans.

His charm and fairness won even the prejudiced. C. W. Bradley tells that before he entered Harding College, his uncle warned him against Armstrong and he came with prejudice against him, but his first day in the Bible class won him completely. Armstrong's sincerity, frankness, and interest in students were irresistible to those who knew him well. He possessed a large measure of the old-fashioned courtesies which came from simple kindness and consideration for others. He always addressed girls as "Miss Mary" or "Miss Jane." In dismissing the young men at the close of the "social hour," he would say, "Good night, young men. Just mark it 'to be continued.'"

He often said it cost nothing to be courteous and kind, and these were among the most beautiful qualities to develop. He told of the congressman who invited a farmer constituent to dinner in Washington, and when the old fellow drank the water from his "finger bowl," the congressman drank his also, and of the old couple on the train who, to the amusement of other passengers, were trying to shield themselves from the sun by holding their hands over their eyes, until a young man stepped over and said, "If you will pardon me, I'll pull the blind down for you."

He was grateful for even the smallest kindnesses, and J. D. Bales records that a speech Armstrong made on gratitude one day so touched him that he surprised and delighted his grandmother by a letter of appreciation for all she had done for him. Bales was not aware that she was on her death bed, but the letter made her so happy she showed it to all who visited her.

Armstrong was a great believer in heredity, and encouraged young people to look carefully at the qualities of each other before deciding on a world-without-end contract. One day he and his grandson, about eight, were trying to drive a calf back into the lot, and the boy said, "Grand-daddy, that calf'll never make a good milk cow."

"Why, Kern?" he asked.

"Look at its background. It hasn't got the right heredity," the child replied.

Despite heredity, however, he often declared that the difference between people is not their stock and blood, for a man can fight his grandfather and overcome heredity. It is not their wealth or poverty, for great men have come from both the rich and the poor. It is not even their mental qualities. "The difference between people lies in their wants. Some are idlers, drift with the stream, and are satisfied with little. Others are dreamers, with visions others never see. It is the men and women who see things that are not, things that seem impossible to others, who make the nation. The mother sees in her boy what no one else sees and works and sacrifices to help him change the vision to reality. The great teacher sees possibilities in her students that they themselves have never dreamed of."

He believed in equality for all men. "It seems that from the beginning God did not intend for man to exercise authority over man . . . and it is only when men depart from God's law that they can exercise dominion over their fellowmen. We on this campus constitute a little world all our own. There are no classes, cliques, clans, or exclusive clubs. There is no 'better than thou' spirit. One teacher years ago declined to go with one of the most attractive girls because 'she is a working girl.' But he was an exception. Working girls and boys are held in as much esteem as others. Many are leaders in all the student activities, among the most popular. We try to follow the ideal that 'He that would be greatest among you, let him be your servant.'"

He had the same feeling for the colored races. He contributed frequently to a Negro college in Mississippi and spoke to the students at Shorter College in Little Rock, encouraging them to educate themselves and prepare for lives of constructive service. "Your hope as a people lies in being yourselves. Develop yourselves and your race to be clean in heart, for 'As a man thinketh so is he.' Establish high standards for your homes, and educate your children to be honest, to want to work, to be independent, to prepare themselves for useful service."

Back in 1916 he had seen the evils of the migrations North. "It is bad for the colored race to move to the North and worse for him to move into the cities. He is ostracized as a skilled employee in Northern cities even more than in Southern.

"I was born and reared in Tennessee, and of Southern parents. Father was a Democrat, one that 'scratcheth not the ticket.' And if I had any prejudice regarding the slave question, it would be wholly Southern. But God has taught me that a Christian cannot be a partisan; that he must know no race, color, or section; that he must love *men, all men;* that God's child must be like his Father, no respecter of persons. So I have interest, much interest, in the advancement of every race of men on the earth; especially does my heart go out to the needy in our own country."

He condemned the laws passed against Japanese landholders in California and Washington during World War II. "These laws are constitutional, but are they Christian? I mean no criticism of the law-making bodies of the Pacific coast. But I am calling attention to the fact that a Christian cannot be true to his Lord and at the same time be responsible for such discrimination against men just because they are yellow, or belong to another race. Christ died for the Japanese just as truly as he died for Americans."

Letters from friends and former students brought happiness in these last years. Boys wrote back from the army.

"I was so young when I came to Harding," Jimmie Frazee wrote, "and my father died before I knew him. You naturally have taken his place with me. I do want you to realize that I sincerely appreciate all that you have done for me. The older I get, the more thankful I am that you were so kind and patient with me."

"To you I am just one of the many boys who 'used to be there,'" wrote Bill Stokes from somewhere on the war front, "but you are just as close to my heart as when I

was right under your wing. The inspiration and guidance
you gave me stands firmly embedded—right where you put
it—undisturbed . . . Those were the four happiest years
of my life. Of course I have happier ones ahead. In years
to come you will see in Harding College a Bill Stokes
again—this time he will be a Junior. This is speculation."
But Bill's speculation proved true, and Bill, Jr., finished
at Harding also.

James F. Patton wrote of the two happy years he had
spent at Harding:

> Seldom a day passes that something does not remind
> me of those good old days. Even the work there seemed
> like taking a vacation from life and being a while in
> heaven. Harding is a good school and probably always
> will be, but it never will be just the same after you are
> gone. Your sincere advice, perfect example of a Christian
> life, and unusual capacity for understanding the prob-
> lems of youth have made you the most loved and cher-
> ished memory that I have carried away from Harding,
> and I am sure I am voicing the opinion of hundreds of
> other students.

W. W. Otey, who had once inclined to Daniel Sommer's
opposition to Christian education, had become a firm friend,
and in a letter in these last years, he expressed his devotion:

> I sincerely assure you that I have long held you in
> that Christian esteem accorded to few in my long life.
> I have regarded you as one of the men of my acquaint-
> ance who were clean in heart and life, trustful of our
> Father, and willing to differ in some measure from
> others and still regard them as brethren in the Lord.
>
> You have served the cause of truth long and dili-
> gently. You have given your heart and life as few have
> done, literally wearing out your body and mind and
> asking less for your earthly reward than most men. I
> have no fear about your reward over there.

After his death countless tributes expressed the gratitude
of friends for the qualities that had so deeply impressed
them. R. N. Gardner, who had known him both as a student and as a fellow teacher since 1896, wrote:

> What has appealed to me most in his life was that
> he faithfully and persistently sought first the kingdom

of God. His whole heart was centered in things spiritual and eternal. His faith in the wisdom and righteousness of such a course was so strong that he never wavered from it. Hardships, adversities, discouraging circumstances nor want never obscured his vision nor swerved him from his course.

Mrs. Mary Shepherd French, J. W. Shepherd's daughter, who had known him from her childhood and had taught with him at Cordell, wrote:

His spiritual life and teaching are one of the very richest blessings of my life. He has made the lives of hundreds rich, and his value in God's kingdom was far greater than we can ever estimate. In his passing Harding College suffered the very greatest loss it has ever or probably ever can suffer again. The whole brotherhood is greatly weakened by his passing.

Miss De Nola Freeman, whose father A. E. Freeman, a prominent minister who served on the board when Armstrong was president at Cordell, wrote shortly after Armstrong's death:

Except my own father I think he was the kindest and best person I ever knew. I can see that thoughtful, tolerant, and sometimes amused smile that he nearly always had. He likely had more influence and was better loved than any other teacher in the colleges during the past forty years.

F. W. Mattox, Professor of Bible and Dean of Students during Armstrong's last years, and later President of Lubbock Christian College, said:

For five years I sat in his classes. Many are the times my soul aspired to greater heights at the inspiration of his stirring speeches. He was a great teacher. Many will say that he has been the moving spirit of the Bible school work in our generation. Harding College could not have existed without him. He was its spirit. When the criticisms grew bitter, he would say, "We must work ourselves over and keep our hearts right." He was always ready to accept all the truth on any question, and wanted the whole truth to be seen on both sides of a debatable question.

T. Q. Martin, a prominent minister of the gospel, who had been a student of his at the Nashville Bible School, wrote: "He always prayed as if he had one hand in the hand of God."

S. P. Pittman, who was formerly a student of his at the Nashville Bible School and later Professor of Bible at David Lipscomb College, wrote:

I doubt that anyone trained and tutored by J. A. Harding achieved what Brother Armstrong did. His silent influence was far reaching. To my mind the success of Harding College was due for the most part to J. N. Armstrong . . .

Wade Ruby, who was a graduate of Harding College and later Professor of English at George Pepperdine College, said:

I do not sorrow at his passing, but glory in his great life of service and in the beauty and triumph of his faith. I know of no one like him left behind. I especially admired his courage. I have come to know that the number of the fearless is indeed small . . . I only regret that many times many of us let Brother Armstrong suffer too much alone instead of rising with indignation to join him in the defense of Christian liberty, of the freedom of men in Christ.

T. H. Sherrill, a student and a prominent minister, who stood staunchly by him during the last persecutions, testified:

He had the best conception of New Testament teaching I have ever heard. His appreciation of its richness and of the spirit of the Christ was too full for the majority of the members of the church. He was great in every way! . . . We loved him beyond words. There is no way to tell how we leaned on his Christian greatness. May his love of principle live on in us! His was the most beautiful life we have ever seen by mere man!

J. C. Shewmaker, a graduate of Harding who has since served for years as a teacher and missionary in Africa, wrote:

I appreciate very much his ability to teach Bible truths with firm conviction and at the same time not force his convictions and conclusions upon his students. He did not try to make his conscience the conscience of his students.

S. F. Timmerman, another graduate of Harding, who later became a missionary in Belgium and later still among the French in Quebec, remembered:

> . . . His cordial friendliness with the lowliest freshman in his classes, his sympathetic concern for the personal problems of his students, his cheerful smile when pressed by his own burdens and anxieties. I remember the kindly manner in which he presented lessons from the Bible, yet coupled with fiery indignation when he felt that some principle of truth or justice was being trampled upon. He was to me the essence of a truly spiritual man.

Dr. Houston T. Karnes, who taught with Armstrong at Harding in 1935-36, and has served on the Harding Board of Trustees and as president of the board for many years, wrote:

> If the author of the Hebrew letter were writing today, Brother Armstrong would undoubtedly be listed with the great heroes of faith. I count myself fortunate to have been with him, even though for a short time. I am a better man for the experience, and I shall always cherish and use the words of wisdom he passed on to me. One remark has been especially helpful to me in my work with young men. It was, in effect, never make a rule which you cannot enforce, and never see everything that takes place.

Houston Prather, who was at Harding during Armstrong's last years and who did not know him at the height of his powers, expressed what many others have said in different words: "There will never be another man like Brother Armstrong. In the pulpit and in the chapel hall, many times under the spell of his voice the roof seemed to vanish and God himself stood in our midst."

The summer of 1941 Armstrong spent with the church at Huntsville, Alabama. It was a full schedule: Sunday morning service, Sunday night service broadcast, Tuesday night men's meeting, Wednesday afternoon women's Bible class, Wednesday evening prayer meeting, and Saturday night broadcast of the Sunday school lesson. Later he preached for a second congregation on Sunday evenings also.

Mrs. Armstrong had gone on to visit the Paines in Atlanta, and wrote him about playing flinch till midnight.

"That reminds me," Armstrong wrote her, "of a good many years ago, when Leon (Harding) and company played flinch down at the Roberson house at Bowling Green all night. That created quite a commotion; somebody thought it was awful. But they were young people, but for 'old people' to play all night, or most of it, is too bad. I don't wonder that you couldn't sleep when you went to bed—your conscience is still functioning!"

The first Saturday evening when he went to the radio station to review the Sunday School lesson, everything was lighted up, the machinery running, but no one was there. At 7:45 a fellow came in and looked surprised, as if to ask, "What do you want?" When Armstrong explained that he had come to broadcast the Sunday School lesson, the man said, "Oh!" Then after glancing at the clock, he said, "I'm sorry. You come back next Saturday evening."

"This is a 'bum' station," Armstrong concluded. "It is in an unoccupied dwelling that looks inside like a barn. If he can broadcast from that studio, then it takes no preparation, and the great studios waste a lot of money, I'm thinking."

He roomed in a good boarding house, but had some difficulty with meals. "I just can't eat vegetables enough to thrive on. The vegetables here are good, but I can't eat quantities." He had never been fond of vegetables nor lightbread. A depot agent in Kansas, seeing he was from Tennessee, once asked him, "How do you put up with this western lightbread?"

"I just endure it when I can't get biscuits," he replied. This was a Southern boarding house and they did have biscuits, eggs, and fried chicken, which were favorite foods.

When Robert Neil came by he wrote, I surely was glad to see him. Anybody that you love and that loves you and the Lord looks good to you in a new town like this." He was always warmly fond of friends, and when Mrs. Armstrong was going to Valdosta with the Paines, he wrote her to greet all his friends, "Just tell them all, anybody that shows up, that I'd like to hug and kiss 'em all."

A sudden storm on June 24 cut off all lights in the city,

the house got dark as night at lunch time, and several trees were blown down. "It beat me out of my piece of pie! . . . Everybody left the dining room—lots of excitement. It never did scare me. It was just a straight wind." He had lived in Oklahoma where twisters really meant business!

On June 29 he became suddenly ill. "When I arose to dress I found myself deathly sick at the stomach. I could walk only by staggers. Three times I tried to dress and lay back on the bed. I finally got back to the bathroom and managed to shave by leaning against something. I drank some water and at once it came back. I thought it would surely pass off so I could preach, but in vain did I wait. At 8:30 I decided I'd be unable to go to church, so I called Mr. Terry in the next room, and he was out. This meant I was alone in the apartment and no phone. I dressed enough to stagger across the hall to Mrs. Harris' room, and asked her son to call Brother Chambers. Brother Chambers said they would manage things. I rolled back in bed for the morning, and I thought for the day. About 11:00 I was feeling better, and I threatened to dress and go to church and preach, but I backed out before I got my shoes on. But I mustered up courage enough to preach at night, and got by all right. I had a bad night—didn't sleep till about two in the morning."

He dropped his knife while opening a bottle of medicine, heard it hit the floor, but could find it nowhere. The maid who came in to clean the room looked and could not find it.

"I told her I believed the room was haunted," he wrote home. "Pataway will have to come down and find it for me." Pataway from childhood was always the "finder" for anything lost in the Armstrong home.

On July 4 he wrote home, "A chemical plant, a war plant, has just been located here. It means an investment of $47,000,000. The people are wild about it! We surely are fools! It will bring everything to Huntsville in the way of crime and immorality. But it will bring business—that mighty dollar!"

He often commented that some sins are respectable, some

disgraceful. "The making and accumulating wealth is always honorable and highly praised by men, but God always condemns it. Every statement in the New Testament discourages and warns against it."

About a month later he wrote: "Every day this week men have been streaming by on their way to the high school where the authorities are assigning jobs for construction of the chemical plant. All kinds of men, eager for work. It is pitiful! These times are pitiful! Why even God does not get discouraged I don't know; maybe He does."

On learning of his grandson Jack Wood's meeting in San Marcos, Texas, with sermon topics, "God Is," "The Unfolding of God's Grace," "The Church," "History of the Church in the First Century," "Religious Conditions in the Dark Ages," etc., he wrote home, "Jack Wood sent me a list of the subjects he is using, subjects that I don't know anything about, most of them. I tell you these 'kids' are brave these days! I am proud of him. I'd like to hear him every night."

On August 11, he wrote a letter he did not intend to write:

Dear Woodson: We have passed over another Sunday and it was a hot one. Saturday was also hot, and today up to noon, but since it has been raining and is cool . . .

There are arrangements for me to go with a carload to Scottsboro tonight . . . As you will remember I spent the summer of '94, '95, or '96, one of those summers, at Scottsboro with the church. It was the first summer we were sweethearts. It was there you sent me your first picture. In some ways it's been a century. My, the changes since then! You and I have surely been through the rub—experiences that were the least of our thoughts. After all, God has been good to us and we have been used to bless thousands. I like our life, not our mistakes, and I'd like to go on and on. I have been mean to you sometimes, but I have never seen another I would have swapped for you, nor has there ever been a time that I could be happy without you or away from you. We are both very positive in make-up, and necessarily we have clashed at times; for this we have our

in character has made us fit for the kind of life we've
lived. Had either of us been weak, we could never have
done the work we have done. We have made a team
and done a work that none of our school-day associates
have done. I am humble when I think about it, for I
was never fitted for my place in our program. Only
God's grace has been sufficient for me in the under-
takings.

Our success, with no money, in a period when money
was the basis of school work has been unique. We could
never explain it save that God has given us the victory.
You have been the greater in the partnership; you and
God have given me victory.

I wish it could be written—the history. Nobody could
write it but you and me. It ought to be done. I tire so
quickly; I feel discouraged about its ever being done.

God has been good to us also in letting us live together these more than forty years. Brother Lipscomb
was opposed to our marrying on the ground of my poor
prospect to live long. I believe, had I lived any other
life, I should not be here. How much longer we know
not, but in the providence of God I'd like to finish out
with you that half century—seven more years. Then I
should be seventy-eight and you sixty nine. Even then,
if I am active and able, I'd like to go on with our
work.

This is a funny letter. I had no notion of writing
this kind of letter when I began. It has been spontaneous—spirit moved. Maybe since I did not purpose such
a letter, but wrote as my heart moved me, I can suggest that you stick it away somewhere. You might want
it sometime . . . I love you, Jack.

Fortunately the letter was "stuck away" and turned up in
time for this biography. It reveals the gentleness and sweetness, the generous nature, and the inner vigor and drive of
the one who wrote it.

Finally the summer at Huntsville drew to a close, and
he made the last payment for his room.

"Mrs. _____ contended for a full month's rent,"
he wrote. "I minced no words with her, and paid her the
$12.50 which she asked. Evidently she expected to have a
fight for a full month's rent. I think I surprised her. After

the settlement she seemed unusually happy—put a clean linen spread on my bed and took down the curtains at the windows and doors to wash and iron, and bragged on how nice I had kept everything . . . ”

Armstrong was always neat and immaculately clean. His “mincing no words” was characteristic of his generosity. He never haggled over money or pinched pennies. He always did more than others expected. His last letter from Huntsville was also expressive of his generous nature.

“I never saw as many cripples,” he wrote, “blind, one-legged, and otherwise distressed people, in a town in my life. You can hardly go on the street that you do not meet some distressing sight of misery and woe, begging for a penny. I can’t help them all, and it distresses me.”

About December 12, 1941, Armstrong underwent an operation and was in the hospital and confined to his home for several weeks. Though he recovered and continued his teaching as usual, the family was aware of his increasing physical weakness. With customary vigor and enthusiasm, however, he revealed to others little, if any, of his decline in health. Clinton Davidson had become concerned earlier and had arranged for special treatments from an outstanding specialist, which gave some additional strength. The college helped pay the expense at the local hospital in 1942. In a note of thanks to Dr. Benson he said, “This gift gave us a real lift in time of need. I feel unworthy of it. In the first place, the school is not able to do it. I hope sometime to be able to do as much for the school in return for this graciousness to me at this time. I am very grateful to you personally for it.”

Clinton Rutherford, a student at Harding, wrote his father Homer Rutherford, a former student of Armstrong at Bowling Green and a lifelong friend, and Homer sent a Christmas gift. Armstrong wrote:

“Dear Homer: I am sorry Clinton wrote you about me and my strain right now. I ought to give to you. Then I remember that even as late as Christmas you sent me a gift, and I think I have not acknowledged it. I am so far behind with my work that my correspondence has been neglected. I have all before me, and meant to get to yours, but before I do you humiliate me with another gift. I cannot say I do not really need gifts, but we have been favored greatly by our doctors, surgeons, and hospitals by being allowed to

FOR FREEDOM

arrange our obligations in small payments, and meant to wipe them all out by early summer, the Lord willing. I can't tell you how grateful your gifts make me, nor could I tell you how unworthy it all makes me feel. I hope I can return all your kindness sometime."

On June 13, he had evidently forgotten he had written in January and he wrote again: "I do this day 'remember my fault.' Many times I have thought of your gift to me last Christmas, and proposed many times to write you my gratitude. I hope you will forgive me for I am ashamed of my neglect. I neglect the very best friends I have in the world."

In December of 1943 Rutherford wrote him: "I often think of you and thank God that you are there over our boys. I don't think I would want my son or daughter to be there if it were not for your wholesome influence in these troublous times. May God bless you and preserve you for many years of usefulness to come. We all love you and Sister Armstrong devotedly."

With growing physical weakness Armstrong seemed to become increasingly aware of the spiritual realities, and as I observed him, I had never been so conscious of the experience the Apostle Paul relates: "Though our outward man is decaying, yet our inward man is renewed day by day. For our light affliction, which is for the moment, worketh for us more and more exceedingly an eternal weight of glory; while we look not at the things which are seen: for the things which are seen are temporal; but the things which are not seen are eternal." Two years before his death he wrote in a student's annual: "In the years to come when you look at these words, remember I will be young then and I will be watching you."

In late 1943 he was notified that his biographical sketch was to be included in *Who's Important in Religion for 1944.* On his birthday, January 6, 1944, he wrote the following Message:

Today, January 6, is our birthday, Mrs. Armstrong's and mine. We have been married forty-five years and seven months. Through the years I have argued with her that since we both have the same birthday we must be the same age, but she comes back with the unanswerable argument that I was born in 1870 and she in 1879, and this closes the argument.

She has been my full partner in these long years—

where I have been lacking she has been strong. And I have said many times she has been worth more to our work than I have been. Largely I have received whatever honor the public has bestowed, and she has been the silent partner. Every true wife always carries the big end of the stick. This cannot be helped, however much men would like to have it otherwise. Woodson and I have loved our work. To us ours has been a rich life—a life full of burdens, hardships, and cares, mingled with joys and satisfactions.

In our love making and courtship we planned for Christian college work. As we approach the end we are happy that we chose that for our job. God has blessed us abundantly. Many times he has chastened us—sometimes because we were disobedient children and sometimes to fit us for greater service, but always, we believe, because He loved us.

No pair of workers, or servants, of the Lord ever had more loyal supporters or helpers; no teachers, we think, were ever loved more devotedly than our students have loved us. We now live in the hearts of thousands of them as they fill their places around the world.

They are our rich legacy. They are more precious than silver and gold.

Yes, we have had our critics, persecutors, and even enemies. But all this has been good for us. I should be ashamed to have lived so long as we in a wicked world like ours, in a world so unfriendly to God's cause, and made no enemies and had no persecutors. They sometimes meant it for evil, but God meant it for good. Had it not been for these "children" of ours scattered throughout the world, these enemies and persecutors would have done us and our work much evil. God has used, we believe, these children to block their efforts many times.

Finally, our health today is fine and both of us are teaching full time. I think I preach with as much vigor and enthusiasm as I have done for years and love it as much as ever. For all this I am profoundly grateful.

Armstrong's tribute to Mrs. Armstrong was not mere gallantry, but a sincere appreciation of the wonderful qualities she had brought with her into his life. In the years when there was no money, with rare art she could make old clothes look like new. Every summer she upholstered school furniture and painted and papered with no thought of pay for her work. She was unashamed to do any kind of necessary service, even to bathing the feet of one of the young women suffering from a mountain hike, much to the embarrassment of the young woman. She taught me once a lesson in humility that I never forgot. Fresh from the university with a Master's degree, I felt it beneath my dignity to haul a load of household goods on a child's little wagon several blocks to a house where we were moving. Before I realized it she had seized the wagon and was pulling it rapidly down the street. I overtook her at once and finished the trip. I have never since shrunk from any necessary task, no matter how menial.

At a county teachers' meeting in Cordell a speaker had ridiculed what he called "yellocution." The next number on the program was a reading from Mrs. Armstrong. As she arose she remarked with a smile that she hoped to show Mr. _____ that not all speech instruction was "yellocution." She then gave simply but touchingly a selection from Tennyson's *Enoch Arden* which moved the audience with its beauty and pathos.

Many students learned their first use of the dictionary in her classes. Forest Moyer wrote her, "I am finding myself unable even to read without both the Collegiate (Dictionary) and the Phonetics book—the first for definition and the last for pronunciation."

But it was not mere instruction in speech that students received in Mrs. Armstrong's classes. Bill Baker wrote her in 1948 after sitting up all night talking with Bill Smith about their college experiences: "We both readily agreed that of all the speakers we heard at Harding none of them could out preach you. In fact your 'sermons' in speech classes were the real classics."

Mrs. Armstrong loved her students and loved the Lord, and she unconsciously revealed to them the beauty of the Christ spirit with its unselfish service which she had known from childhood and had seen lived by her father and mother,

her husband, and a host of other great teachers in the Christian schools.

Shortly before Christmas of 1948 she received an unusual letter from R. L. Hart, a saintly preacher of her father's generation, whose affection for the Harding family breaks into sincere but flowery imagery. He expressed his admiration for her, whom he first met as a child, for Armstrong and his great work, and for her father, who was his "favorite preacher." But he closed: "Finally, may your last days be your happiest and best days; may your skies be ever bright; may no dark clouds o'ershadow you; may the grass spring fresh and green beneath your elastic tread; may lovely flowers bloom along your path, while lovely songbirds trill forth their merry lays to the beauty of your countenance and the glory of your song."

With the infirmities of age steps lose their elasticity and voices their song, and Brother Hart's glowing wish for her last years could not be realized, but as those years have stretched on past ninety they have been free from clouds and have been given peace and security by the affectionate care of a daughter who has tended her like a child.

Armstrong once remarked that "Death is so humiliating." I was surprised, for I had never thought of it in that way. But he had seen more suffering than I. It was not the pain or the separation which he feared, but the helplessness. He had always cared for himself and been able to help others. He dreaded being helpless and a burden in age.

But he was spared this humiliation, for his last year was one of the most active. He taught his classes through the year. On April 19 he taught his Bible class at the College church, preached to the church Downtown, and in the evening gave the baccalaureate sermon at Russell. The preceding Sunday he preached at the College church in the morning and at Little Rock in the evening. Called to preach a funeral in the country one day, he found they wanted a funeral service at the home and another at the cemetery.

"If funerals are valuable to the dead," he wrote, "this woman is doubly blessed. But I'll tell you this, it's not easy to preach two funerals in one day to the same crowd and for the same person, but somehow I like these unique experiences. They give a kind of thrill."

At seventy-four, what a zest for life and for unexpected crises! He had said many times he would far rather preach a funeral than marry a young couple! How can anyone explain that? In the one case, perhaps, he felt the struggle was ended and peace and joy lay ahead; in the other, the "trial" was just starting, and no one knew the end. Often as he looked down at a baby he would say, "Poor little thing; there is so much he'll have to learn." Yet he himself enjoyed learning! Enjoyed the challenge of two funerals for the same person, the same audience, the same day!

In May, A. B. Barrett, one of Armstrong's roommates at Nashville, and the man who really started Abilene Christian College, came by for a visit and spoke at chapel. It was a happy reunion. Thinking of the service Barrett had given to the church, and perhaps his own long service in Christian education, he wrote:

The value of money is so extravagantly over-rated that we are all prone to lose sight of greater and better things. If one makes a gift of a million dollars to some great cause, his name, his picture, and the amount of his gift get on the front pages of the great dailies, and he becomes the subject of comment throughout the country. If he makes that gift to a college, a building is names for him, or some permanent monument is placed on the campus.

On the other hand, if one gives himself to a cause, his power and influence—literally wearing out his body and mind without money and without price—and die a "pauper," the little circle in which he serves may rise up and call him blessed, but he will die in comparative obscurity, while that part of the public that happened to know about him and his life regard him as a fanatic or a fool.

Barrett's letter to Mrs. Armstrong immediately after Armstrong's death reveals his appreciation of the brief visit: "I have dearly loved Brother Armstrong all the years that I have known him, and I have ever resented the harsh things that so many have said about him . . . I am so happy that I had the privilege of being with this man of

God while at Harding recently. He was so happy, apparently, and wondrous kind to me. I am the happier for it."

All the years of his evangelistic work, though Armstrong enjoyed preaching, he was always unhappy at being away from home. When Mrs. Armstrong was away, he was completely lost. In 1940 she had attended a convention of the Phi Beta National Professional Fraternity of Music and Speech in Washington, D. C. Though she was there only two or three days, he had a letter awaiting at her hotel: "If you have had a good trip you are now in your meeting and have experienced a "Tea" at the White House. I imagine that was a thrill. But I miss you. I don't like for you to be away."

But in spite of his loneliness he urged her and Pataway to visit her mother in Atlanta in August of 1944, because Sister Harding was not well and they were uncertain how long she could live. He and I drove them to the train, and the next day he sent her the last letter he ever wrote. It failed to reach her in Atlanta because she had been suddenly called home by his death just three days after she had left, but it reflects vividly his cheerfulness and his fine sense of humor:

Dear Woodson, twenty-four hours since you left in the heat at Kensett. I made my appointment with the doctor only five minutes late. I had a good supper last night and rushed to prayer meeting. Had a good night. Cool here at night. Hot today.

This morning I put buttermilk in my Post Toasties, sugar in my boiled eggs, and salt in my breakfast food! Now there!!

At dinner I couldn't find any preserves open, so I hunted up a jar in the shelves. I didn't know what they were, but they are good. Then when I was through dinner, there sat on the stand a jar already opened. So now I have two cans. Like Lavern (a student who helped them) I'll eat up all your preserves. You had better hurry home. Anyway I'm not suffering yet!

I went up to Cline's (the author of this biography) twice yesterday, but the house was empty. Just a little while ago he came down to see if I were still living . . .

Give my best regards to the folks and tell mother

(Mrs. J. A. Harding) nothing would have been a greater pleasure to me than to have gone with you. Hope
you'll have a good time. I'll have a big time here, you
know it! With love to you and Pataway, Jack.

Through the summer he had preached each Sunday over
the radio, then taught his Bible class at the College church,
and had rushed from it to the Downtown church to preach
both morning and evening. He had also conducted the
Wednesday evening meetings, and had spoken a number of
times at the college chapel. He had never preached better
in his life. His mind was alert, his memory perfect, and
the years of experiencing the goodness of God, even with
bitter persecution, had brought to him a spiritual growth
few men ever attain and had given him a large measure of
the patience God must have with human frailty.

His last day was a busy one. Students were finishing
examinations, the summer school was closing, and many
were leaving for home. A constant stream stopped to say
goodbye. James Bales, who was to begin teaching in the
fall and was on his way to Nashville, spent most of the
morning with him. After dinner he spent about an hour
talking with Weldon Casey's parents. After supper he visited
with Mrs. Benson and her mother, Sister Hockaday, whose
husband had been such a rock of strength as Chairman of
the Board at Cordell years before. The Hockadays were
always among his dearest friends. After leaving the Bensons
he got his mail and stopped by the house for a visit with
me. A little later Bales and Joe Pryor visited with him a
while as he sat on his front porch. Then as Brother Taylor,
Earl Priest's grandfather, walked by, he called to him to
come over, and the two had a good visit.

Finally, sitting in his favorite chair by the window, with
his lap-board across the arms and his Bible open before
him, he worked on his radio sermon for the following
Sunday. Shortly before nine o'clock the Basfords, who had
an apartment above, heard him reading, and at the usual
hour of ten he evidently retired. It had been a happy day
filled with pleasant visits with many friends.

The next morning Mrs. Basford slipped downstairs quietly
not to disturb him, and re-locked the door as she went back

up. About 11:30 I went down to take him with me to the restaurant, for I thought both of us had fared long enough on our own cooking. When I found the front door locked, I was uneasy, and when I found the back door also locked I was alarmed. I rushed around to the window of his bedroom, and a single glance told me he was gone. I called Mrs. Basford, who unlocked the door. He was lying as if quietly asleep.

Some time before, he had said, "Woodson, I have a feeling that before the end comes to me I may have a good deal of pain, and I don't want to suffer." And with a whimsical smile he added, "It hurts me so much to hurt." Then as his face grew serious again he said, "So I'm praying that in God's mercy some day he will let me preach two sermons or conduct my Bible classes, then go to sleep and wake up 'over there,' and I want you to pray for this with me."

On August 12, 1944, the birthday of his grandson Jack Wood Sears, his prayers were answered, for with no evidence of struggle or pain, he fell quietly asleep to awake in another world, and a great and unselfish life had closed.

A photograph of the letter from A. S. Croom to J. N. Armstrong (referred to on page 204) is reproduced here in full.

Morrilton,Arkansas.
19 January 1924.

Dear Bro.Armstrong:

A little deliberation and thought sometimes convince us of a lack of clearness in something previously said or written. In my last letter,I told you I did not want to promise unconditionally that I would remain here after this year,and then switched off to the salary question without giving the things that concern me most at this time.

The Board is standing behind me here in the fight I am having to make against teachers who have broken confidence and are indirectly doing their best to oust me by catering to all the whims and complaints the students have or can make against me. In other words they are doing all they can,it seems,to nourish a student grudge again against me for enforcing the regulations in the fall. Perhaps,I have made mistakes,but for a teacher to sit in a faculty meeting,helpmake regulations,and pretend his hearty cooperation and support of the same, to turn and knife you from the back by working among the students, is an inexcusable outrage in a school that calls itself Christian. Now, if at any time the Board should fail me in what I consider being true to Christian principle,you might easily understand why I should dislike to be bound to you by my word that I would stay. Whether I stay or not,the field is open to you and I am more than glad for you and your coworkers to enter. The teachers above referred to are Hinds, Sullivan,and Sullivan's wife. Strangely enough Sullivans never showed any disposition but to love me and cooperate heartily with me until Bro.Hinds went there to room this year. And Bro.Hinds did not until I tried to choke him off his high salary. He gained his point in regard to salary by secretly working on some of the members of the Board by correspondence,onemember,I know of. The majority of the member would pppose his getting it,but acquiesce to maintain peace. Bro.Barber has told me so. To be plain here is another point I should be unyielding on and that is I will not teach another year in a school with a man of that principle posing as Bible teacher,if I know it beforehand as in this case.

Now,I pledge you to secrecy on a matter. I have good evidence that a man is going to give us $10,000 in a few days to finish the auditorium with. This man is not Sgroggin and I shall not disclose his name. He wants it kept strictly and for that reason please keep it so. We want to raise our $20,000 before this is given.

Again I say,let's not cut the teachers salaries until it is necessary. The teachers can make a good donation to# the drive and that will give it a good impetus and us a good pull. The amount given by each one could be distributed over the 5-year period.

Very fraternally,

A. X. Croom

Also, a good salary gives better standing with the State as you know.

IN CHAPTER 14 reference is made to the defection of a Professor Wright, a matter which might easily have been adjusted locally and in quietness except for outside interference. But since it became a pretext for unfair and even vicious attacks on Armstrong and the college, and since many do not know the facts back of it, the following information is given.

In the summer of 1934 the head of the art department at the college unexpectedly resigned, and his place was filled by Professor Earnest Madison Wright, who had applied twice before, saying that he wanted to teach in a Christian school where he could also study the Bible and prepare to preach. His father had been a student with Armstrong at the Nashville Bible School, a very conscientious, faithful minister.

Wright proved an excellent teacher, but at the opening of school he asked me if he might use college girls as nude models in his classes as the art school did in Los Angeles. He believed it would build enrollment in his courses.

"No, certainly not," I said. "You may have used nude models in Los Angeles, but in a school like this, it simply cannot be done." As a precaution I reported the request to President Armstrong because I was leaving immediately for the University of Chicago. But nude models were never mentioned again.

Later, students became disturbed by some fanatical ideas Wright had presumably obtained from Amy Semple McPherson, a popular preacher in Los Angeles, and several concluded he was a little unbalanced. But knowing and loving his father, Armstrong and other teachers hoped they could bring him back to sensible views. Students, however, were becoming so disturbed that Armstrong finally asked Wright to cease agitating his ideas or resign. In a letter of February 9, 1935, he resigned, and the resignation was publicly announced at chapel. Then on February 16 he wrote Armstrong a second letter pleading to stay:

> I make this one last appeal to you. I do not want to leave Harding. I would gladly give all my energies to putting Harding on a solid and lasting foundation . . . I have ability and I cannot sit idly by and let it fall into decay.
>
> You can very well see that the brotherhood is riding for a fall . . . The old lines are holding no longer. The power of God is sweeping the forts and taking them by storm. Church after church is finding God and the Holy Spirit. The antagonists of the Holy Spirit are fighting their last desperate battle, but it is a losing one.
>
> I am appealing to you, Brother Armstrong, to show what great things He can do for Harding College by opening the channels for the spread of the truth, and fear not for one moment what man can do against us because of our stand upon this matter . . .
>
> You very well know that people put their trust in their leaders. They are truly as sheep about their shepherd. When we cannot convert the shepherd to the truth, the only other avenue of approach to the sheep . . . is to substitute other shepherds. They must be weaned from the one and drawn to another who teaches the truth. This process discredits the former teacher and causes his followers to lose confidence in him . . .
>
> O I wish to God I could show you what can be done in training evangelists for powerful service in the field. I wish I could have a class of these young ministers

. . . My, what wonders could be worked if only they were given the proper training!

Instead of the leaders here at Harding trying to convey the impression that I am deranged on religious matters to protect their teaching and prestige, how much more Christian would it be if they would cooperate to the fullest extent . . .

Since Wright's resignation had already been announced, Armstrong made no reply. But shortly after, when Armstrong was absent from the campus, Wright arose in the student assembly and denounced Armstrong for accepting his resignation. Professor Bell replied that he was sure Armstrong would be properly capable of defending his action if he were present and that Wright was out of place in bringing such accusations in his absence. But on February 21, two weeks after his resignation, Wright wrote both the *Firm Foundation* and the *Gospel Advocate:*

As a minister of the gospel of Jesus Christ and as head of the art department of Harding College, Searcy, Arkansas, let me say that I both believe and teach the premillennial advent of Christ and also the baptism of the Holy Spirit and divine healing . . . As to Brother Armstrong's position on these matters let me suggest that as far as I can learn he is very flexible in his belief, adapting himself to whatever seems to be the more likely to yield the greater enrollment for the school.

I believe that he considers the *Word and Work* group to be in a position to ultimately triumph in the contest now raging and it is the part of wisdom to leave the way open to adopt the policy of the school to suit the situation that may develop, Respectfully,

Earnest Madison Wright,

Since Armstrong had asked for his resignation and had ignored his pleas to be retained, Wright was evidently taking the steps he had recommended in his letter—trying to "discredit" Armstrong and "cause his followers to lose confidence in him."

When John T. Hinds of the *Gospel Advocate* received the letter, it was so clearly a misrepresentation that he immediately sent it to Armstrong, who wrote him a full explanation. The letter was never published in the *Advocate*.

Armstrong immediately telegraphed the *Firm Foundation,* but the letter was already in the issue of March 12. The editor commended Wright for his "candor in the statement of his creed and doctrine," but sarcastically commented that "Fools rush in where angels fear to tread." The Term "fools" reflected a suspicion that something was wrong with Wright, but his letter, nevertheless, was published, with the comment that the editor understood that Harding had four teachers who were not Christians, and the college ought to let the brotherhood know whether this was true or not.

How Wright's letter could be published without an effort to learn the facts is hard to understand. Even reputable scientific journals refuse to publish criticisms of other scientists without first sending the article to the one criticized and permitting him to reply in the same issue. But all the religious journals, as well as the colleges, had for months felt the pressure of the group who wanted to exclude from the church all who believed in a millennium or even tolerated those who did. The *Foundation* might honestly have felt that it was befriending the college by compelling it to "speak out" once again.

On March 19 it printed Armstrong's telegram: "In fairness to Harding College tell readers Wright's letter completely misrepresents Harding College. Resignation secured from Wright because of faulty teaching and perfectly accepted to take effect in the winter quarter days before date of published letter. Being disgruntled he wrote the letter. Article containing full explanation follows."

The editor commented that, if the college had informed him of Wright's teaching, "This would have obviated the necessity of publishing Brother Wright's letter." But "Wright's teaching" was merely a local irritant which the college was quietly correcting. As Hinds had recognized, there was no "necessity" to trouble people off campus about it. Wright was already a dismissed teacher, and no longer "head of the art department."

Armstrong's explanation of the incident in the *Firm Foundation* was as kind to Wright as he could make it. To Armstrong's knowledge Wright had never mentioned the millennium and had referred to divine healing only once; his constant interest was the Holy Spirit:

> His charge that I am "flexible," were it not for its setting, would be ridiculous. Truly I have many faults, but that is not one of them. I would leave even my enemies who know me to clear me of this charge . . . Brother Wright is gone, and as he departed, we at Harding had, as I imagine, many of us, kindred feelings to those of our Lord as he wept over Jerusalem. We would have saved him, but he would not . . . From first to last we dealt gently with the young man . . .

The publication of Wright's letter brought some sharp protests. One letter sent to the *Firm Foundation* "for publication," said:

> I am not a Premillennialist. I have studied the matter for years and I do not hold with those who teach that Christ will return to earth in person and set up a kingdom and reign a thousand years.
>
> On the other hand, I think you and the publishers of the *Leader* and *Advocate* are making a serious mistake in giving so much space to brethren with hot heads and cold hearts who wish to abuse those who do not understand the scriptures just as you do.
>
> In my judgment you made a very serious mistake when you published the note from Earnest Wright in this week's paper. I do not know Earnest Wright, but I do know J. N. Armstrong, and I know he is not the kind of man he is pictured to be in that note, and I believe you know it as well as I do . . . Had you remembered the Golden Rule, you certainly would have sent Brother Armstrong a copy of the note and awaited his reply before giving it such a prominent place in your paper . . . It pays to be fair when opposing a true man of God as we both know Brother Armstrong to be. As I see it, some of you brethren have lost your hearts as well as your heads, and I suggest that you slow down a little.

This incident aroused across the country new sympathy for Armstrong and Harding College. Five years later Earnest's father, Madison Wright, wanted to visit the college to correct the impressions made by his son. Armstrong extended him a warm invitation, but said there was no need for corrections. It was all "passed and forgotten . . . Earnest never had any damaging influence on the campus, and we would have smoothed it out without any break with Earnest if he had not written that letter to the *Firm Foundation* . . . I hate it very much for Earnest's sake and for your sake as well."

The pitiful truth, which no one at the time recognized was that Wright's mind was evidently slipping. Relatives said years later that in 1932 during an earthquake in California he had been trapped under the debris of a school building. He had refused medical attention and had grown progressively worse. His father died in 1945, and his mother was finally convinced he would have to be confined in a mental institution. She had telephoned another son, who promised to come over in the morning, but that night Earnest killed his mother, sat with her body till morning, and then calmly telephoned the police. "I wish to report a little matter. I killed my mother last night at 2816 Osceola Ave. My name is Earnest Wright. The body is here and I will remain until you arrive."

Wright greeted the police at the door, took them to his mother, whom he had laid on the bed, and then explained the crime. On the lid of an old-fashioned stove was the number "709" written in crayon. Wright explained that he charted his life by calculus, that when he wrote the number on the stove a month before he did not know its meaning. But last night as he was reading his Bible the meaning suddenly came to him; it was "to kill."

"When a number comes up, I act immediately," he said. "I never hesitate or argue. The number suddenly told me to kill her."

She was standing by the stove, he said, and he knocked her to the floor with his fist, then twisted her neck, and finally grabbed the iron footrest from the stove and beat her over the head. He showed police pieces of the broken footrest wrapped in a towel.

Armstrong had died three years before this tragedy. He would have been deeply grieved, for he had always remembered Brother and Sister Wright with affection. Had the *Firm Foundation* known Wright's mental condition in 1935, of course, it would never have published his letter.

Though the publication of Wright's letter brought a flood of unfair criticism from various journals, Armstrong always regarded it as only an unfortunate mistake in editorial judgment. His affection for the editor was as strong as ever, and the attitude of the *Firm Foundation* toward him was even kinder and more considerate than before.

INDEX

Hall, S. H., 216, 239, 278, 283, 296, 298
Harding College, 199-262
Harding, James A., 33-35, 84, 142, 154, 185, 192
Harding, Dr. Leon K., 31-35, 94, 95
Harper College, 188-207
Harper, E. R., 110, 282-291
Hinds, John T., 199, 204-206, 328
Hockaday, W. D., 97, 98, 108, 109, 157

Instrumental music, 22, 23, 61, 62

Karnes, Houston, 228, 239, 312

Kieffer, George W., 129, 136, 221, 227, 245
Kurfees, M. C., 68, 69, 192, 202, 203, 213, 285

Lewis, John T., 292, 293
Lipscomb, David, 31, 34, 78, 193, 215, 271, 276
Living Message, 171-187, 214, 215, 264, 276, 281

McCaleb, J. M., 181, 271
McQuiddy, J. C., 193-196
McMillan, E. W., 298, 299
Merritt, Dow, 89, 131, 132

Nashville Bible School, 26, 28-53, 149
Nichol, C. R., 148, 149, 249, 280, 285, 290

Octographic Review, 82-85, 128
Otey, W. W., 86, 290, 291, 309

Pepperdine, George, 261-263
Phillips, Jesse, 20, 21, 207, 260
Pool, Clem Z., 285-287
Potter Bible College, 67, 68, 142
Preaching, 35-41, 54-63

Premillennialism, 213-218, 275-299

Reese, John G., 239, 243, 244, 284
Rhodes, B. F., 71-73, 78-81, 110, 150, 191, 215, 247, 253-255
Rutherford, Homer, 304, 317, 318

Salaries, 54, 66, 67, 144, 203, 226-228
Searcy, Arkansas, 240-242, 250, 251
Sewell, Jesse P., 143, 149, 250-253, 264, 282, 289, 299
Shepherd, J. W., 133, 159
Shepherd, Mary, 127, 133, 137, 310
Showalter, G. H. P., 148, 214, 250, 290, 304
Smith, Earl C., 215-217
Smith, F. W., 217
Smoking, 133, 134
Sommer, Daniel, 74-85, 109, 128, 145, 215, 297
Special Providence, 121-125, 176-178
Srygley, F. B., 85, 174, 194

Thompson, C. Ray, 207, 210
Thorp Springs Christian College, 35, 110, 111, 148-150
Tornadoes, 106, 112-114

Unity, 182-187, 281-299

Western Bible and Literary College, 73-90
White, R. C., 31, 35, 93
Whiteside, R. L., 23, 42, 110, 125, 141, 280
Wilson, R. L., 208, 209, 283, 284
Woodbridge, Judson, 285-287
World War I, 152-160, 193-196
World War II, 267-274
Wright, Earnest, 252, 327-332